contents

ACKNOWLEDGMENTS

Now that which is given to a truly honest and grateful person is paid us in the acknowledgement he makes, and in the good will that is got by it from the rest of the world . . .
—Cicero, *The Offices*, 44 B.C.

I could not have done this book alone. There are many people who assisted in making this happen, and particular among them are the folks listed below.

My most heartfelt thanks go out to Lauren Dundon for giving so much of her time and talents to provide the great photos for this book. She went way beyond what anyone could expect of a photographer or of a friend. Special thanks also to Joe Schmid and Joe Heslin who literally had a hand in almost every photo. Additional photo thanks to Robert Oliver, Park Tool, and Schwinn Bicycles.

Thank you to Zack Miller of MBI Publishing Company for proposing this book, and to the MBI staff for assistance, encouragement, and financial support. Thanks to Felix Magowan for leadership in creating a joint effort between Velo Press and MBI, and to Mark Saunders and Jack Savage for working out the myriad details of the copublishing agreement. Thank you to Erin Johnson, Chas. Chamberlin, and Nate Cox of Inside Communications for scrounging up photos, illustrations, and text that I requested; to Schwinn for photos; to Charles Pelkey for editorial eagerness, skill, and sensitivity; and to Inside Communications for flexibility with my schedule. Thank you Dag Selander and Steve Torrente for handling critical details in the final frantic weeks.

For assistance with the technical details, thanks go to Doug Bradbury, Wayne Stetina, Paul Morningstar, Arlo Englund, Steve and Anne Hed, Wayne Lumpkin, Bob Gregorio, Wendell Walker, Dan Garceau, Scott Boyer, Steve Boehmke, Dave Wiens, Jeff Cole, Steve Driscoll, Calvin Jones, Zach White, Tom Ritchey, Tom Eagleton, Tom Armstrong, Portia Masterson, David Reid, Park Tool, Wrench Force, Shimano, Answer Products, Rock Shox, Magura, White Industries, Hed Design, Cannondale, Bontrager, Bianchi/Time Sport, Vivo Sport, Louisville Cyclery, and Sports Garage.

The support of my family through this process has been more than anyone could ask for. Thank you Sonny, Marlies, Ron, Rex, Mom, and Dad for taking over innumerable responsibilities of mine so that I could have long uninterrupted stretches to write. Thank you Emily and Sarah for allowing your father to be unavailable, busy, and grouchy so much. And thanks to everyone else on both sides of my family for encouragement.

—Lennard Zinn

DEDICATION

To my wife, Sonny, for always being there to support me no matter what, for giving me a swift kick here and there when I needed it, and for *not* giving me the boot sometimes when I deserved it. I love you and cannot thank you enough.

First published in 1998 by MBI Publishing Company, 729 Prospect Avenue, PO Box 1, Osceola, WI 54020-0001 USA

The information in this book is true and complete to the best of our knowledge. All recommendations are made without any guarantee on the part of the author or Publisher, who also disclaim any liability incurred in connection with the use of this data or specific details.

We recognize that some words, model names and designations, for example, mentioned herein are the property of the trademark holder. We use them for identification purposes only. This is not an official publication.

MBI Publishing Company books are also available at discounts in bulk quantity for industrial or sales-promotional use. For details write to Special Sales Manager at Motorbooks International Wholesalers & Distributors, 729 Prospect Avenue, PO Box 1, Osceola, WI 54020-0001 USA.

Library of Congress Cataloging-in Publication Data

Zinn, Lennard.
Mountain bike performance handbook / Lennard Zinn.
p. cm. -- (Bicycle books)
Includes index.
ISBN 0-933201-95-8 (pbk. : alk. paper)
1. All terrain bicycles--Parts. 2. All terrain bicycles--Performance. I. Title. II. Series.
TL414.Z55 1998
629.227'2--dc21 98-23791

On the front cover: Cross-country ace Carl Swenson at speed. *Robert Oliver, courtesy* VeloNews

On the back cover: Top: Downhill racing's punishing conditions require radical solutions. Middle: Though often neglected, chains play a key role in your bike's performance. Bottom: Aftermarket brakes like Avid's Arch Supreme can offer superior stopping power and feel compared to your bike's stock brake set up.

Edited by Charles Pelkey
Designed by Katie L. Sonmor

Printed in the United States of America

MOUNTAIN BIKE PERFORMANCE HANDBOOK

LENNARD ZINN

INTRODUCTION

Mountain bike mechanics and component design engineers must ride. If they do not ride, they cannot fathom the stresses the stuff is exposed to.
—Bob Gregorio, John Tomac's long-time mechanic

WHAT IS THIS BOOK, ANYWAY?

To best express what this book is, it is important to distinguish what it is not. This is *not* a maintenance book. A maintenance book can tell you how to keep a bike as close to its original design specifications as possible after use and abuse. This book, on the other hand, instructs you in ways to *improve* your bike. This book is intended to bring your bike to a higher level of performance and let you get much more out of it than you could in its original design.

I have written a very thorough and up-to-date maintenance book entitled *Zinn and the Art of Mountain Bike Maintenance,* to which this book serves as a companion manual. This book, however, goes into much more depth on a number of subjects. If you want to fix a part that is broken or adjust it so it works properly, consult *Zinn and the Art of Mountain Bike Maintenance*. If you want to upgrade and modify your bike, consult this book.

A good way to understand this distinction is by looking to the automotive world. If you had just bought an old Porsche, you could buy a Porsche maintenance manual so that you could adjust, lubricate, replace, and fix its parts. If you want to get more performance out of the car than it originally offered, however, you would need something more. You would want a *performance manual* that would instruct you on how to bore the cylinders to get more displacement, how to replace steel valve springs with titanium, or how to upgrade the suspension and chassis for your particular application. This book is the mountain bike equivalent of such a performance manual.

I wrote this book for the racer or performance rider who is constantly striving to get the most out of his or her equipment and body. This book will allow you to make your bike uniquely *yours*. The suspension will be adjusted to your weight and riding style. The position on the bike will be set up to fit *you* for the type of riding you most enjoy. Component upgrades on your bike will be appropriate for you and not for someone 50 pounds heavier or lighter or who rides differently from you.

Using this book could also save you a lot of money. With the rapid growth in mountain bike technology, parts become obsolete almost as quickly as computer hardware. You can upgrade your bike to the performance standard of the latest bikes without going out and buying a new one every year. I am a lot more committed to encouraging your love of cycling and the self-reliance of being able to improve your own bike than I am to that vitality-robbing suggestion that you must lay out big bucks in order to "keep up" with other riders.

WHAT'S INSIDE

This book not only covers how to enhance performance of suspension, drivetrain, tires, etc. for specific conditions, it also explains *why* these changes make a difference. That way, you can gauge the relative value of a new widget for your application or can decide for yourself a way to approach a problem.

The procedures in this book go well beyond the work of most shop mechanics. This book is about squeezing the most out of your equipment. This is exactly the world within which professional team mechanics and component designers live. Therefore, I include tips from team mechanics, who do precise work all the time and under extreme conditions of weather and time pressure. You approach a problem differently if one of the top riders in the world is breathing down your neck to get his or her bike done and then expects the bike to perform flawlessly! You also learn shortcuts! I also include suggestions from the top component designers in the industry, who know better than anyone how to make their parts work the best they can for a certain course.

To illustrate and clarify the benefits and/or problems often encountered while performing a specific procedure, I have included case studies of changes made to specific bicycles and how it worked out when the rubber hit the dirt. While riding, you may not be currently able to distinguish the kind of minutiae of a bike's operation that top pros can, but if you never experiment with those minutiae, you will never develop the ability to tell the difference, either. This sort of work is beyond the level of "do this, do that"; it is in the realm of: "try this, and see how it works." If you love tinkering and experimenting, you will love using this book!

The book is divided into chapters devoted to specific parts of the bike. Each chapter includes detailed photographs illustrating specific steps described in the text.

In addition to delving into upgrading the performance of your existing bike, this book also deals with how to build a great bike from scratch.

In the back, the appendices offer supplemental information specific to the text. There are appendices on troubleshooting; frame sizing and bike positioning; gear development; and recommended tightening torques for specific bolts. There is also a glossary of specific terms related to working on high-performance mountain bikes, so you will know what those words mean that tech geeks throw around with such wild abandon.

WHY READ IT?

This book is about having *fun*! It is for people who love riding all-out as well as goofing around with their bikes. This book makes no attempt at preaching about things you *should* do to your bike. Everything in here is optional. You can go as far as you want with it, or not at all. This is about the last 10 percent or so in the bike's performance, which, for some of us, makes all of the difference.

This book is meant to elicit a higher mechanical standard from you. Creating an exceptional bike from one that was less than that requires performing exceptional work and having the ability to understand how and why to perform it. There are great rewards in raising your expectations of yourself and attaining them. You will be training yourself to tell the difference between mediocre and great mechanical work and in noticing subtle performance differences while riding. It is that last little bit of performance that can make all the difference in your joy and satisfaction while riding.

I love working on bikes as well as riding them, and I find that doing each enhances the experience of the other. When I can make an improvement to my bike and feel the difference when I ride, it is very satisfying. Similarly, when I can identify something lacking in how my bike rides, I get excited to get back in the shop (or get out some tools on the trail) and make it do what I want.

If you are someone who demands a lot out of your equipment and yourself and appreciates those times when your body and bicycle work harmoniously together, this book is for you. Similarly, if you are someone who finds sheer pleasure in making something work better than it did before, read on!

1

TOOLS

If your only tool is a hammer, everything starts looking like a nail.
—Anonymous

Obviously, tools are central to upgrading your bike. Beyond the normal requirements of maintenance, high-performance work on the bike requires specialized tools. Tools you can ordinarily do without (by depending on a shop once a year or so) become important to own if you want to switch forks, build up a frame, or even dial in your tire pressure accurately.

The good news is that working with good tools can be as fun as riding on good parts, and you need some cool ones for working on high-performance bike equipment. You now have a great excuse to buy some nice new tools, and you can tell those eye-rolling spouses and housemates that I made you do it.

1.1 WHAT TO LOOK FOR WHEN OBTAINING TOOLS

The first step in tool procurement is to determine exactly what type of tool you need. A really cool, expensive tool is just a paperweight if it is for an application different from yours. The specific task you intend to perform needs to be distinguished, and then the tools that make that task possible start to reveal themselves. Consult the applicable section of this book (or *Zinn and the Art of Mountain Bike Maintenance*, if it is a maintenance operation) to see what tools you will need.

Once the particular application and the type of tool for it have been identified, the question then becomes which brand and model to get. Generally, the more frequently you work on your bike, and the more concerned you are about not damaging bolts on the bike, the higher the quality of tools you will require. Most tools are good enough to turn one bolt once, but some are not good for much more than that. For example, many inexpensive flat wrenches are stamped out of sheet steel that is either very brittle or very soft. The fit on the bolt will not be good, because the ripped edge created when the wrench opening is punched out simply cannot be that precise. A soft wrench can "mushroom" out on a tight bolt, rounding off the straight sides of the wrench opening, and a brittle wrench can snap off. Wrench failure can be quite dangerous. When a tool gives way with your weight on it, you can smash your nose into the bike or at least peel skin off your knuckles. Shattered tool pieces flying around can endanger you and onlookers.

It is not my intention to promote any particular brand of bike tool. I do recommend becoming an educated consumer and finding out about how the tools you are considering buying are made. Generally, production processes like heat treating, laser cutting of wrench openings, forging, and investment casting indicate better tools. Certainly, a good warranty is something to look for, as is the reputation of the tool company, and any feedback you get from knowledgeable mechanics can be invaluable.

1.2 THE BARE NECESSITIES

The tools in photos 1-1 to 1-11 (and in 1-12, if you have air shocks) are the tools you cannot realistically do without if you expect to be able to set up your bike for a particular ride or race or be able to install high-performance up-grades on your bike. You can expect to do 90 percent of the work on your bike with this set of tools. With *only* these tools, you will not be able to check wheel dish (or even build wheels without a lot of trouble), install or remove a headset, or prepare a frame for assembly.

1-1

Standard metric tools and bike-specific tools

- Standard flat-bladed screwdrivers: small, medium, and large.
- Phillips-head screwdrivers: small and medium.
- Set of metric Allen wrenches (hex keys) that includes 2.5-mm, 3-mm, 4-mm, 5-mm, 6-mm, and 8-mm sizes. Folding sets work nicely to keep your wrenches organized, although they sometimes bend when loosening a stuck bolt. I also recommend buying extras of the 4-mm, 5-mm, and 6-mm sizes.
- Set of metric open-end wrenches or combination wrenches that includes 7-mm, 8-mm, 9-mm, 10-mm, 13-mm, 14-mm, 15-mm, and 17-mm sizes.
- Set of metric socket wrenches that includes 7-mm, 8-mm, 9-mm, 10-mm, 13-mm, 14-mm, and 15-mm sizes.
- Ratcheting torque wrench (rather than a standard socket wrench ratchet handle). A torque wrench can ensure that you are tightening bolts to their proper tightness. A torque wrench is not an absolute necessity, but it takes some experience and feel to know how tight to tighten a bolt, depending on the size of the bolt, what the part is, and what the bolt is threaded into (e.g., steel, aluminum, magnesium, or plastic). Following torque recommendations is a sure method.
- Hex-key bits to fit on a socket handle or torque wrench.
- Crow's-foot wrenches to fit on a socket handle or torque wrench. *Note*: the offset of the crow's-foot wrench opening from the socket hole reduces the torque. Multiply desired torque setting by 0.85 to determine wrench setting.
- 13/14-mm and 15/16-mm cone wrenches. Two of each is even nicer. These are thin, flat wrenches. Some are only single-ended, in which case you need one of each size.
- Splined cassette cog lock ring tool for removing cogs from the rear hub.
- 15-mm pedal wrench. This is thinner and longer than a standard 15-mm wrench and thicker than a cone wrench.
- Splined pedal-spindle removal tool.
- 14-mm socket/8-mm hex combination crank bolt wrench (or equivalent separate tools).
- Crank puller for removing crank arms.
- Splined bottom bracket tool for Shimano cartridge bottom brackets and clones of them.
- Bottom bracket pin spanners, including adjustable one.
- Bottom bracket lock-ring spanners and lock-ring spanner/fixed-cup wrench.
- Chainring nut wrench.
- Pairs of headset wrenches. Be sure to check the size of your headset before buying these. This purchase is unnecessary if you plan only to work on threadless headsets.

1-2

Tire stuff

- Tire pump with a gauge and a valve head to match your tube valves (either Presta or Schrader). This pump is oversized to pump mountain bike tires faster.
- Accurate tire pressure gauge for Presta valves. Race mechanics gauge tire pressure separately, rather than depending on the gauge on a pump, which can be inaccurate. Pumping once to too-high pressure can ruin a pump gauge.
- Set of three plastic tire levers (or a telescoping "Speed Lever").
- Tire and tube.

1-3

Chain tools

- Chain rivet tools for breaking and reassembling chains.
- Chain elongation gauges. The Rohloff gauge or the Park CC-2 can quickly determine if a chain needs replacing. An accurate 12-inch ruler will substitute adequately.
- Cog wear-indicator gauge to determine if cogs are worn out.
- Shimano TL-CN24 chainplate spacing tool, for checking that the chain's inner width is sufficient that it can release from the chainring teeth and not "suck" into the frame.

1-4

Pliers and cutters

- Cable cutter for cutting brake and shifter cables without fraying the ends/Cable-housing cutter for cutting index-shifting-specific coaxial cable housing. If you purchase a Shimano, Wrench Force, or Park CN-24 housing cutter, you won't need to buy a separate cable cutter, since these cleanly cut both cables and housings.
- Needle-nose or alligator-nose pliers.
- Side cutters. These are not appropriate for cutting cables, though they can cut housings.
- Cable-tensioning pliers (not a necessity, but convenient).
- Pair of snap-ring pliers for removing snap rings from suspension forks, derailleurs, pedals, etc.

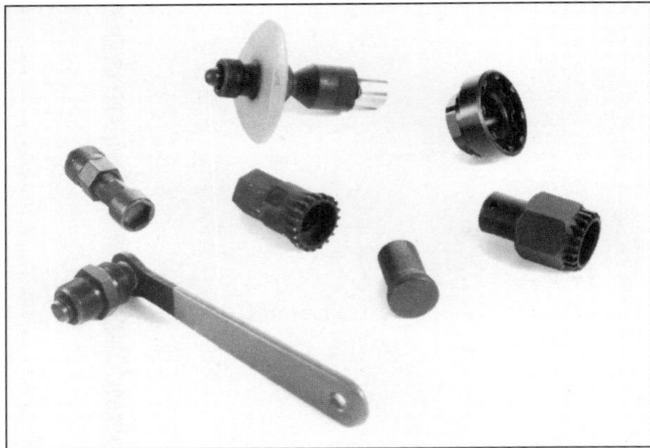

1-5

Crank arm tools

- Crank pullers for removing crank arms.
- Splined bottom bracket tool for Shimano cartridge bottom brackets and clones of them.
- Shimano crank lock-ring-removal tool for removing the spider from post-1996 Shimano cranks with removable spiders. This tool also holds the adjustable cup on post-1996 XTR and Dura-Ace bottom brackets. The female-threaded knurled nut, which threads onto the crank bolt, holds the lock ring remover in place for removing the XTR spider.

1-6

Spoke wrenches

- Spoke wrenches of different sizes to match the nipples used on various wheels. The wrench in the foreground fits on splined, rather than square, nipples.

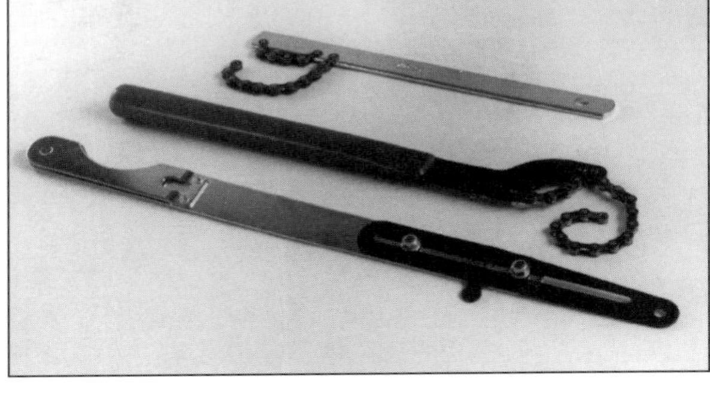

1-7

- Chain whips for holding cogs while loosening the cassette lock ring.
- Chain-line indicator.

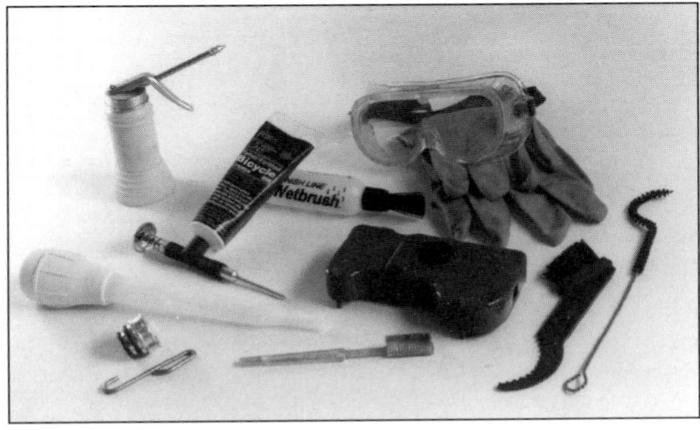

1-8

Freehub tools

- Morningstar "Freehub Buddy" for cleaning and lubricating freehubs. A poor second best to the Freehub Buddy is the process of frequently flowing lubricant into the freehub (after removing the hub bearings). This method does not allow you to apply the pressure the Freehub Buddy allows, though.
- Morningstar "J" tool for removing the hub dust seal in order to lubricate the freehub.
- Turkey basting bulb for injecting solvent into a freehub via the Freehub Buddy.
- Thin grease gun (allows you to inject grease into a freehub via the Freehub Buddy.)
- Oil can for injecting chain lube into a freehub via the Freehub Buddy.
- Chain cleaner (which has nothing to do with freehubs).
- Safety glasses to keep solvent out of your eyes.
- Rubberized gloves to protect your baby-soft skin.
- Brushes, including solvent-filled brush bottle.

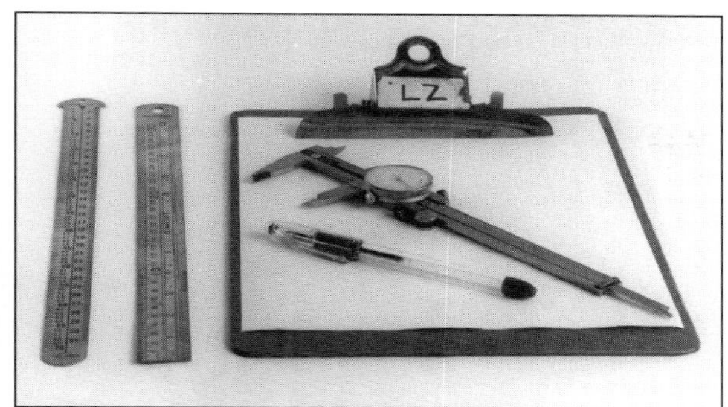

1-9

- Rulers for measuring things.
- Notebook or clipboard and pen to store by your bike. This may be your most important tool! Unless you are always willing to drop everything and work on your bike immediately after every ride, you will usually be doing work on your bike some time after noticing things during a ride that you want to improve. If you note it down in the notebook after your ride, you can get it out of your head, and you will remember what to do when you have time to work on your bike in the days and weeks following.
- Vernier calipers (this one has a dial gauge) for measuring inside and outside of things.

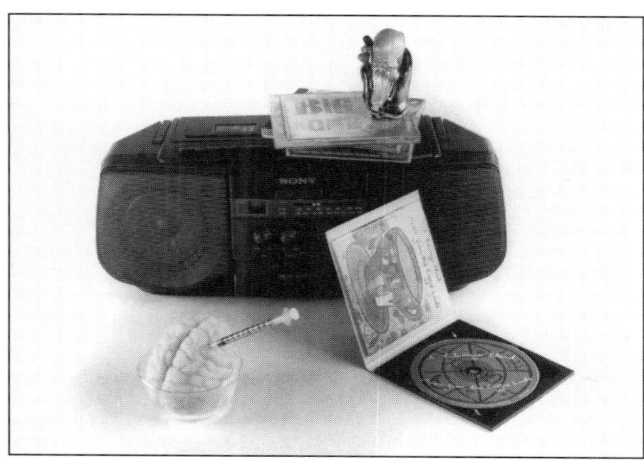

1-10

- One stereo and some good tunes. This is especially important if you plan on spending a lot of time working on your bike.
- Patience.
- Common sense.
- Syringe (for injecting alcohol under grips to remove them). Duh.

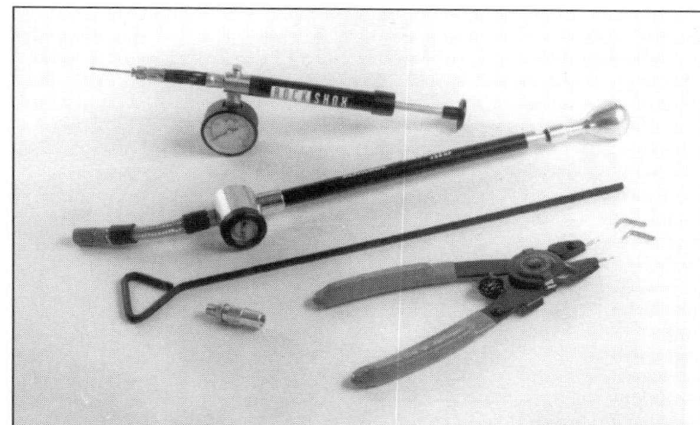

1-12

Suspension tools

- Shock pump(s), if you have air-sprung suspension. Air-sprung forks and rear shocks require small air pumps equipped with the appropriate gauge and head. Generally, a rear shock requires higher pressure than a fork, so the same pump for both is inappropriate. Remember that pressure gauges are most accurate in the middle of their range, so pumping a low-pressure fork with a high-pressure rear shock pump introduces inaccuracy. Similarly, don't pump a rear shock with a low-pressure fork pump; you wreck a gauge by pumping it to pressures at the top of its range or above. Pre-1999 Rock Shox air forks have ball valves and require a ball-inflating needle on the pump. Rear shocks and other air forks, including Englund retrofit fork air cartridges generally have Schrader valves.
- No-leak shock pump fitting (some shock pumps, like the Schwinn pump pictured here, have integral no-leak fittings). For Englund Total Air retrofit fork cartridges and small, high-pressure rear shocks, it is advisable and, in some cases mandatory, to ensure that no air escapes when removing the pump. The internal volume of these shocks is so small that a tiny amount of air lost will result in a large drop in pressure.
- Long 5-mm hex key useful for disassembling some types of suspension forks.
- Pair of snap-ring pliers with different bits for removing snap rings with different types of accessibility.

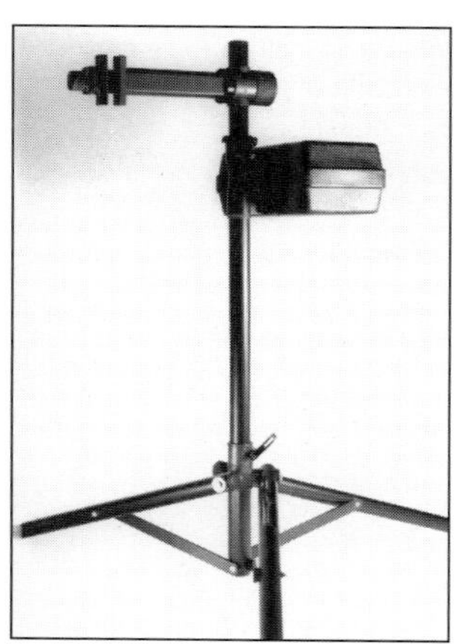

1-11

Portable bike stand suitable to use at home and to take with you to races or Moab. A toolbox or shelf to keep tools and parts out of the dirt is nice.

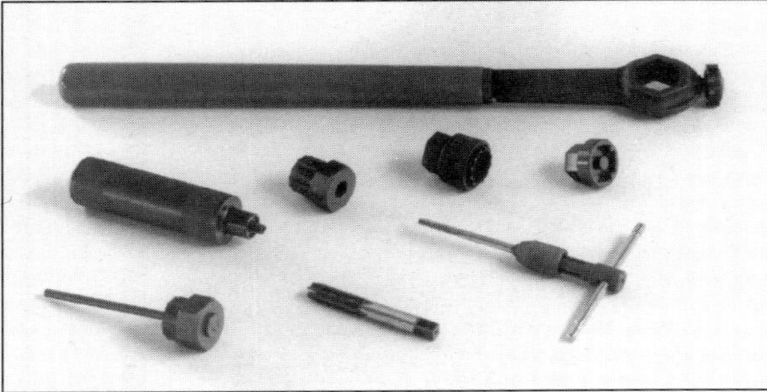

1-13

- Long handle to turn a cassette lock-ring remover.
- Special splined cassette cog lock-ring tools with mechanisms for keeping them straight when removing a stuck lock ring. One is investment-cast with a flange to keep it flat against the lock ring; the other has a shaft to keep it aligned with the center of the axle.
- Splined freewheel remover, in case you have a really old rear hub with a freewheel.
- Star-nut installation tool for threadless headset star-nut insertion into steering tube.
- Pivot-bearing removal tool for Avid brakes.
- Metric taps (you need 5 mm x 0.8 for water-bottle bosses, 6 mm x 1 for brake bosses and seat binders, and 10 mm x 1 for rear derailleur hangers.

1-14

- Headset cup remover.
- Headset press used to install headset bearing cups. The press should fit all three cup sizes. Chris King headsets need a press that does not contact the pressed-in bearing. King sells inserts for regular headset presses to install his headsets.
- Fork crown race-setting tool (a.k.a., slide hammer) for installing the fork crown headset race.
- Hacksaw guides for cutting fork steering tubes off straight. Pictured are both threaded versions for all sizes and a one-size-fits-all version for threadless steerers.
- Electric drill with drill bit set for customizing.
- Dropout spacing caliper.
- Derailleur hanger alignment tool to straighten the derailleur after you shift it into the spokes or crash on it.
- Dishing tool for checking if that set of wheels you just built is properly centered.
- Dropout alignment tools (a.k.a., tip adjusters).
- Willingness to work and rework jobs until they are complete (not pictured).

1.3 ADDITIONAL TOOLS FOR A FULL-BLOWN TOOL SET

The tools in photos 1-13 to 1-22 will allow you to do almost anything on a bike, including building wheels, preparing and assembling frames, and even dialing in a pro's bike for a race.

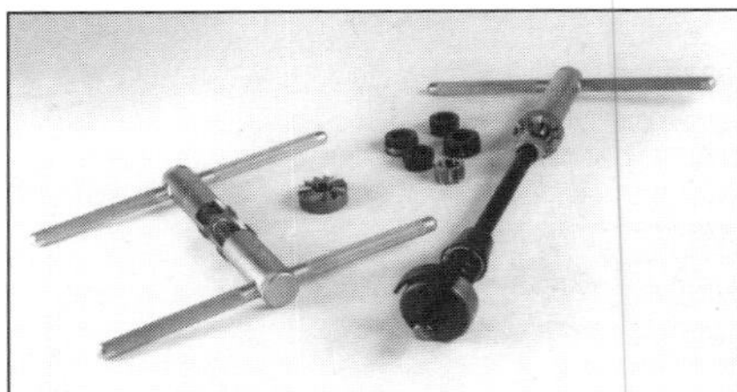

1-15

Frame prep tools

- English-threaded bottom bracket tap set. This cuts threads in both ends of the bottom bracket while keeping the threads in proper alignment.
- Bottom bracket shell facing tool. This tool cuts the faces of the bottom bracket shell so they are parallel to each other.
- Head tube reamer/facer. This tool keeps both ends of the head tube perfectly parallel and reams the ends of the head tube out to fit the headset cups and line them up.

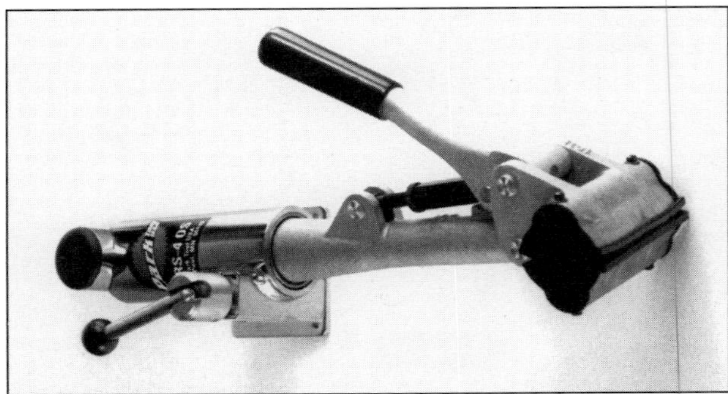

1-16

Fixed bike stand. This one is a sturdy and stable bench-mounted unit. Get a stand with a clamp designed to fit any size frame tube.

1-17

Truing stand with spoke wrenches for truing and building wheels. For added accuracy a dial indicator from X-IT design can be added to one of these Park TS-2 stands.

1-18

For the mechanic who has everything: Park's totally dialed, cast truing stand slides on machined rods and indicates round and true with dial gauges. The stand also checks wheel dish.

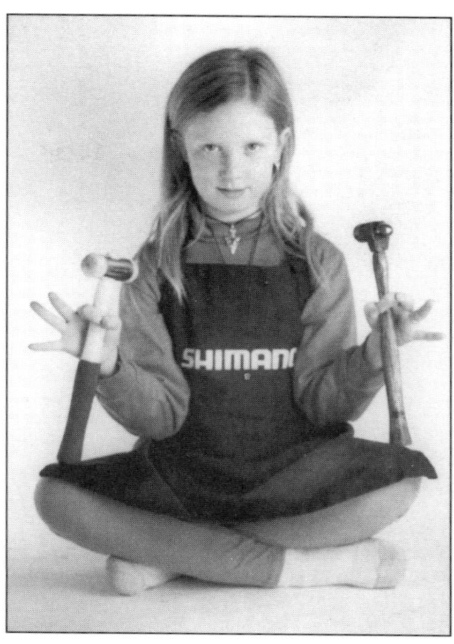

1-19

- Soft hammer. Choose a rubber, plastic, or wooden mallet to prevent damage to parts.
- Medium ball-peen hammer.
- Shop apron (to keep your nice duds nice).
- A calm demeanor.

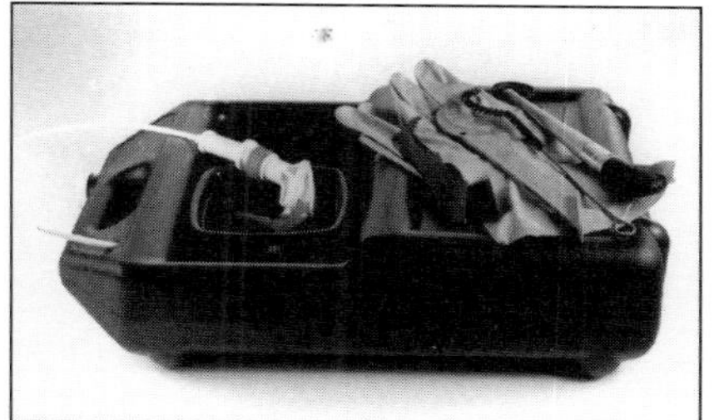

1-20

- Parts washing tank with basket, reservoir, and spray nozzle. Either recycle dirty solvent or use an environmentally safe degreaser and dispose of it responsibly; check with your local environmental safety office.
- Rubberized gloves.
- Cleaning brushes.

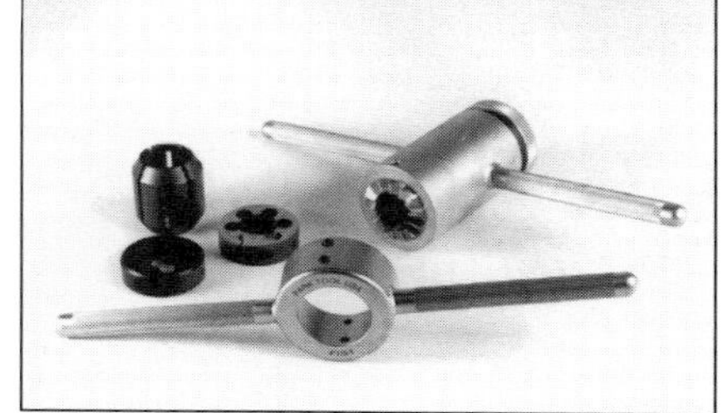

1-21

Fork prep tools

- Fork crown race cutter (faces and sizes crown race seat on rigid forks).
- Fork threading die for chasing damaged fork threads.

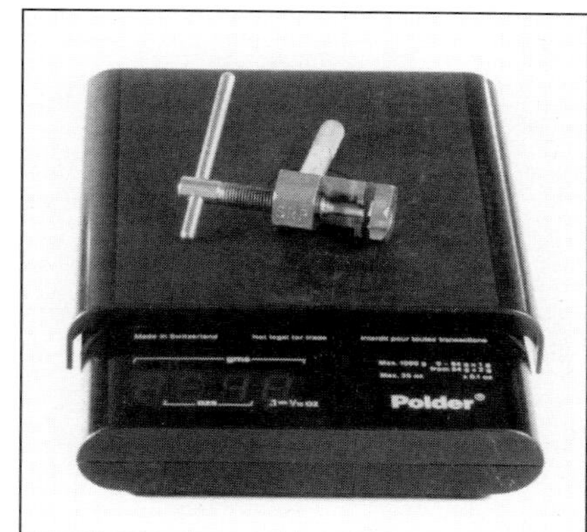

1-22

Gram scale. Gotta weigh those trick light parts (or titanium chain tools).

1.4 SPARE PARTS

Having the parts pictured in photos 1-23 and 1-24 on hand will save you from last-minute runs to the bike shop for common spare parts. Any well-equipped home shop requires several sizes of ball bearings, spare cables, cable housing, and a lifetime supply of those little cable-end caps. You should also have a good supply of spare tires, tubes, chains, as well as some cog sets and chainrings. For suspension forks, be sure to have a few spare elastomers and/or coil springs on hand.

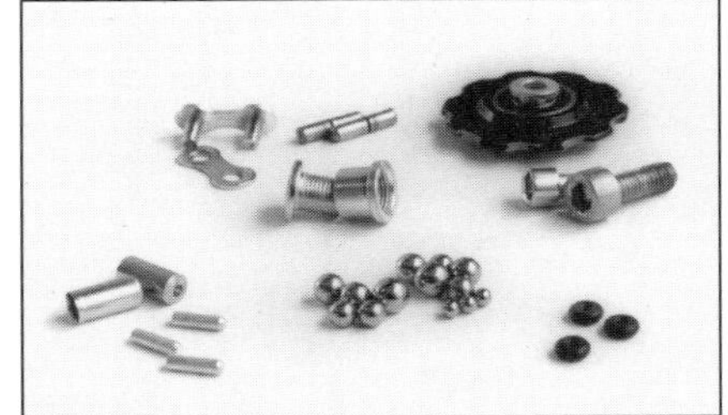

1-23
- Spare Shimano chain subpins.
- Spare master links.
- Spare ball bearings of various sizes.
- Spare cable crimp ends.
- Spare cable doughnuts.
- Spare cable housing caps.
- Spare binder bolts and brake bolts.
- Spare chainring nuts and bolts.
- Spare derailleur jockey wheels.

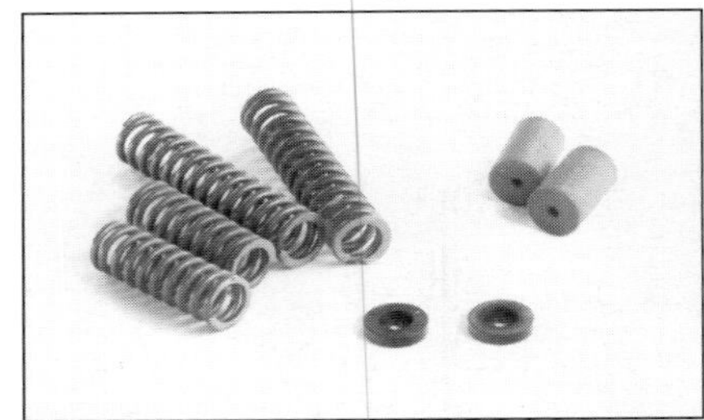

1-24
Spare fork coil springs and/or MCU springs.

1.5 SETTING UP YOUR HOME SHOP

I recommend keeping this area clean and very well organized. Make it comfortable to work in and easy to find the tools you need. Hanging tools on peg board or slat board (photo 1-25) or placing them in bins or trays are all effective ways to maintain an organized work area. Being able to find the tools you need will increase the enjoyment of working on a bike immensely. You will not be tearing up the bed at night dreaming about trying to find the 14-mm socket! Placing small parts in one of those bench-top organizers with several rows of little drawers is another good way to keep chaos from taking over.

1.6 TOOLS TO CARRY WITH YOU WHILE RIDING

1.6A For Most Riding

Keep all of this stuff (photo 1-26) in a bag under your seat or somehow attached to your bike. Some people may prefer a fanny pack or backpack. The operative words here are *light* and *serviceable*. Many of these tools are combined into some of the popular "multi-tools." Make sure you try all tools at home before depending on them on the trail.

1.6B Tools to Carry in a Cross-Country Race

With the vast majority of mechanical problems, taking a small subset of the items in photo 1-26 will save you from having to walk or to cheat by accepting mechanical assistance. You can stuff them in your jersey pocket, your Camelbak pack, or in a small bag under your seat.

Bring:

- Spare tube. Two is not a bad idea, since you sometimes screw one up replacing it under terrible conditions while in a panic.
- Tire pump or CO_2 cartridges with valve fitting.
- Chain tool/multi-tool. Get a lightweight one that really will assemble a chain and has at least a screwdriver and 4-, 5, and 6-mm hex keys on it. If you are using a Taya chain or a Sachs Super Link, bring along a spare master link. If you are using a Shimano, remember to bring along a spare pin or two.
- Optional: tire levers. Not everyone needs these to change a tire. If you do, bring some.

1.6C Extra Stuff to Carry Along on Long or Multi-Day Rides:

These items are, of course, in addition to the items above in 1.6A. You also will need lots of food, water, and extra clothes.

- A lightweight aluminized folding emergency blanket.
- Rain gear.

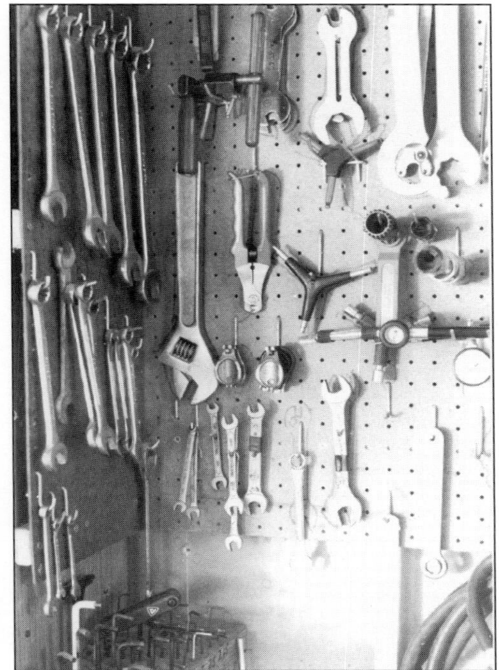

1-25
An organized home shop is necessary for efficient-work.

1-26

- Spare tube. This is a no-brainer. Make sure the valve matches the ones on your bike. If rarely needed, keep it in a plastic bag to prevent deterioration.
- Patch kit. You'll need it after you've used your spare tube. Choose a kit that comes with sandpaper instead of a metal "cheese grater" for roughing up the tube. At least every 18 months, check that the glue has not dried up, whether open or not.
- Tire pump and/or CO_2 cartridge inflator. The bigger the pump the better. Mini-pumps are O.K., but they're slow. Make sure the pump is set up for your type of valves. CO_2 cartridge inflators either accept the thread-in type of cartridge, or they have a cup that holds the unthreaded BB-gun-type cartridge; the cup threads into the valve head. Either way, you get more use out of the cartridge if you get an inflator with a shutoff valve. Carry extra CO_2 cartridges, if you do not carry a pump.
- At least two plastic tire levers, preferably three.
- Chain tool that works.
- Spare chain links from your chain. If you're using a Shimano chain bring at least two "subpin" rivets. Alternative: instead of carrying chain links, bring some "master links" that are opened and closed by hand.
- Small screwdriver for adjusting derailleurs and other parts.
- Compact set of Allen wrenches that includes 2.5-mm, 3-mm, 4-mm, 5-mm, and 6-mm sizes. These can be part of a multi-tool. (Some of you might need to bring along an 8 mm for crank bolts, too.)
- 8-mm and 10-mm open-end or box wrenches.
- Properly sized spoke wrench (can be part of a multi-tool).
- Pedal wrench and headset wrench.
- Small containers of grease and oil.
- Hand cleaner.
- Spare spokes. Innovations in Cycling sells a really cool folding spoke made from Kevlar. It's worth getting one or two for emergency repairs on a long ride.
- Spare brake pads.
- Spare binder bolt.
- Matches, because you never know when you can be stranded overnight. Check them frequently for lighting ability.
- Taillight.
- Identification.
- Cash: for obvious reasons as well as to boot sidewall cuts in tires.
- Credit card. Don't leave home without it.

Note Read Chapter 3 of *Zinn and the Art of Mountain Bike Maintenance* on emergency repairs before embarking on a lengthy trip. If you are planning a bike-centered vacation, you may want to bring along as much of the "bare necessities" tool set as you can fit in your tool kit, as well as some spare parts.

1.7 LIGHTING

Although lights are not normally considered tools, they really are the tools that make riding at night possible. There are many lighting systems available, so how do you choose?

1.7A Lights to Be Seen

If you are riding on automobile roads, at minimum use a bright red taillight so that you can be seen from behind. Flashing LED lights are a good solution for this, as they are small, portable, cheap, run a long time on a set of batteries, and can be seen from a great distance (photos 1-26 and 1-27). Bring lots of 'em. Other reflectors (white on front, red on back, perhaps some in the spokes) are also a good idea. I have bolted a rear reflector to a toe strap so that I can carry it along easily and strap it anywhere I want on the bike when I need it.

A really cheap headlight so you can be seen from the front can save your butt sometimes when a car pulls out of a side street ahead of you or a runner or inline skater comes the wrong direction toward you.

1.7B Lights with Which to See Ahead

If you are not on lit streets or riding under a full moon, you will need a headlight to be able to see enough to ride at a significant speed (photo 1-27). I recommend at least a 6-watt light. Anything smaller than that is only to warn other road users; you won't see squat with it. Any light this big will have a separate battery pack, as a couple of standard batteries inside a light will be insufficient to provide that much power for any length of time. The battery pack will usually either fit in a water-bottle cage or will Velcro onto the frame. Some types also have waist belts or attach to the back of the helmet.

I recommend getting a rechargeable battery pack. A Ni-Cad battery pack will be the most durable (and expensive).

For straight, wide roads, a handlebar-mounted light is sufficient. On single track or when turning into dark side roads, a helmet-mounted light (photo 1-27) is a necessity. The light will turn with your head and automatically point where you are headed. The best setup is a combination of both bar-mounted and helmet-mounted lights. To see on the darkest night and with heavy undergrowth, a 12-watt handlebar light with a 20-watt high beam and a 10- or 12-watt helmet-mounted lamp will be awesome. Do not be offended when people avert their gaze when you look at them with that light on your head.

Burn times longer than two hours are rare with most of these systems, especially after they have been recharged a few times (which shortens their run time). If you need more time than this, plan on bringing along spare batteries in your pack. Also, make sure to let Ni-Cad batteries run completely out before recharging them, or they will develop a "memory" and run a shorter time. Just leave the light on when you get home until it dims out before plugging it into the charger.

1-27
- Flashing taillight that clips to a pocket.
- Flashing taillight that clamps to a seat post.
- Headlight with high and low beam and rechargeable Ni-Cad battery pack.

2

CHAINS

Pardon me . . . I have broken our chain; we are both destined to die of grief.
—*Alexandre Dumas,* The Man in the Iron Mask

Why is there an entire chapter devoted to chains in a performance manual? Well, for one thing, the chain is *the* critical link in your bike's power transfer system. If the chain is not doing its job well, investing time and money in other components will be for naught, as the bike won't work worth beans.

This performance handbook assumes you know how to assemble and disassemble a chain, so what else is there to say about chains? (If you don't know how to open and close a chain, no problem; you can look it up in *Zinn and the Art of Mountain Bike Maintenance* or any other instruction manual.)

The chain is taken for granted by most riders, yet it is essential when it comes to propelling or shifting the bike. If you are saying, "A chain is simple; I don't need to read about chains," just shut up and read. You may learn something that will make an unexpected difference in the performance and durability of your bike. If you do not take proper care of your chain and replace it before it is worn out, your shifting will suck (literally *and* figuratively), you won't go as fast as you could, and you will fry your other drivetrain components. You will have to replace sprockets at much greater expense than a chain or two would have cost.

Many World Cup racers have a new chain put on their bike for every race. They understand that the performance of the chain is so critical to *their* performance that they are not willing to run any risks of a chain breaking, not shifting effectively, or not running freely. While replacing a chain that frequently is excessive for almost everyone else, most riders and their bikes would benefit from focusing more attention on chain performance.

FIVE REQUIREMENTS FOR THE CHAIN

The chain needs to be functioning smoothly in order to transfer your power effectively. If it is not, your most precious commodity, your energy, gets gobbled up by friction. Using leg power to heat up a chain is very unproductive!

1. The distance from roller to roller has to be precise in order to properly engage the sprockets and minimize wear while maximizing power transfer.
2. The chain needs to have minimal side play, so that it will shift easily. A chain that is too laterally flexible will not respond quickly to the shifting pressure of the derailleurs. Too flexy, and it can engage teeth on two separate chainrings at the same time and become a wrapped-up, jammed, and tangled mess.
3. Modern chains have shaped side plates to ease shifting. Photo 2-1 shows chains by Shimano, Sachs, and Taya, illustrating different plate shapes.
4. The chain needs to be clean and well lubricated to move smoothly from cog to cog as well as to minimize wear and reduce friction.
5. Finally, the chain needs to have the proper number of links to be the right length for a particular bike. The chain needs to be short enough so that the derailleurs can control it and keep it from jumping off, and it needs to be long enough that it can reach all of the gear combinations. You don't want to have an accidental shift to the big-big combination rip your rear derailleur apart.

2.1 CHAIN CLEANING

The chain needs to be kept clean, or it will wear out very quickly. Grinding compound, which is used in automotive applications for grinding steel off valves and other parts, is a mixture of grease and sandy grit. This is exactly what you mix together on your chain every time you ride through dirt, mud, and/or sand. The grit sticks to the chain lubricant, mixes with it, and forms an extremely abrasive compound that grinds away at chain parts, cogs, chainrings, and derailleur pulleys.

To avoid ruining parts at an accelerated rate, while simultaneously impairing the performance of your drivetrain, you need to keep the chain clean. While better than nothing, just adding more lube without cleaning simply creates *lots* of grinding compound.

Cleaning is not difficult, nor does it take much time, especially if you do it regularly.

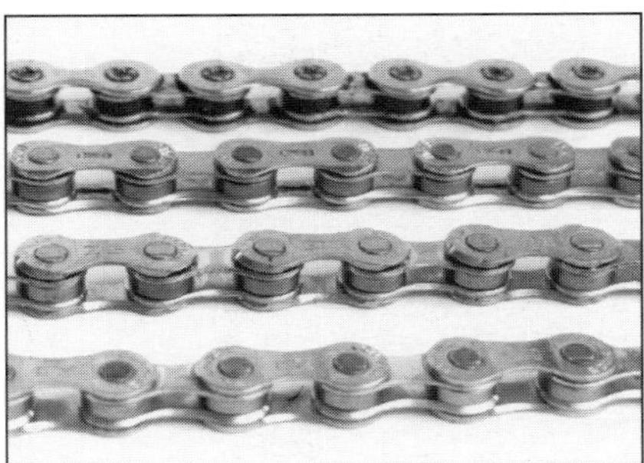

2-1
From bottom: Shimano HG, Shimano IG, Sachs, and Taya chains. To facilitate shifting, Shimano chains have bent outer plates (the IG has an additional bevel at opposite corners, more visible in photo 5-3), Sachs chains have beveled outer plate corners, and Taya chains have thinned center edges on each outer plate.

2-2
If the Shimano TL-CN24 tool will insert fully into the chain, the plate spacing is sufficient for good shifting between front chainrings.

2.1A Do I Need to Remove the Chain to Clean It?

Unless you have a master link, I recommend keeping the chain clean and well lubricated *on the bike,* removing it only rarely (once in its life is a good idea: see "Chain Tip" sidebar below) or not at all, since opening a chain creates a weak link. Any time you push a rivet out and back in (photo 2-4), the hole the rivet passes through in the outer link plate gets slightly enlarged. Since the chain manufacturer mushrooms out the rivet heads to prevent them from pulling through the link plates, pushing that mashed-out rivet head through an outer plate enlarges the hole in the link plate. If you shift a reassembled chain with the front derailleur while pedaling hard, you can flex the chain enough to pop the link plate with the enlarged hole off the rivet. The plate opens, breaking the chain, often tearing your front derailleur to shreds when the opened link hooks the derailleur cage on its next time around.

Whenever you install a non-Shimano chain (or a Shimano chain without using the special connecting pin), you should always check that the connecting link moves freely and that the rivet ends are protruding at least 0.2 mm, in order to prevent the plates from opening. Using the Shimano TL-CN24 tool (photo 2-2), check that the inner link spacing is wide enough not to pinch chainring teeth and cause chain suck. The TL-CN24 has a thin tab 2.38 mm thick. If the tab will not fit down into the inner links (be especially careful about checking the link plates adjacent to the replaced rivet), the chain will likely suck.

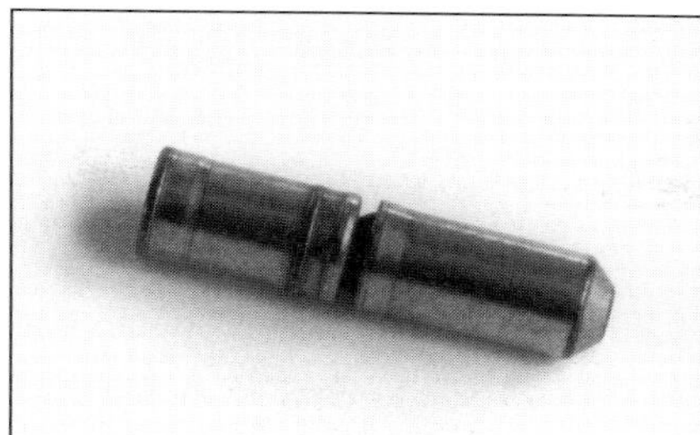

2-3
Shimano's chain assembly subpin has an extra, pointed tip on the leading end with a gradual flare and an enlarged tail end.

2-4
Chain tool at work on a rivet.

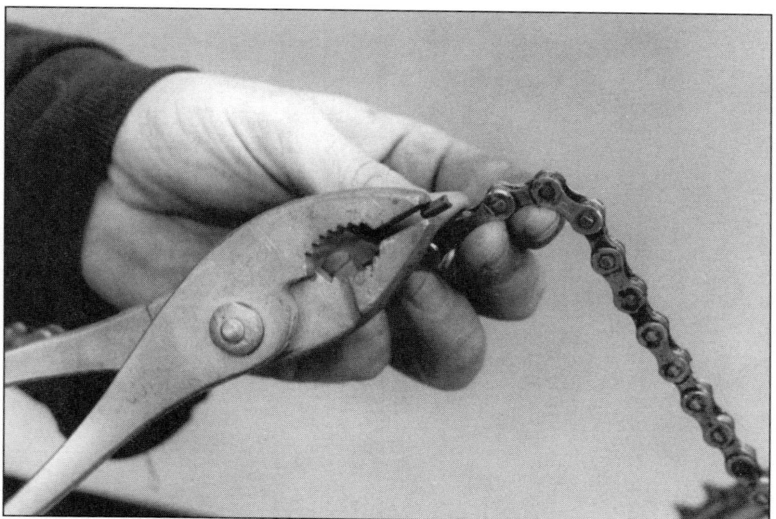

2-5
Breaking off the leading section of a Shimano chain assembly subpin with a pair of pliers.

One condition in which it is unavoidable to open the chain is when installing an XTR differential-plate front derailleur on the bike. As the XTR cage has no tail screw and does not open, you must open the chain to pass it through the cage. As long as you are at it, replace or flip the chain over (see "Chain Tip" sidebar). With other derailleurs, both front and rear, install them by opening the derailleur and not the chain (unless you are putting a new chain on at the same time).

While some chains use disassembly methods that mitigate chain weakening, no disassembly method other than opening a master link actually does no damage to the chain. Shimano chains require completely removing the old pin and substituting a new "subpin" to put the chain back together (photo 2-3). The subpin is mushroomed at its tail end, and it has an extra, pointed tip on the leading end with a gradual flare to gently stretch the link plate hole as the pin pushes through. After pushing it into place (photo 2-4), you break off the leading section with a pair of pliers (photo 2-5). This leaves you with a link that is *almost* as strong as the other links in the chain. Problem is, only one or two subpins come with the chain, so you cannot open the chain frequently without buying more subpins. Sachs SC-M55 mountain chains have a single black link plate at which all disassembly and assembly is to take place.

Rohloff makes a "Revolver" chain tool, which minimizes chain breakage when replacing the original rivet. Instead of simply pushing the rivet back through, the Revolver has a back plate that mashes out the end of the rivet again (photo 2-6). The plate rotates and clicks into position with a rivet end pattern to match your chain.

A master link allows you to open the chain frequently without damage. The new Sachs/SRAM chains for 1998 all come with a Sachs version of Lickton's Super Link (photo 2-7) and KMC has its own version of this link. Taya chains have a different type of master link (photo 2-8).

If you are using a master link, be aware that it wears out along with the chain. *Do not* replace a chain and use the same master link; get a new one!

One very good application for a master link is for on-trail repair. If you break a chain, popping in a master link is a great way to get going again. Carry a couple along in your spare bag.

2.1B Cleaning Methods

There are many ways to clean a chain, and you should choose one that works for you. It needs to be convenient and efficient enough that you will do it frequently and effectively.

Wiping: If you use a lubricant that does not attract dirt, your chain will stay in decent shape if you just wipe it down and lube it after each ride. Turn the crank while grabbing the chain with the rag. Keep lubricating and wiping it until the rag stops getting as black with each revolution. You should wipe the chain down like this after every time you lubricate it, no matter what cleaning method you use, since you do not want lubricant on the outside of the chain to pick up grit. The only lubricant that is doing any good is down inside

2-6
The Rohloff Revolver has a back plate that flares out the end of the rivet upon reassembly. The back plate can be turned to different positions to line up a die to mash out the end of the rivet in a pattern matching the original pattern on the rivet. One position is a cutaway to allow the rivet to pass through when disassembling the chain.

2-7
A Sachs master link. Each half of the link is hooked into one end of the chain. The ends are pushed together so the pins pop through the enlarged part of the hole in the opposite master link half. Pulling the chain locks the narrow end of each hole into the groove in each pin.

2-8
Taya chain master link. Once the pins are pushed through the two ends of the chain, the plate is flexed so that the tops of the pins move closer together. The plate with the two holes is popped over the rivets, once the pins are flexed toward each other enough to line up with the holes. Pulling the chain pops the hole edges into the grooves in the pins.

the chain, between the rivets, rollers, and link plates. Pinch the rag against the rear derailleur jockey wheels to clean them as you turn the crank (photo 2-9).

Car wash: You can clean the chain quite effectively on the bike in a number of ways. One is to blast the grit out with a high-pressure hose at a car wash. But be careful. First, make sure that you only direct the spray vertically: down through the chain and radially inward at jockey wheels and cogs. If you direct it horizontally toward the bike, you will be replacing some very expensive parts soon. The seals on bottom brackets, hubs, and freehub bodies were never intended to take high-pressure water blowing straight in at them.

Dawn dish soap: Many World Cup team mechanics clean chains with Dawn dish soap and a brush. Mix the Dawn with hot water in a bucket and scrub the chain with a brush. Rinse (straight down) with water from a small hose nozzle.

Bio degreaser with air or water pressure: Similarly, you can smear a biodegradable degreaser (Simple Green, for example) all over the chain, scrub it with a brush, and blast the semi-dissolved goop out with compressed air or water from a garden hose with a high-pressure nozzle on it. Make sure you blast from a vertical angle.

Chain cleaner unit: A solvent-filled rotary-brush chain cleaner can clean the chain while it is on the bike (photo 2-10).

2-9
Wiping jockey wheel by pinching a rag against it while turning the crank.

2-10
A solvent-filled rotary-brush chain cleaner cleans the chain while it is on the bike.

Remove and scrub: If you *do* remove the chain, clean it with a brush in a solvent tank, or shake it up in a plastic jar with diesel fuel, or similar combination of solvent and lubricant.

More detail on chain cleaning is in Chapter 4 of *Zinn and the Art of Mountain Bike Maintenance.*

2.2 CHAIN WEAR AND REPLACEMENT

If you want to avoid needlessly spending a lot of money on your bike, replace your chain *before* it is worn out, at least every 50 hours of riding on dirt or 100–200 hours on pavement. The replacement interval is highly dependent on weather and maintenance.

2.2A What's Wrong with Riding with an Old Chain?

Using a worn-out chain causes three major problems:

1. As a chain wears, more space is ground out between chain parts, and the chain lengthens. Using an excessively worn chain accelerates the wear on cogs and chainrings. The chain links are no longer that precise distance apart that they need to be to properly engage the teeth on cogs and chainrings, and the load is not distributed over all the engaged teeth. Instead, *all* of the load is concentrated on a single gear tooth at a time, eventually causing each tooth to become hook-shaped.

Once this goes on for a while, replacing the chain is insufficient, because the cog is shot. A new chain will skip all over the place, since it cannot engage the worn teeth properly. The cogs, chain, and often the chainrings all need to be replaced. Bummer.

Chain elongation can be dangerous, because the chain will skip when you are putting a big load on the pedals, and that could land you on your nose . . . or worse (but you didn't *really* want children anyway, did you?)

2. A worn chain will also have more lateral play from being pushed sideways by the derailleurs so many times and that will cause shifting to deteriorate.

On the rear, a worn chain will not shift as well, because it will simply flex laterally when the upper jockey wheel forces it sideways. Good index shifting requires a chain that is stiff laterally so that a side force immediately pushes it off the cog and onto the next one. A chain with a lot of side play will have to be overshifted past the intended cog and the derailleur will need to be recentered under the cog after the shift.

3. A worn chain can break easily. The side plates will get worn at the rivet holes, particularly at the connector link, and the plate can lift off the rivet.

2.2B Checking for Chain Wear

To avoid the heartbreak of complete drive-train replacement, check your chain for wear frequently. A rule of thumb is to replace it before chain elongation reaches 1 percent, (about 1/2 *an inch* per 100 links or 50 *inches* of chain).

A brand-new chain, even if all of the lubricant got washed off on a wet ride, will run smoothly over the cogs when you pedal it backward with your hand. After it is halfway worn out, it will only feel smooth when clean and well lubricated, but when dry it will feel notchy and lumpy to turn. When totally worn, it will feel rough and bumpy to turn even when it is clean and lubed.

You can see wear in your system, although you cannot tell how much of it is gear-tooth wear and how much is chain wear, by lifting the chain at the top when it is engaged on the large chainring. If you can lift it enough to make one entire tooth visible, your chain, your chainring, or both, are shot.

A good way to check chain wear is with Rohloff's "go/no-go" chain-wear indicator (photo 2-11). You hook one tooth of the tool on a roller and rotate the tool down into the chain. If it goes all the way in, the chain needs to be replaced. The "A" (for "aluminum") side of the tool indicates aluminum cogs, which wear out much faster. The closer tolerance (0.075 mm elongation per link) of the "A" side of the tool is important to use if your small cogs are titanium. The "S" side is to be used on steel cogs and allows 0.1 mm of elongation per link.

Another chain-wear indicator is Park's redesigned "CC-2 Chain Checker." The "0" on the lever is centered in the tool window, and the pin on each end of the tool is inserted between chain rollers. When you can fold the lever enough that "1.0" shows in the window, the chain has 1 percent or more chain wear and is due for replacement (photo 2-12). By periodically noting the number in the window, you can track chain wear over time. Keeping a log is useful, so you know on average how long you can go with a given type of chain (and which ones get you the most miles per dollar). With the CC-2 tool, you can also check initial play in the chain links with new chains. Chains are built with some play to move easily, so you will see at least ".25" show in the window.

A ruler can also serve as a chain-wear indicator. There should be an integral number of links in 12 inches. If measuring link-to-link shows the chain to be more than 1/8 inch longer than that (or 0.125 *inch,* which is about 1 percent of 12 *inches*), replace it.

You can also compare your old chain next to a new chain to see how much it has lengthened. If it is a quarter-link longer, you have waited too long.

If a new chain is still skipping, check the cogs for wear using methods described in Chapter 5, section 5.1D. Also, check the derailleur adjustments (Chapter 3, sections 3.2 and 3.3) and the chain line (Chapter 4, section 4.1).

2.2C Chain Line

The chain line, or angle of the chain relative to the frame, strongly affects

CHAIN TIP

from Wayne Stetina, Shimano North America R&D Manager

If you remove the chain when it is only halfway worn out and flip it over, you will double your chain life. In other words, your chain will be turned inside out. The other side of the rollers will now contact the gears, and the derailleurs will now be laterally bending the chain the opposite direction. Stetina says that Shimano engineers discovered this phenomenon quite by accident.

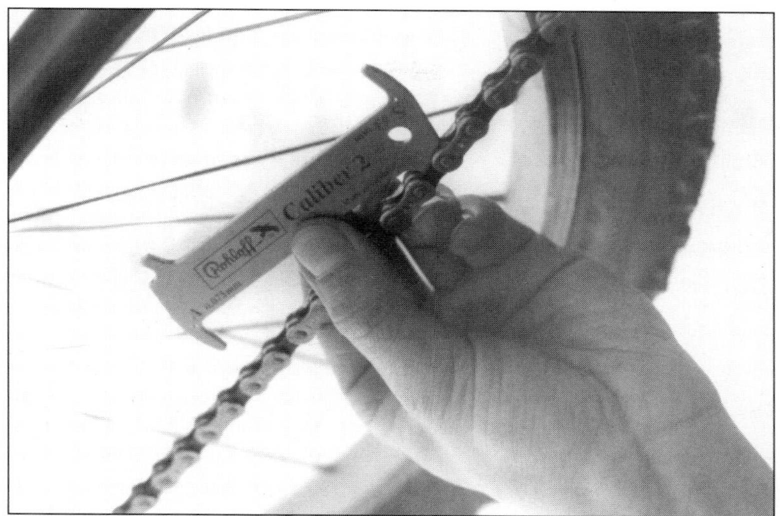

2-11
Rohloff's go/no-go chain-wear indicator. If the curved tip can be inserted completely into the chain so that the tool is flat against the chain, the chain is shot. The "A" edge of the tool (against the chain in the photo) has a tighter tolerance for use with light-weight cogs. The "S" edge of the tool is for a chain running on steel cogs.

2-12
Park "CC-2 Chain Checker." A pin on each end of the chain—one on the right-hand end in the photo, and one on the bottom of the pivoting wedge—goes into the chain. Rotating the wedge increases the distance between the pins. Turn the wedge until it stops, and read the number showing through the diamond-shaped window in the top of the tool. If it says "1.0" or more, replace the chain.

front derailleur performance. If the chainrings are set outward too far from the frame, the chain will tend to fall off to the inside frequently and to rub the front derailleur in low gear. It will also be hard to shift out to the big chainring. If you are having these types of problems with your front derailleur, read the chain-line section in Chapter 4, section 4.1.

Along these lines (pun intended), avoid using cross gears unless you have to. In a race, sometimes you will have to use the big-big combination to get over a hill in a hurry, but it causes excessive wear on the chain (and the cog). When you are riding less frantically, use your front derailleur more and avoid extreme cross gears.

2.2D Chain Suck

While usually blamed on the front derailleur, chain suck is often caused by a worn chain. As I mentioned above, if the chain is so laterally flexible that it can still hang onto teeth on the chainring it is leaving when the shifting initiation point reaches the bottom, the chainring will just keep carrying the chain up and around, tangling it in the frame, front derailleur, and the part of the chain coming into the top of the chainring.

A stiff link can also cause chain suck, as can an extremely dirty or rusty chain.

Chain suck can also be caused by a chain that is too narrow to release easily from the chainring teeth. Shimano offers a go/no-go chain-plate-spacing checking tool called the TL-CN24. The tool is inserted into the chain, as shown in photo 2-2, to see if the link plates are far enough apart to release from Shimano-spec chainring teeth (see Chapter 4, section 4.4C).

2.3 CHAIN LUBRICATION

Rather than squirting lube all over the entire chain, which attracts dirt with the excess and adds no lubricating benefit, drip lube on each chain roller. Pick a lubricant that is appropriate for the conditions. Some work better in wet, muddy conditions, others in dry, dusty conditions, and others in the cold.

As I said before, you should wipe the chain down with a rag after every time you lubricate it, since you do not want lubricant on the outside of the chain picking up grit. The only lubricant that is doing any good is down inside the chain, between the rivets, rollers, and link plates.

Lubrication frequency depends on the type of riding you do. If you ride through puddles and creek crossings, you need to lube the chain every time you ride. Just be aware that if you keep putting a thick oil or automotive oil on every time, the grit mixed with it will create grinding compound and will wear out your chain rapidly. On the other hand, almost any lube is better than none.

I recommend leaving the factory lubricant on a new chain for as long as you can. The lubricant is down deep in the chain exactly where it needs to be. You can never assemble the chain with grease again, so avoid cleaning a new chain with solvent before installation.

2.3A Chain Waxes

Your chain can stay really clean if you use one of the new chain-wax products on the market. White Lightning is the best known, but Schwinn, Pedro's, Wrench Force, Cannondale, and others also offer them. Usually, there is a solvent mixed with the wax that cleans up some of the old guck on the chain and then evaporates, leaving just the wax.

Unfortunately, unless you live in a dry, sandy area, I do not recommend any of the waxes, because they do not stay on as well as oil. Most waxes tend to dry hard and flake off, which is why the chain stays so nice and clean. One ride in the rain can wash the wax off, and your chain will start squeaking and rusting. If you *do* use one of these products, use it a lot, because it will not stay on long. Check your chain frequently for rust and listen for squeaks.

If, however, you ride in sand deep enough that it actually contacts the chain, there is *nothing* better than chain wax to avoid picking up those abrasive chunks.

2.3B Dry, Hard-Packed Conditions

Under dry, hard-packed conditions, almost any good lubricant will do. There is no water to wash it off, and there is little dirt to gunk it up.

2.3C Dry, Dusty Conditions

Under dry, dusty conditions, you need a lubricant that does not attract dirt. That fine dust will wear your chain out in a flash if it gets into the rollers and small spaces. Chain wax (White Lightning, Pedro's Ice, Schwinn Factory Wax, Wrench Force Dry Lube, etc.) will work well. Apply it daily.

2.3D Muddy, Wet Conditions

In wet conditions, especially on long rides, water mixed with grit is constantly washing off the chain lube. You need something heavy-bodied and tenacious that fights off water and stays on.

In really nasty, wet races, teams often apply grease to the chains rather than oil. Grease attracts dirt like crazy, but it is not a concern in wet conditions, because the chain immediately gets covered with mud and grit no matter what you have on it. The grease will stay on better, whereas lighter lubes are likely to wash off before half of the race is over.

2.3E Rehabilitating a Squeaking Chain

A chain that still squeaks after lubrication is dry or rusted deep down inside places where lube just can't penetrate. This usually happens after cleaning very thoroughly with a strong solvent, like kerosene or acetone. It can also happen after riding in the rain, particularly with a chain wax/solvent on the chain. Try soaking the chain in diesel fuel or another solvent/lube combo. Lubricate it again after drip-drying. If it *still* squeaks, throw it away (into the scrap metal recycling bin). Life is too short for riding with that squeak.

2.3F Optimal Chain Length

How long should your chain be?

The answer to this question depends on the riding conditions. The requirements of cross-country, hill-climb, downhill, and dual slalom riding are different, and ideal chain length varies.

1. For cross-country racing and riding, follow the recommendations of the derailleur manufacturer. This usually means making sure that the chain can reach the big-big combination (i.e., from the largest chainring to the largest cog). While riding in this cross gear is not recommended and is very hard on the chain, it is nice for your derailleur *not* to be torn apart if you do shift into this gear. Check that your bike can do this. To find this length when installing a new chain, first circumvent the derailleurs and wrap the chain only over the large chainring and the large cog and bring the ends together. Note the spot where the ends of the chain meet and remove the excess chain beyond a single link of overlap (photo 2-13). (One chain link is an inner/outer pair—photo 2-14.)

On Ritchey 2x9, this method may make the chain slightly too long to be retained properly. You may need to run a shorter chain and avoid using the big-big combination.

2-14
One chain link includes both an inner section and an outer section.

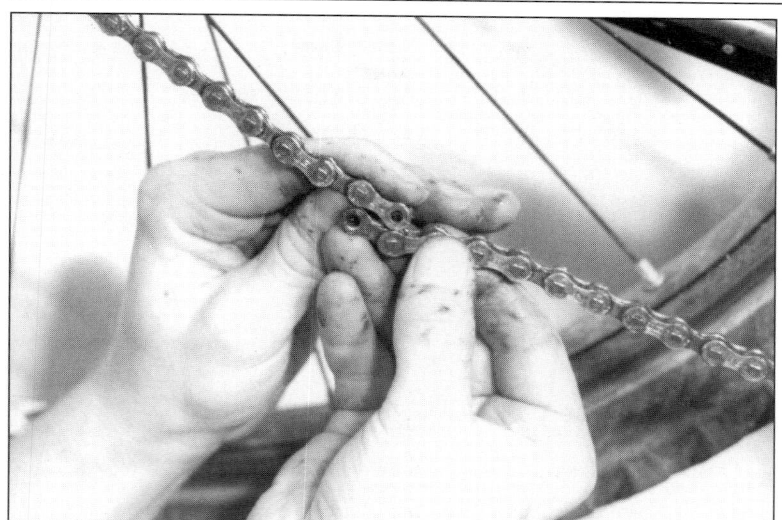

2-13
Determining chain length: with the chain on the big-big combination, have one link of overlap.

2-15
1997 winner of the World Cup South Africa downhill Elke Brutsaert uses top and bottom chain retainers to keep her chain on.

If you have rear suspension, deflate or disconnect the shock and find the position in which the distance from the bottom bracket to the rear hub is greatest and only then determine the proper chain length in this position. This way, the operation of the suspension will not rip apart your drivetrain.

2. For most hill climbs, if you are willing to take the time to do it, you can reduce chain friction somewhat by adding a couple of links to the chain. The derailleur jockey wheels will not be forced against the chain as hard, and the cranks will turn more easily. (You can also reduce derailleur knuckle-pivot spring tension to accomplish the same thing—see Chapter 3, sections 3.2G and 3.2H.) Chain retention will be compromised, so experiment with it long before trying it on the night before an important race!

3. For downhill and dual slalom, you need to keep the chain as short as possible in order lessen the chance that it will jump off when things get rough. The bike will generally be set up with a single chainring with retention rollers and chain guards. Photo 2-15 shows how Elke Brutsaert, winner of the 1998 World Cup downhill in South Africa, keeps her chain on.

You want the minimum length of chain you can get away with and still reach all of the rear cogs. With some full-suspension bikes, this may require deflating the rear shock and operating the suspension through its full range while checking the chain length, as the distance from bottom bracket to rear hub may vary when you hit bumps. An extra rear derailleur pull-back spring and chainstay and chainring rollers will improve chain retention.

3

DERAILLEURS AND SHIFTERS

Stand fast, good Fate, to his hanging; make the rope of his destiny our cable, for our own doth little advantage.
—William Shakespeare, *The Tempest*

This chapter is devoted to the parts that move your chain from gear to gear: the shifters, shift cables, and front and rear derailleurs (photo 3-1). The gears themselves as well as the rear cogs and front chainrings are dealt with separately in Chapters 4 and 5.

3.1 THE DERAILLEUR/SHIFTER CONNECTION (E.G., CABLES)

Like they do the chain, people generally neglect their cables. They are low-tech items, but I am willing to bet that 90 percent of shifting problems are caused by low-tech items like sticky cables, worn or dry chains, worn cogs, and worn chainrings—not by bad derailleurs! You can have the best shifters and derailleurs in the world, but if the cables connecting them are sticky, your shifting will stink. Probably the most important thing you can do to improve your shifting system

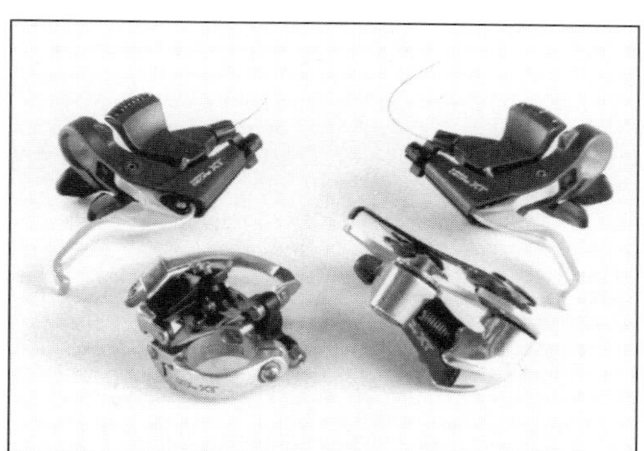

3-1
Shimano XT shifters, shift cables, and derailleurs.

is to improve the cables and housings and sealing systems for it. The good news, of course, is that this is the lowest-priced improvement you can make to your bike, and it's likely to be the most noticeable.

Sticky cables prevent the derailleurs from behaving consistently. Good rear shifting, for instance, requires that the upper jockey wheel of the rear derailleur lines up directly under the cog. If the cable is sticky, the derailleur will not move all the way under the cog, because the spring in the derailleur cannot overcome the cable friction. The derailleur will line up short of center on one side or another, depending on which side of the cog it is coming from. Consistent shifting requires very low-friction cable movement so the derailleur will always line up directly under the cog, regardless of which side the shift is coming from.

Shimano builds side play ("Centeron," in Shimano-ese) into the upper jockey wheels of its rear derailleur to allow for some deterioration in cable performance. The floating pulley provides a little adjustment range on derailleur position (dictated by cable tension), so that there is not just one precise "sweet spot" to which it must be adjusted. It also allows for a misaligned derailleur hanger. If there were not the lateral free movement of the top pulley, the derailleur would be noisier with sticky cables. The derailleur would have to move the full distance to center the upper jockey wheel exactly under the cog, and sticky cables would not allow that. The floating top pulley can drift sideways to line itself under the cog without the derailleur moving all the way there.

3.1A Cable Service

If your cables and housings are not kinked, frayed, or split, the best place to start is with cleaning and lubrication, which is covered in detail in Chapter 5 of *Zinn and the Art of Mountain Bike Maintenance.* In brief, you pull the cable housing sections out of the cable stops, wipe the cable down and smear it with a lubricant wherever it was inside the housing (photo 3-2). Re-insert the cable housing sections into the cable stops. Use a lubricant that will not get dry or gummy inside the housing. A good lube for this is the molybdenum disulfide grease that comes with some shifters from Shimano; many chain lubes work well, too.

You may need to check the way the cable runs through the cable guides under the bottom bracket if your bike has a bottom-pull system. Some of these plastic cable guides are very cheap and create quite a bit of friction as soon as the top shiny surface has been worn off, even when well lubricated. The cable can also cut a V-shaped groove into the guide, which restricts its movement. You can lube it all you want, but the cable still will not slide well, and your shifting performance will be poor. Keep these guides clean and lubricated (photo 3-3), and replace them whenever they look worn.

3.1B Cable and Cable Housing Replacement

You will be amazed at how much improvement you get in your shifting by installing new cables and housings. Again, installation is covered in detail in Chapter 5 of *Zinn and the Art of Mountain Bike Maintenance.*

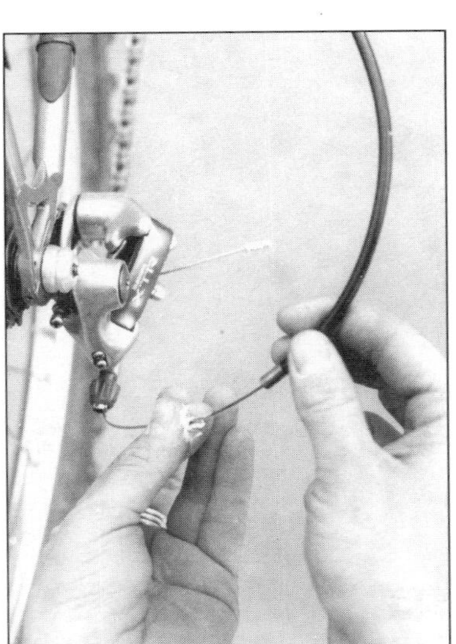

3-2
Smear the cable with lubricant wherever it runs inside housing.

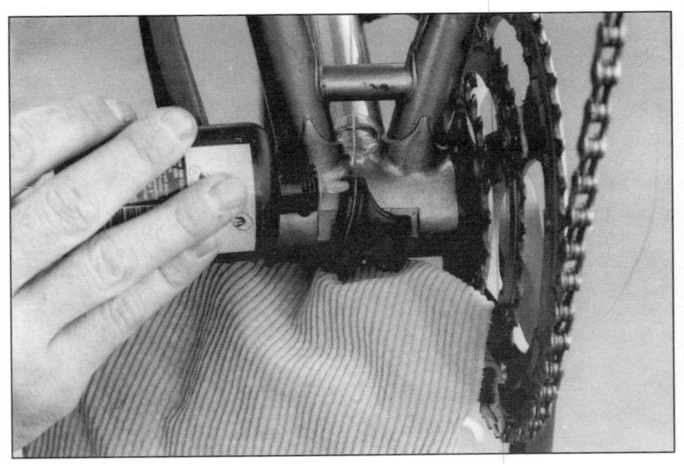

3-3
Keep the cable guides under the bottom bracket clean and lubricated.

Reducing friction is a combination of good cable routing and low-friction cables and housings. Cut compressionless housings with cutters designed for that purpose (photo 1-4) to avoid fraying and splitting (and friction). Avoid sharp bends, places where the housing's movement is restricted by pressing against the frame, and housing loops that are too short (your derailleurs will shift when you turn the bars sharply, or the rear derailleur cannot swing freely around its mounting bolt) or too long (there is more cable to stretch and housing to compress, the cable bends are tighter, and there is more cable/housing contact length to cause friction).

3.1C Low-Friction Cables

All cables and housings are not created equally. A low-friction system is made up of stiff, noncompressible housings with low-friction liners and smooth cables.

The housing must be coaxial derailleur cable housing, rather than the spiral-wound type (e.g., brake cable housing), which can compress lengthwise. A Teflon housing liner is a must.

Cables are smoother if they are "die-drawn," a process in which the cable is pulled through a small hole in a hardened "die" to flatten the outer cable strands. The smoother surface is obvious to the eye as well as to your fingers.

Coated cables will move more freely yet. Shimano makes a plastic-coated cable, and the benchmark for low-friction cable is Gore-Tex RideOn cable and housing. The Shimano cables are easy to install, but the Gore-Tex are not. The Gore-Tex coating must be stripped from both ends, wherever it runs inside the shifter and where it is clamped at the derailleur cable-fixing bolt. The cable slides inside of a continuous plastic tube that runs the full length from the shifter to an inch from the derailleur cable-fixing bolt. A little rubber accordion-shaped seal called a "grub" is required to cover the single exposed end of the plastic tube to keep it dry and clean. Make sure you follow the instructions that come with the cables, or you will have some very expensive cables that will not move because of wadded-up Gore-Tex inside the housing.

3.1D Cable Seals

If you installed Gore-Tex or other low-friction cables properly, you will probably notice a big improvement in shifting performance. Unfortunately, this performance improvement will be fleeting as dirt and grime get into the housings. A method of sealing the ends of the cable housings is required for the performance enhancement to endure.

As I mentioned above, Gore-Tex accomplishes this by using a plastic tube over the cable from end to end and covering its one exposed opening with a rubber seal. It does not matter if dirt gets inside any of the housing segments, since the cable is actually sliding inside of the continuous tube. Eventually, though, the plastic tube breaks and separates at the ends of some of the housing segments, and performance deteriorates, eventually requiring replacement of the whole cable system.

Shimano's high-end coated cables come with little rubber seals for every housing end (photo 3-4). These are quite effective and well worth using, so don't throw them out with the rest of the cable packaging.

3-4
Shimano's little rubber derailleur cable seals.

"Gritlock" cable seals made by Vivo (photo 3-5) cost a bit, being a combination of machined aluminum and accordion-shaped rubber tubing. They will protect your investment in cables and housings. Replacing cables monthly if you ride a lot in mud can add up.

SRAM's "Bassworm" is a stretchable cable seal made out of surgical tubing (photo 3-6). It protects the final housing segment at the rear derailleur from contamination as well as giving the cable an additional return spring to help the rear derailleur get to the smallest cog. You slide the cable through the tube, secure the hook-shaped cable housing stop into the frame's cable stop with a tiny screw, stretch the tube, and secure its top end by tightening a set screw onto the cable.

3.1E Eliminating the Rear Derailleur Housing Loop

Shifting performance can be improved by replacing the last loop of cable housing at the rear derailleur with a roller. A roller reduces drag by reducing sliding friction with rolling friction, and it is not sensitive to the entry of dirt. In the aftermarket, Avid's Rollamajig (photo 3-7) and other similar designs are available. In original equipment, the Sachs Di.R.T. and Shimano XTR Rapid-Rise rear derailleurs (photo 3-8, left) both have eliminated the cable loop and its potential for becoming clogged with dirt. But for 1999, Shimano once again eliminated the roller in favor of an ultra-low-friction housing and cable. As of press time, however, I have not yet had the chance to test the new design.

3-5 Vivo's "Gritlock" cable seal.

3-6 SRAM's "Bassworm" stretchable surgical tubing cable seal doubles as a cable return spring.

3-7 Avid's Rollamajig replaces the cable loop on a rear derailleur.

3-8 Standard Shimano XTR (right) and Shimano XTR Rapid-Rise (left) rear derailleurs. The Rapid-Rise has no rear cable loop and has a reversed parallelogram spring direction. Notice how the relaxed standard derailleur is compressed to the small-cog configuration, while the relaxed Rapid-Rise is extended to the large-cog configuration.

3.1F Hydraulic Shifting

A few years ago, S.A.F.E. pioneered hydraulic shifting with Hydrashift, which replaced the rear derailleur cable run with hydraulic tubing. A master cylinder at the shifter and a slave cylinder at the rear derailleur are attached to short cable segments connected conventionally to the shifter and rear derailleur.

Unless a hydraulic line is broken, there is no possibility for water or dirt to work its way into the derailleur control system. Extra tubing length, as on a tandem, adds little extra resistance, unlike with a cable system.

Disadvantages I experienced with this system were that it had more overall resistance than coated cables and required a larger derailleur spring to get quick movement to the smallest cog. It also performed sluggishly in cold weather, since the hydraulic fluid increased in viscosity as the temperature dropped.

The S.A.F.E. system seems to no longer be available, but I would expect more attempts at hydraulic shifting in the future.

3.1G Air Shifting

Shimano, with its "Air Lines," is pioneering compressed-air-powered shifting. The system is incredibly fast but is only available to a few pros in its second season of field testing. A flick of a toggle lever (photo 3-9) lets a puff of compressed air shoot the derailleur from cog to cog. Currently, it is only used on bikes with a single front chainring (like downhill and dual slalum bikes), since the left and right hand both operate the rear derailleur only: One controls downshift, while the other controls upshift.

3.2 THE REAR DERAILLEUR

The rear derailleur is certainly one of the most important parts on a bike for proper performance and riding enjoyment. A good rear derailleur performs dependably even when your shifting technique is poor and hurried. The goal here is shifting that is absolutely flawless, even under hard efforts. If you get it working this way, that sweet feeling of confidence knowing that you can always get the gear you need will be yours on even the trickiest climbs or during full-out efforts. Remember that, even though you *can* shift a good rear derailleur under full power (assuming it is well adjusted), there is much less chance for missing a shift, and your chain, cogs, and derailleur will last longer if you back off your pedaling power every time you shift.

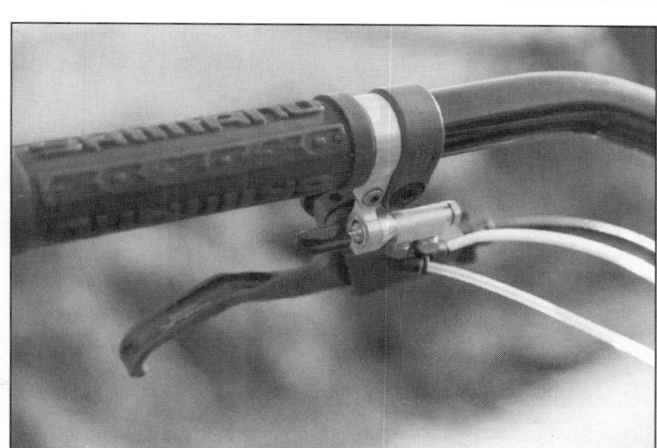

3-9 Shimano Air Lines air toggle shift lever.

This section begins with ensuring that the derailleur is aligned properly, followed by lateral movement adjustments, spring tension adjustments, and upgrading.

3.2A Rear Derailleur Alignment

The performance of the rear derailleur is dependent on the proper alignment relative to the other parts of the drive train. The best derailleur in the world will not work well if it is mounted on a bent derailleur hanger.

The derailleur hanger on the dropout can be checked for alignment with a tool that aligns it relative to the rear wheel. This is shown in Chapter 13. The tool threads into the derailleur hanger and the arm is swung around next to the rear wheel. You check the distance from the tool arm to the rim at various points (photo 13-6). If the spacing from the rim to the tool arm varies around the rim, you bend the hanger, using the tool arm as a lever. I recommend pulling outward on the tool at the point where it is closest to the rim (photo 13-7). Be careful not to overdo it.

If the hanger is really bent, it may need to be replaced. Some frames have replaceable bolt-on derailleur hangers, making replacement a snap. Others require a framebuilder to weld or braze another dropout on. If the threads are screwed up in the hanger, you can try retapping the hanger with a 10 mm x 1 tap. If the threads are totally shot, Wheels Manufacturing offers a "dropout saver," a nut insert you slip into the hanger from the back side after drilling the hole out big enough to accept it.

3.2B Rear Derailleur Cage Straightening

Sometimes the derailleur hanger is not the reason for misalignment of your rear derailleur. The jockey cage may be bent. If it is only mildly bent, sometimes you can straighten it by hand, eyeballing from behind when in a big gear and from above when in a small gear. Make sure you hold the derailleur body with your hand so that it and the derailleur hanger do not get bent in the process. If this does not fix the alignment problems, replace the derailleur and recheck the hanger alignment.

3.2C Fine-Tuning Adjustment of Rear Derailleur

The entire adjustment of derailleurs is discussed in Chapter 5 of *Zinn and the Art of Mountain Bike Maintenance*. Sections 3.2D to 3.2G below address the finer points to go from good shifting to great shifting.

Before starting, make sure the chain is in good condition and well lubricated.

3.2D Cable Tension

Cable tension determines whether the derailleur moves to the proper gear with each click. After making sure the high-gear limit screw allows the derailleur to move out to the smallest cog, tune the cable tension first at the smallest cog. Make these adjustments with the chain on the big chainring as well on the middle one.

Keep clicking the shifter until it will not let any more cable out. The chain should now be on the smallest cog. Shift back and forth one click. If the derailleur is sluggish or overshifts in either direction, the cable tension is off. For faster inward shifts and to prevent overshifting to the outside, increase the tension by backing out (counterclockwise) either the barrel adjuster on the derailleur, or the barrel adjuster on the shifter. To speed shifts to the smallest cog and to prevent jumping past the second cog on inward shifts, decrease the cable tension by tightening (clockwise) the barrel adjuster. Fine-tune the cable tension similarly on other cog pairs.

Note **The chain should move in to center under the cog regardless of the side it is moving in from. If it does not, or you get inexplicable "ghost shifting," first look at the cables and then at the bottom bracket guides for cable drag. Only if these items are all fine should you check whether the shifter is worn out.**

If shifting both directions is slow, the derailleur may be too far from the cogs and/or the chain is too worn (Chapter 2, section 2.2). To get the derailleur closer to the cogs, you need to adjust the tension in the p- and b-pivots (sections 3.2G and 3.2H).

If relieving cable tension still does not let the chain drop quickly to the smallest cog, you need to do more work. First, back out the high-gear limit screw a bit (section 3.2F) to make sure it is not stopping the derailleur's outward movement. Secondly, replace or lube your cables for smoother operation. If it still won't drop, yet your derailleur alignment is good (3.2A and 3.2B above), you need more derailleur return spring tension (3.2E) and/or a derailleur with tighter pivots.

On a Shimano Rapid-Rise reverse-spring rear derailleur (photo 3-8), cable tension is adjusted the opposite of traditional derailleurs. Unlike traditional derailleurs, the return spring moves the derailleur inward to larger cogs, instead of outward to smaller cogs. If the derailleur moves in to the second cog slowly, *decrease* the cable tension. If it comes out to the smallest cog slowly or not at all, increase the cable tension.

3.2E Increasing Derailleur Parallelogram Spring Tension

I am talking here about the spring in between the parallelogram plates of the rear derailleur, not about the spring in either pivot knuckle. This spring moves the derailleur laterally. On most derailleurs, it moves the derailleur toward smaller cogs.

More spring tension can be had by: (a) putting a washer on the mounting bolt between the derailleur hanger and the derailleur to move it farther outward, (b) putting a Grip Shift "Bass-worm" on the rear derailleur cable to pull the cable down more (see section 3.1D above), (c) installing a bigger return spring in the rear derailleur, and finally, if all else fails, (d) replacing the rear derailleur. Try these individually or in combination to solve shifting problems. Some derailleurs have an adjustment cam on the return spring attachment. Turn the cam screw to tighten the spring.

Replacing the return spring is often required for good derailleur action with Grip Shift combined with a Shimano rear derailleur. The Shimano rear derailleur has a weak return spring tuned to work with Rapidfire shifters. You can get an aftermarket return spring to upgrade a Shimano rear derailleur. Be aware that changing this spring can be a real bear. Getting the end to pop over the second pin takes lots of time and patience.

Rear derailleur without lateral return spring: White Industries' Linear Pull rear derailleur has no return spring (photo 3-10). The cable forms a continuous loop. The shifter is always pulling the derailleur along the two tracks, no matter which direction you shift.

Note **If the shifter barrel adjuster does not hold its adjustment, shifting will steadily get worse as you ride. If you have this problem, there are a couple of things you can do, besides getting a new shifter. One is to put Finish Line "Ti-Prep" on the threads to create a bit more friction; I have found this to be a temporary fix only. Scoring across some of the threads with a screwdriver may increase friction enough. A foolproof solution, though it eliminates adjustment while riding the bike, is to keep the shifter barrel adjuster turned all of the way in and make all cable tension adjustments with the barrel adjuster on the rear derailleur (Rapid-Rise has no barrel adjuster at the derailleur, though; the shifter barrel adjuster is a must).**

3.2F Limit Screw Adjustments

With a traditional indexed derailleur with the cable tension set properly, you need not worry about the high-gear limit screw; the cable stops the derailleur from over-shifting the smallest cog. On the other hand, the low-gear limit screw is imperative to protect your rear wheel and derailleur by preventing shifting into the spokes. It is never pleasant to see your expensive equipment turned into shredded metal. However,

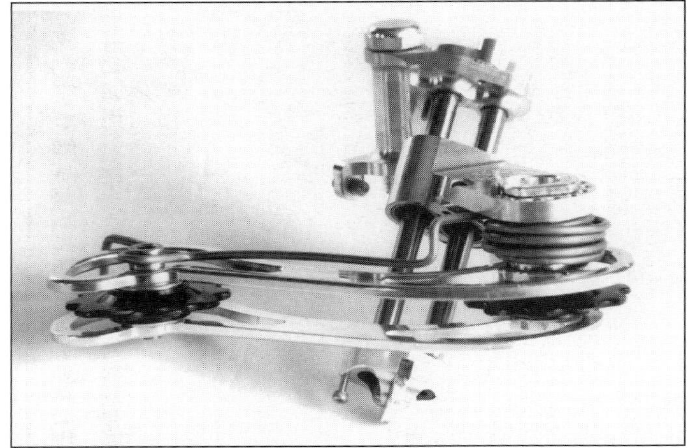

3-10
White Industries. Linear Pull rear derailleur.

3-11
Adjusting the B screw so that the upper jockey wheel is close to the cog.

with Shimano Rapid-Rise reverse-spring derailleurs, the high-gear limit screw must also be set to prevent the chain from going into the dropout, since the thumb lever can keep pulling the derailleur outward until it is stopped by the screw.

The low-gear screw is sometimes labeled "L," and is usually the bottom screw. You can check which one it is by shifting to the largest cog, maintaining pressure on the shifter, and turning the screw. If the derailleur moves, you have found the low-gear screw.

1. Shift the chain to the inner chainring on the front. Gently shift the rear derailleur to the largest cog.
2. If the derailleur touches the spokes or pushes the chain over the largest cog, tighten the low-gear-limit screw until it does not.
3. If the derailleur cannot bring the chain onto the largest cog, loosen the screw a quarter turn and try again.

3.2G "B" Screw (Upper Knuckle Pivot Spring Tension) Adjustment

The small "B" screw contacts against the tab on the underside of the derailleur hanger on the right rear dropout. It increases or decreases the tension in the upper knuckle pivot spring. This is one of the two adjustments (most people think it is the *only* one!) affecting the spacing between the upper jockey wheel and the underside of the cogs (a.k.a.: "chain gap"). Keeping the chain gap to a minimum makes shifting more precise. You want the upper jockey wheel as close as you can get it to the cog so that any lateral movement of it puts a sharper lateral bend on the chain and forces a quick shift.

Adjust the B screw (photo 3-11) so that the upper jockey wheel is close to the cog, but not pinching the chain against the cog. Check it in the lowest gear and in the highest gear. You'll know that you've moved it in too closely when it starts making noise.

On SRAM ESP derailleurs, set the B screw when the chain is on the middle chainring and largest cog. Turn the screw so that the length of chain across the chain gap is 1 1/2 links (photo 3-12) (one link is a complete male-female segment pair, so 1 1/2 links is three chain segments).

Sachs specifies two different chain gap measuring techniques with its Di.R.T. rear derailleur, depending on whether the largest cog is a 32-tooth or if it is 28 teeth or fewer. With a 32, put the chain on the 32, and make sure that the vertical chain gap from the bottom of the cog to the top of the jockey pulley is 10 to 12 mm, or 1 1/2 to 2 chain links when viewed from the side (photo 3-13). If the cogset has a largest cog of 28 or less, set the chain on the 11 or 12, and make sure that the vertical chain gap from the bottom of the cog to the top of the jockey pulley is 10 to 12 mm, or 1 1/2 to 2 chain links.

When the B screw is not enough: Sometimes, you cannot get the chain gap very small using only the B screw. This is particularly a problem with a closely spaced cogset or with a long derailleur hanger on the frame's dropout. In either case, the derailleur starts well below the cogs, so the jockey wheel cannot get close without considerable reconfiguring of the derailleur. See section 3.2F to correct this problem.

Note on shifting trouble: If, despite your best efforts, you cannot get the rear derailleur to shift well or it makes noise in even mild cross gears, go on to the discussion on chain line in Chapter 4, Section 4.1.

3-12
Set the B screw on a SRAM ESP rear derailleur with the chain on the middle ring/large cog combination. There should be 1 1/2 chain links bridging gap between the top of the jockey wheel and the bottom of the cog.

3-13
The proper chain gap on a Sachs Di.R.T. Plasma derailleur is 1 1/2 links when set on a big cog (this is a 33-tooth Ritchey cog).

3.2H Lower Knuckle Pivot Spring Tension ("P" Spring)

The lower pivot spring also affects the chain gap. It twists the derailleur forward and puts pressure on the chain through the jockey wheels. You want to dial in the balance between the upper and lower pivot springs. You can bring the upper jockey wheel 1/4 to 3/8 inch closer to the cogs and increase chain retention by increasing the lower knuckle pivot spring tension.

On recent Shimano XT, LX, and STX rear derailleurs, there is a screw on the side of the lower pivot that makes it possible to disassemble the pivot without even removing the derailleur from the bike. The set screw engages a groove in the pivot shaft to keep it from pulling apart. Remove the screw with a 2-mm hex key (photo 3-14), and pull the jockey cage away from the spring. Put the spring in the other spring hole to increase its tension (photo 3-15), push the pivot assembly back together, and replace the set screw. Shimano derailleurs always come with the spring in the low-tension hole.

While the set screw assembly makes it possible to perform this change with the chain and cable hooked up on the bike, I don't recommend it. You will have to unscrew the mounting bolt anyway, and the derailleur will get so twisted around that it will be hard to tell which

3-14
Removing the P knuckle set screw with a 2-mm hex key.

3-15
Increasing the P spring tension by putting the spring end in the other hole.

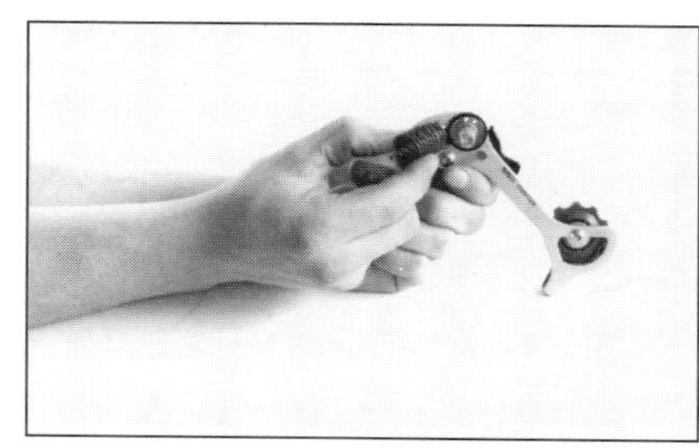

way is up with the cable and chain connected. You can end up turning the jockey cage the wrong direction and deforming the spring so it will not fit back in the knuckle. Just remove the derailleur before you open the P knuckle.

Increasing P spring tension on XTR, older model, and road Shimano derailleurs is more complicated because there is no set screw on the lower knuckle housing. You need to remove the derailleur from the bike and remove the stopper screw that stops the jockey cage from twisting all of the way around (photo 3-16). Remove the upper jockey wheel and unscrew the pivot bolt from the back side with a 5-mm hex key (photo 3-17). Pull the derailleur cage off the end of the spring and move the end of the spring into the other spring hole to twist the spring further when reassembled (photo 3-18). Wind the jockey wheel cage back around, screw it all back together with the pivot bolt, and replace the stopper screw.

REAR DERAILLEUR TIP

from Wayne Stetina, Shimano North America R&D Manager

Increasing the P spring tension is always a good idea for better chain retention and closer cog tracking. The downside is that there will be more resistance in the drivetrain; spin the crank backwards, and you will see. The higher spring tension forces the jockey wheels against the cogs more. With higher P spring tension, though, you will lose your chain less, which can cost you a lot more time than a little extra resistance in the drivetrain.

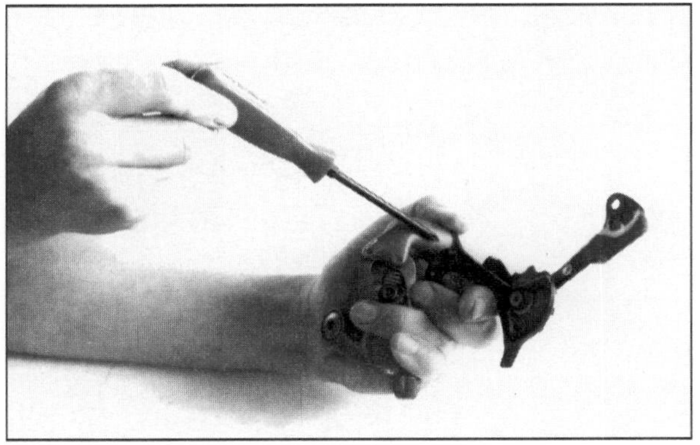

3-16 Removing the thin stopper bolt that stops the jockey cage from twisting around on an XTR derailleur.

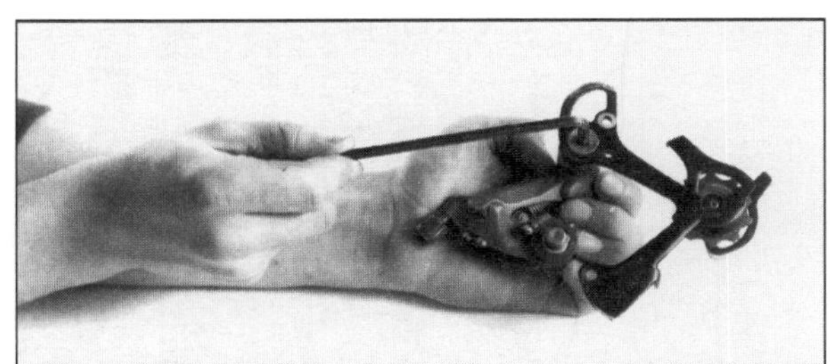

3-17 Unscrewing the pivot bolt to pull the derailleur cage off the P spring.

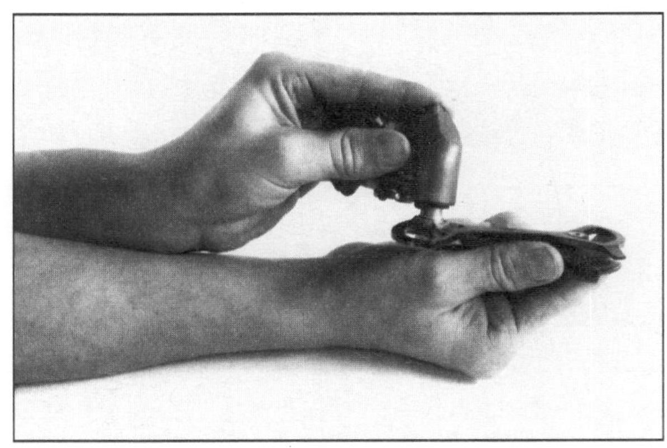

3-18 Increasing the P spring tension on an XTR derailleur by putting the spring end in the other hole.

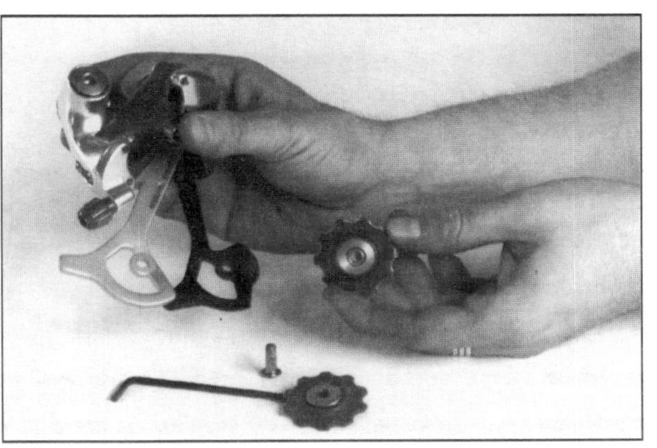

3-19 Replacing a plastic bushing-core jockey wheel with an aluminum sealed-bearing jockey wheel.

3.2I Jockey Wheels

Jockey wheels must be in good condition and turning freely for good derailleur performance. If the teeth are worn, replace the wheels. Check the spinning of the pulleys. If they do not turn well, overhaul or replace them (this is covered in *Zinn and the Art of Mountain Bike Maintenance*).

Drivetrain friction can be reduced and longevity increased by switching to sealed-bearing jockey wheels (photo 3-19). Especially with Shimano derailleurs, you want to make sure if you use aftermarket jockey wheels that the upper one has some free lateral movement, which allows the chain to line up under the cog better. On high-end Shimano derailleurs, the ceramic bushing inside the top pulley actually gets quite slick over time and can spin as well as a cartridge bearing. The resistance you feel in clean Shimano jockey wheels is generally the rubber seals. These can be removed to reduce friction for big races (especially road).

3.2J Derailleur Pivot Maintenance

As the derailleur pivots wear, the play in the derailleur increases. There are the two main upper and lower knuckle pivots, and then there are four pivots on the parallelogram: one on each corner. Pivot play (looseness) decreases shifting performance, since pull from the cable first twists the derailleur before moving it laterally.

The upper and lower knuckle pivots can be disassembled on most rear derailleurs. They should be at least lubricated with grease periodically.

Most derailleurs do not have serviceable parallelogram pivots, so the derailleur must be replaced when they get too loose. On derailleurs that do have replaceable parallelogram pivots, the derailleur can be returned to its original performance level after it gets loose. Usually, all you need to do is pull off the snap rings on the pivot pin heads, push the pins out, put new ones in, and replace the snap rings.

3.2K Replacing Derailleur Bolts with Lighter Ones

The upper and lower pivots can be disassembled on most derailleurs, and replacement aftermarket aluminum and titanium pivot bolts are made by many manufacturers. Replacing the lower pivot bolt can be done after disassembling the pivot as described above in section 3.2H (photos 3-14 to 3-18). The upper pivot can usually be disassembled by removing a snap ring. See *Zinn and the Art of Mountain Bike Maintenance*, Chapter 5, for more detail on this.

For around 40 bucks, you can get a complete lightweight bolt kit that includes the cable-fixing bolt, upper and lower pivot bolts, and the jockey wheel mounting bolts.

3.2L Muddy Conditions

If you ride in really muddy conditions, your derailleurs will get exceedingly filthy, will wear faster, and will not shift as well. If you can seal the derailleur from the muck, it will work better and require less frequent service and replacement.

Vivo makes "Grunge Guard" rubber covers for front and rear derailleurs (photo 3-20); they conceal the pivot points, springs, and the last inch or so of exposed cable. Grunge Guards are cheap,

3-20
Vivo "Grunge Guard" covers a rear derailleur to protect it from muck.

easy to put on (they secure with a zip tie), and do not seem to restrict derailleur movement. The barrel adjuster is still accessible. The limit screws can be reached by opening the back flap, which clips shut over a rubber nub. The downside is that Grunge Guards cover the whole derailleur, including the logo, so you cannot show off that brand-new XTR derailleur that you just scored. Bummer.

Vivo also makes an "Enduro" derailleur that has an integral accordion seal.

3.2M A Note on Compatibility

Not all derailleurs are compatible with all shifters, chains, and cog sets. Generally, most manufacturers of aftermarket mountain bike drivetrain parts make their equipment to be compatible with Shimano, since Shimano parts are pretty much the standard.

One glaring exception to this surprising amount of compatibility throughout the bike industry is the SRAM ESP derailleur and SRAM ESP shifter (photo 3-21). The SRAM ESP shifter pulls twice the cable length per shift as Shimano, and it only works with the SRAM ESP derailleur (photo 3-12). The greater cable pull is meant to reduce cable tension and hence cable friction.

Otherwise, most Sachs shifters and Grip Shift work with Shimano derailleurs; most hub cassette bodies accept Shimano and Sachs cogs; most cog sets fit on Shimano and Sachs cassette bodies and are spaced to shift with Shimano derailleurs, and most mountain bike chains are of the proper width and lateral flexibility to work on Shimano eight-speed systems. This does not mean that there will not be performance decreases (and sometimes improvements) when mixing components.

If your parts mix is not working, experiment with other parts combinations to bring performance up. Start with the least-expensive component, the chain, and work upward from there.

It is also important to remember that in the 1999 product line, Shimano rolled out its first 9-speed mountain-bike group. As on the Shimano road groups, this involves narrowing the distance between cogs to about 2.5 mm, which will require an especially narrow chain. The new nine-speed systems will not work with eight-speed chains.

3.2N Chain Tensioning for Downhilling

Downhill and dual slalom require more chain retention. You can get springs that pull back on the rear derailleur, idler arms, or guides with rollers to secure and tighten the chain (photo 2-15), and rollers or guides to keep the chain from coming off the front chainring (photo 3-22).

3.3 THE FRONT DERAILLEUR

The front derailleur may very well be the most complained-about part on mountain bikes. It can be extremely finicky, and if it misshifts, you can get your chain jammed or tangled but good.

3.3A Front Derailleur Shifting Method

The front derailleur has a harder job than the rear derailleur, because it is shifting chain that is under tension. The chain going through the rear derailleur is relaxed and only has tension applied to it by the jockey wheel cage return springs,

3-21
SRAM ESP shifters.

3-22
Mr. Dirt adjustable downhill chain retainers.

but the chain going through the front derailleur carries your full pedaling load. This makes the front derailleur very sensitive to pedaling force during shifting. If you do not back off on the pedals a bit when shifting, you are greatly increasing the likelihood of getting everything jammed up. Margarita Fullana of Spain had the 1997 World Championship cross-country silver medal wrapped up until she got overly excited and tried to shift to her inner chainring while pedaling hard up a steep climb just before the finish line. The chain jammed, she got it unstuck, and then it broke when she started pedaling again. Without a chain, she had to run through the Swiss town of Chateau d'Oex and up the last hill. She was passed on the climb and lost the silver medal. That was a high cost to pay for not taking another fraction of a second to slightly back off on the pedaling force during the shift!

Even if you do not actually jam or break your chain while doing it, you are also rapidly wearing out your chainrings and chain by shifting under load. Just *don't* do it.

3.3B Front Derailleur Position Adjustments

The entire adjustment of the front derailleur is thoroughly described in Chapter 5 of *Zinn and the Art of Mountain Bike Maintenance.* Below are the fine details to optimize its performance.

3.3C Front Derailleur Vertical Position Adjustment

A front derailleur should generally be set so that the cage is about 1 mm to 2 mm (1/16 to 1/8 inch) above the outer chainring. Shimano front derailleurs have attached to their bottom edge a little piece of tape with this adjustment range and the outline of some chainring teeth printed on it. This makes it very easy to set the height. Just make sure that you set the height 1–2 mm above the *tallest* teeth, since HG and IG chainrings have teeth of varying height.

Sometimes, the bottom edge of the derailleur cage may not match the curve of the chainring over its length and consequently will not shift ideally. For example, the forward tip may be a millimeter above the chainring while the tail might be 6 mm above it (this can be caused by a chain-suck incident that bent the front derailleur linkage). The various shifting ramps inside the cage will not hit the chain properly, and the cage cannot control the chain movement as tightly.

Another cause for this type of misalignment can be a seat tube that does not meet the bottom bracket shell on center. In this case the derailleur is rotated relative to the crank. If the tail is spaced high above the outer ring when the front tip is close, using a compact-drive front derailleur (assuming you are not using a compact-drive system already) can help. The tighter curvature of the derailleur cage will bring the tail closer to the rings. The reverse is also true: On a compact-drive system, if the derailleur's front tip is too far above the outer ring when the tail is close, use a derailleur for full-sized rings, which will have a higher tail. Another solution could be to use a braze-on type of front derailleur with a separate band clamp made by Sachs or Shimano. You can take a piece of beer can and then

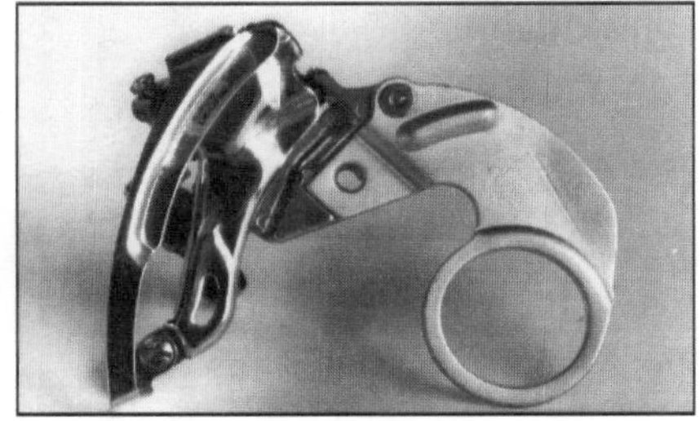

3-23
Shimano XT front derailleur with bottom-bracket-mounted flange. The flange mounts the derailleur, sets its height, and prevents the chain from falling down and wrapping around the bottom bracket spindle.

3-24
A Third Eye Chain Watcher is set next to the inner chainring and prevents the chain from falling off to the inside.

FRONT DERAILLEUR ROTATIONAL TUNING TIPS

from Wayne Stetina

Triple front derailleur (keep it straighter than a double):

1. heel out: stronger downshift top to middle, weaker downshift middle to small, stronger upshift small to middle, weaker upshift middle to top
2. heel in: opposite of above

Double front derailleur:

1. heel out: stronger downshift, weaker upshift
2. heel in: weaker downshift, stronger upshift

shim the bottom or top edge of the derailleur face where it meets the inside of the clamp to tilt it up or down.

3.3D Front Derailleur Horizontal Twist Adjustment

Usually, you want the outer plate of the derailleur cage parallel to the plane of the frame. You can check if the cage is parallel to the frame by measuring the space between the outer cage plate and the inner side of the crank arm at either end of the cage, when the derailleur is on the big ring.

Sometimes, this adjustment does not give you the best shifting, though, and some subtle position changes will make a difference. The cage of some derailleurs flares wider at the tail (Shimano XTR is one example). The outer tail of the derailleur cage on these models needs to be out a bit, so it parallels the chain in highest gear. Make sure you do not have the tail out so far that it hits the crank arm.

Similarly, when in low gear, the inner cage plate should also parallel the chain, making the tail a bit *in* from parallel with the plane of the frame.

3.3E Bottom-Bracket-Mount Front Derailleurs

Shimano makes some derailleurs the primary mounting point of which is a flange that is held pinched between the bottom bracket cup and the face of the bottom bracket shell (photo 3-23). These derailleurs are available from the low end up to the high-end XTR differential-plate version with a carbon-fiber bottom-bracket-mounted flange. The flange mounts the derailleur, sets its height, and prevents the chain from falling down and wrapping around the bottom bracket spindle. High-end front derailleurs (XTR, XT, LX, STX), have a secondary mounting screw directed straight inward into either a band clamp adapter or a brazed-on threaded boss on the seat tube. These derailleurs have little or no vertical height adjustment. For instance, the XTR flange-mount front derailleur just has two height adjustments to accommodate either a 46-tooth or a 48-tooth chainring. You *can* adjust the horizontal twist of these derailleurs a bit, though.

On low-end derailleurs, the flange mount is called "Easy Set," since there is no secondary bolt and no height adjustment. You just slap the flange onto the cup, slide the centering clips around the seat tube, tighten in the cup, and the derailleur is set and adjusted.

3.3F Front Derailleur Cage Straightening

You can straighten a bent cage a bit with a pair of pliers. Also, you can sometimes improve shifting by bending the tip of the cage in a bit if it is not initiating the shift well. Or you can bend the cage out at a point where it might be rubbing the chain despite your best adjustment efforts. Be careful, because it is easy to make the derailleur *worse* this way.

3.3G Front Derailleur Cable Tension

Dial in the cable tension with the shifter barrel adjuster so that the derailleur begins to move as soon as you move the shifter. Set it so that the derailleur shifts easily to the granny gear but does not drop the chain to the inside or rub the chain in low gear.

You can also trim the indexing of the derailleur over the middle ring to avoid chain rub in cross gears by fine-tuning the cable tension.

3.3H Front Derailleur Limit Screws

If you have the cable tension set properly, you need not worry about the inner limit screw. Just have it loose enough that it allows the chain plenty of clearance in low gear. The cable tension will prevent the derailleur from dropping the chain off to the inside.

If you *do* have trouble with dropping the chain to the inside, try a Third Eye Chain Watcher (photo 3-24). This plastic part attaches around the seat tube below the front derailleur and will nudge the chain back onto the inner ring when it starts to come off. Any tendency for the chain to come off to the inside (or to not reach the outer ring) should lead you to read the chain line section in Chapter 4, section 4.1.

3.3I Front Derailleur Spring Tension

It is by spring tension alone that the front derailleur forces the chain to a smaller chainring. If the tension is too low, the derailleur will not shift unless you pedal *very* softly, while everyone else rides away from you. If the tension is too high, it will be hard to twist or push the shifter.

Shimano front derailleurs have a spring that opposes a twist on itself, like the spring in a mousetrap. Some Shimano front derailleurs have an adjustment cam that pushes against the tip of the spring to vary its tension. You can adjust spring tension by turning the cam with a screwdriver.

FRONT DERAILLEUR TIPS

from Wayne Stetina

I always either use a plate-mounted front derailleur (photo 3-23) to prevent the chain from dropping down to the bottom bracket, or I use another physical barrier (like the Third Eye Chain Watcher—Chapter 3, photo 3-24) to keep it from doing so. If you shift to the inner ring while you hit a bump and get the chain oscillating just right, the chain's going straight to the bottom bracket. The only thing that is there to stop it is the front derailleur cage, but you have to set the limit screw to allow the cage to move inward enough to get quick shifts and not rub the chain in the granny gear. Even on an elite level, I have seen too many races lost this way.

Always avoid front shifts under full power. Even though Shimano's new front derailleur designs are intended to allow full-power front shifting, it does not mean it is a good idea. Your system will wear out much faster if you do.

While cross gears create lots of chain wear because of the side loads on the chain, there are other reasons to avoid them, too. Chain retention is insufficient when bouncing over bumps in small-small combinations. Avoid big-big combinations, because stretching the rear derailleur out so much puts more spring pressure against the chain and adds drag.

Sachs Di.R.T. front derailleurs have a simple linear return spring (photo 3-25), which will probably lend itself well to aftermarket spring upgrades.

White Industries offers a "Linear Pull" upgrade for a Shimano top-swing front derailleur, which eliminates the return spring. The spring and the little plastic piece that connects the two linkage

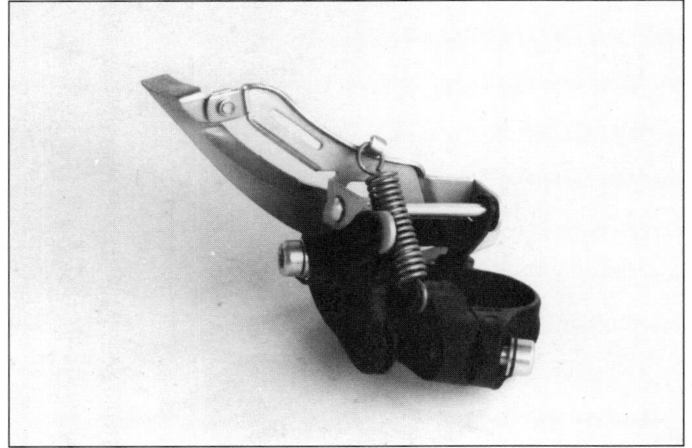

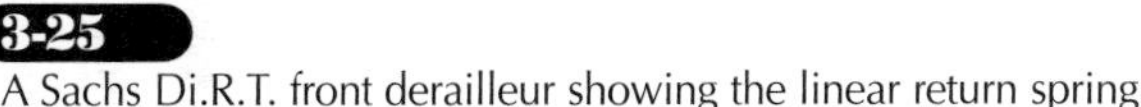

3-25
A Sachs Di.R.T. front derailleur showing the linear return spring.

3-26
Grunge Guard installed on a bottom-pull front derailleur to keep dirt out of the mechanism.

pins and covers the spring are replaced by an aluminum disc with two holes in it to go over the pivot pins. The cable wraps around the disc and is fixed to it with a clamp bolt. As on the White rear derailleur (photo 3-10), the shift cable is a continuous loop that pulls the derailleur in either direction.

3.3J Chain Line

The chain line, or angle of the chain relative to the frame, strongly affects front derailleur performance. If the chainrings are set outward too far from the frame, the chain will tend to fall off to the inside frequently and/or rub the front derailleur in low gear. It also will be hard to shift out to the big chainring. If you are having these types of problems with your front derailleur, read the chain line section in Chapter 4, section 4.1.

3.3K Front Derailleur Won't Go Inward Enough

Some frames have such a fat seat tube that the front derailleur's inward movement is stopped by it. The lower derailleur pivot will hit the frame, and any amount of loosening the cable and the limit screw will not move it inward any farther. Sometimes you can twist the tail of the front derailleur in slightly and then bend the outer cage slightly to eliminate the resulting rub. Your other options are moving the crankset outward, which makes the chain line less than optimal; replacing the front derailleur with one that does not hit; or replacing the frame.

3.3L Front Derailleur Upgrades

One improvement in front de-railleur design is the Shimano XTR differential-plate front derailleur. The two cage plates are not rigidly fixed together; they move independently like a pair of chopsticks to lift and move the chain. They also drop down over the chainrings to retain the chain better.

Tips for adjusting these derailleurs are above in sections *3.3C* and *3.3D*.

Shimano's low-mount "top swing" front derailleurs offer some of these features with a standard one-piece cage.

Using the White Industries linear-pull system with a Shimano top-swing derailleur eliminates waiting for the return spring to make shifts, although the cable can jump out of the groove it rides in.

A modest upgrade to your existing front derailleur is to replace the cable fixing bolt and seat tube clamp bolt with titanium ones. It'll cost you about 12 bucks and save you 10 or 15 grams.

3.3M Chain Suck

Chain suck is not usually caused by the front derailleur. See Chapter 2, section *2.2D*, and Chapter 4, section 4.4C, for solutions to chain suck.

3.3N Sealing Front Derailleur from Dirt

Vivo makes rubber Grunge Guards for top-pull as well as bottom-pull front derailleurs. The Grunge Guard covers all the pivots and springs and is affixed around the seat tube with a zip tie and clipped around the derailleur with rubber nubs (photo 3-26). You still have easy access to the adjusting screws by opening the nub.

3.3O Front Derailleur Downhill/Dual Slalom Chain Retainer

Downhilling and dual slalom do not require a front derailleur, but they do

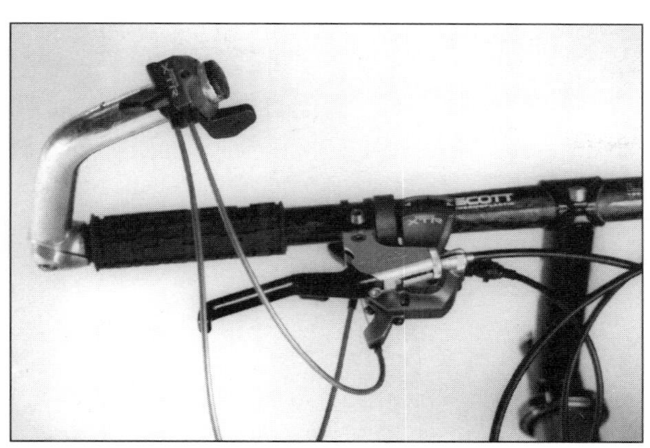

3-27

Shimano XTR Rapidfire SL shifters mounted on separate band clamp offer more positioning options and brake choices. The XTR Rapidfire Remote shifters allow shifting from the bar end.

3-28

Leave a little space between the grip and the twist shifter to reduce friction.

require a lot of chain retention for a single chainring (photo 3-22). A derailleur with long Teflon plates replacing the cage can make an inexpensive chain retainer.

3.4 THE SHIFTERS

The shifters must be in good shape or good shifting will not occur. "In good shape" means different things with different shifters.

3.4A Shifter Service

Grip Shift and other twist shifters have large cylindrical plastic surfaces inside bearing on each other. They will perform poorly if there is any grit between those surfaces. Disassembly, cleaning, and lubrication of Grip Shift is discussed in Chapter 5 of *Zinn and the Art of Mountain Bike Maintenance*. Cable replacement in various shifters can be found in the same chapter.

Shimano Rapidfire shifters are sealed fairly well from the entry of dirt and are complex enough that they rarely reward disassembly. Small parts are also not available for them. They do well with no service or an occasional drop of chain lube inside.

3.4B Shifter Tuning Tips

Shifter tuning for reliable shifting is integral to derailleur and cable adjustment, which is already covered above, but it also depends on good ergonomics and low friction.

You should set the shifters in a position that is comfortable for you to access. Just because many bikes are set up with the shifters, brake levers, and grips all butted right up against each other is no reason you have to set yours up this way. If it is more comfortable to have the shifters farther inboard from the grips, then put them there. The same goes with the rotation of the shifter positions around the bar; turn them so that you can reach them most easily and shift with the least wrist and hand strain. Also be aware of shifter positions that limit your grip options or braking options.

If you have Rapidfire shifters on their own separate band clamps (photo 3-27), you have more positioning options than with Rapidfire shifters that are integral to the brake lever (as well as more choice of brake levers). Comfortable positions for braking and for shifting are not necessarily the same.

Grip Shift, Sachs, and other twist shifters need to be positioned at least far enough inboard that they do not drag on the grips. The shifters usually come with a separate plastic ring to separate the shifter from the grip and reduce friction. Leaving a little space between the grip and the shifter is even better (photo 3-28). You also may find that the length of grip that came with the shifters is not right for you; in that case, cut some to the length you like. Set your bike up for *you*, not for the generic bike rider.

If it is too hard to twist your twist shifters (a problem for kids and small adults), you can make it easier. Pull the shifter apart (by removing the screw in the triangular piece that holds the inner and outer pieces together). Bend the "Snoopy"-shaped spring that clicks into the notches a bit flatter. When replacing the spring, note that Snoopy's nose faces forward, and he needs Gripshift-compatible grease on him.

3.4C Shifter Upgrading

Quick, effective shifting is the name of the game. If you are not getting that, a change in shifters can sometimes give it to you. For instance, many riders find a surprising improvement in shifting speed and reliability by switching from old twist shifters to Shimano Rapidfire SL. The performance of all shifting components goes up every year, and upgrading to a new version of your current shifters will almost certainly make an improvement. Shifters and derailleurs of the same brand and model often will perform better than a mix of shifter and derailleur brands, even if they are claimed to be "compatible." Companies work harder to make their components work best together as a system. Also, be aware that SRAM ESP rear derailleurs will *only* work with SRAM ESP Grip Shift shifters (photo 3-21), which are made especially for them; the amount of cable pull required for each shift is about double that of other systems.

A simple upgrade is to get a $20 (!) titanium shifter pod mounting bolt for Shimano Rapidfire and save a couple of grams. Careful when removing the old bolt! (See section 3.4G below.)

3.4D Remote Shifters

As of this writing, shifters on the bar ends are limited to one system: Shimano Rapidfire Remote (photos 3-27, 3-29). If you ride a lot on the bar ends, you may appreciate having the option to shift out there as well. The remote shifter consists of two levers that twist about the bar end and are connected to the bar-mounted shifters by thin, double-headed cables in thin housings. They can only be used on standard-diameter, round cross-section bar ends. Sorry, those trick, ergonomically shaped, ovalized carbon, hexagonal titanium, or extra-fat bar ends will not accept Rapidfire Remote.

Rapidfire Remote can only be used with Rapidfire SL shift levers that have holes drilled in them for the remote cables. There is otherwise no difference between these Rapidfire SL levers and older versions.

The Rapidfire Remote cables disconnect and connect very simply. After turning the lever to release tension on one remote cable, you can push the cable head out of the lever on either end of the little cable. Pull the plastic cap off the side of the cable head (photo 3-29), and the cable head can then pull back through the hole in the lever. Do this process in reverse to hook up the cables.

3.4E Ritchey 2x9

Ritchey 2x9 consists simply of a compact-drive crankset with only two chainrings (usually 42x29), Sachs-made twist shifters, and a dish-shaped 33-tooth titanium cog that installs inboard of any Shimano-compatible eight-speed cassette. Installation of this system is covered in the second edition of *Zinn and the Art of Mountain Bike Maintenance*, Chapter 5.

If a 29–33 gear is low enough, this system might constitute an upgrade for you. There is certainly some benefit to simplifying the front shifting. No matter how much improvement has been done on front derailleurs, front shifting is never as quick as rear shifting, nor can it be done under load as easily. When you are stupid from oxygen-deprivation on a hard climb during a race, it can be nice *not* to have three shifting options in the front. Your mind can handle "easy" or "hard," but an option in between can cause confusion—as can figuring out which chainring you are currently using in the first place.

The Ritchey (Sachs) shifters can also be used with standard 3x8 systems.

3.4F Optical Gear Displays

Some people love 'em, and some people hate 'em. Most recent Shimano optical displays are removable, if you really do not like them. Similarly, if one jams up, you can unscrew the little Phillips screws (photo 3-30), pull it off, and discard it.

If you have twist shifters that do not tell you which gear you are in, but you would like to be able to see that without looking back, you can paint the numbers on the shifter body adjacent to the twist grip at each click.

3.4G Moving Integral Rapidfire Plus Levers to a Band Clamp with Brake Upgrade

If you have Rapidfire Plus levers that are an integral part of your brake levers, and you want to upgrade your brakes, you do not need to get rid of the shifters. The shifters can be moved to an aftermarket band clamp so that you can use whatever brake lever you want.

For instance, if you have Shimano cantilever brakes with integral brake/-shift levers and you want to use V-brakes or hydraulic brakes, you will have to dispense with the brake levers. Rather than junking the shifters, you can mount them on a separate band clamp adjacent to the new brake levers.

Unbolt the shift lever from the brake lever body (photo 3-31). You need to do this carefully, turning back and forth, as you are breaking the thread-lock compound on the bolt threads. Be aware that the female socket nut that the bolt is tightened into can turn. The socket nut is rectangular on the bottom end and is held in place by a rectangular recess under the shifter body. When you unscrew the bolt, it initially unthreads, but then it will start turning the nut and galling the aluminum shifter body unless you pry

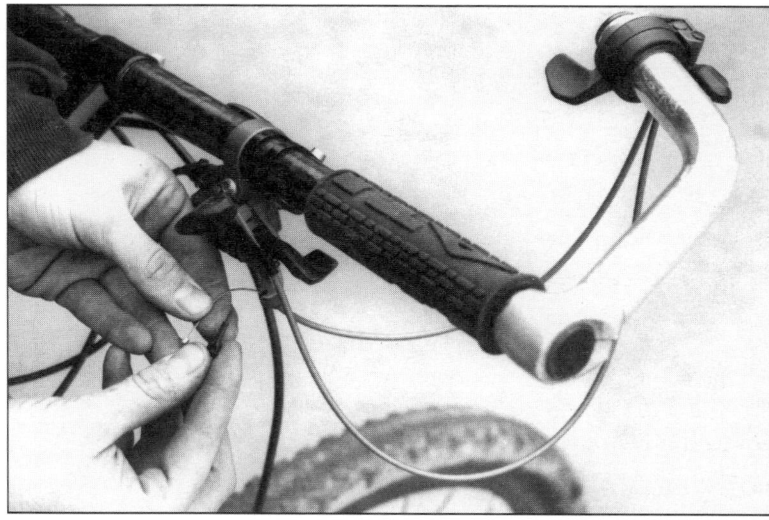

3-29
Shimano Rapidfire Remote shift cable change. A plastic cap secures each cable head in its hole.

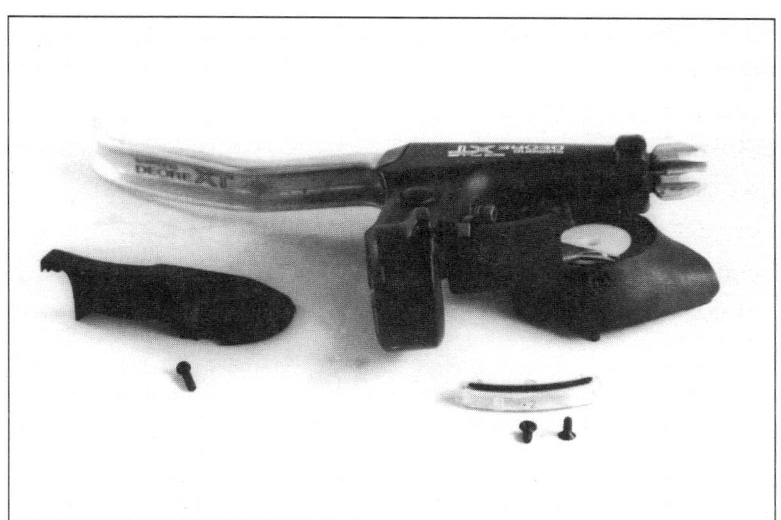

3-30
A Shimano optical gear display can be removed with a small Phillips screwdriver.

upward on the bolt head with a screwdriver as you unscrew it. This keeps the rectangular nut end seated into its recess in the lever body.

Run the cable out through the new clamp (photo 3-32), line up the pin on the shifter with the hole in the shifter band clamp, and bolt the shifter on. Screw the barrel adjuster from the old shifter body into the band clamp. When mounting the band clamp onto the handlebar, you can orient it to get the angle you want for most comfortable shifting.

If you have an optical gear display, you will not get to use it on the aftermarket band clamp.

3.4H Air Shifting

Shimano Air Lines is described above in section 3.1G (photo 3-9). It is certainly an upgrade in terms of shifting precision, although it takes both hands to operate the rear derailleur, which eliminates multiple front chainrings.

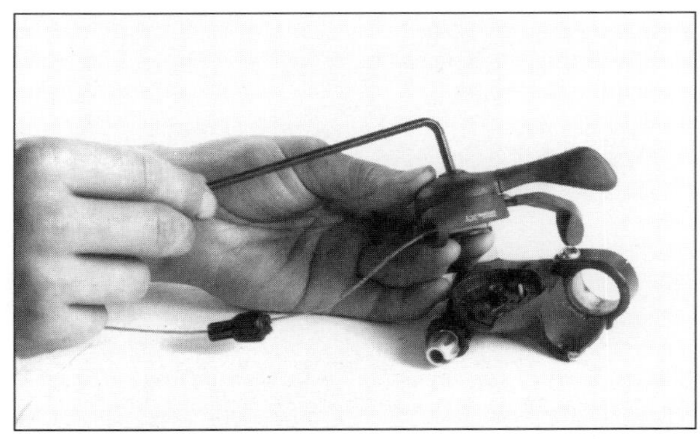

3-31
Unbolting the shift lever from the brake lever body.

3-32
Installing a Shimano Rapidfire Plus shifter on an aftermarket band clamp. The cable exits the band clamp, and a pin on the shifter must be lined up with a hole in the bottom of the band clamp next to the bolt hole.

4

CRANKS, BOTTOM BRACKETS, AND CHAINRINGS

"At least it cannot be your health," said he, as his keen eyes darted over her, "so ardent a bicyclist must be full of energy."
—*Sir Arthur Conan Doyle,* The Adventure of the Solitary Cyclist

Since any energy that you apply to propel the bike must first pass through the crankset, it is important to have the components of the crankset, namely the bottom bracket, crank arms, and chainrings (photo 4-1) working properly and aligned relative to the rear cogs.

An optimal crankset will be stiff and light and will rotate with little resistance. Its chainrings will be sized for your riding and will be centered with the rear cogs for the ideal chain line. The chainring teeth will be clean,

4-1
The crankset, bottom bracket, crank arms, and chainrings.

unworn, and shaped to hold the chain well and release it at the bottom. The chainrings will also have shifting ramps of the proper size and location to facilitate smooth chain movement from chainring to chainring.

With your existing crank, the three most useful things you can do to improve overall performance are: set the chain line accurately, replace worn chainrings, and overhaul or replace the bottom bracket, if it is no longer freely rotating.

4.1 CHAIN LINE

Chain line is the relative alignment of the front chainrings with the rear cogs; it is the imaginary line connecting the center of the middle chainring with the middle of the cogset (Fig. 4). This line should in theory be straight and parallel to the vertical plane of the bicycle.

Chain line is often way off due to mismatched cranks and bottom brackets. Many shifting (and autoshifting) problems blamed on derailleurs, chains, or chainrings are actually caused by poor chain line. Your entire drivetrain will work better and last longer if you set the chain line correctly.

Chain line is adjusted by moving or replacing the bottom bracket to move the cranks left or right.

4.1A Chain Line Measurement

You can roughly check the chain line by placing a long straight edge against either side of the middle chainring and back to the rear cogs; the two lines should be centered about the middle of the rear cog stack. You can accurately measure the chain line with the method below.

The position of the middle chainring, measured as the distance from the center of the seat tube to the center of the middle chainring, is often called the chain line by bike companies and crank manufacturers. The position of the middle chainring is actually only the front end point of the chain line (CLF). The rear end point of the chain line (CLR) is the distance from the center of the plane of the bicycle to the center of the cogset.

FIGURE 4. MEASURING CHAIN LINE

1. Find the front end point of the chain line (CLF in Fig. 4):
   - **A.** Using the outside-measuring arms of a caliper, measure from the left side of the down tube to the outside of the large chainring (photo 4-2). This will give you dimension d1 in Fig. 4. (Measure from the down tube, not the seat tube, as seat tubes are often ovalized or tapered.)
   - **B.** Using the inside-measuring prongs of the caliper, measure the distance from the right side of the down tube to the inside of the inner chainring. This will give you dimension d2 in Fig. 4.
   - **C.** To find CLF, add these two measurements, and divide the sum by two.

     CLF = (d1 + d2)/2
2. Find the rear end point of the chain line (CLR in Fig. 4):
   - **A.** Measure the width of the cog stack, end to end (t in Fig. 4).
   - **B.** Measure the space between the face of the smallest cog and the inside face of the dropout (S in Fig. 4).
   - **C.** Measure the length of the axle from dropout to dropout (W in Fig. 4); this dimension is also called "axle overlock dimension," referring to the distance from locknut face to locknut face on either end. Generally, on any mountain bike made since 1989 or so, this will be 135 mm.

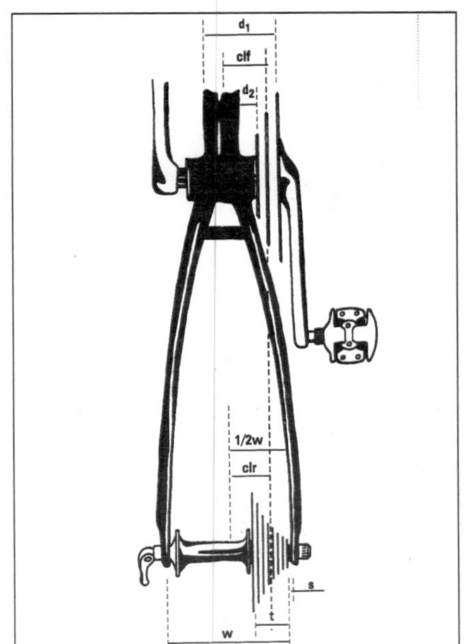

Figure 4
Chain line measurement.

4-2
Measuring from the left side of the down tube to the outside of the large chainring with a caliper to determine chain line.

D. To get CLR, subtract from one-half of the rear axle length: one-half of the thickness of the cog stack and the distance from the first cog to the inside face of the right rear dropout.

CLR = W/2 - t/2 - S

3. Compare CLF and CLR:

If CLF = CLR, your chain line is perfect. This, however, almost never occurs on a mountain bike, due to considerations about chainstay clearance, prevention of chain rub on large chainrings in cross gears, and inward movement range of the front derailleur. Shimano specifies a "chain line" (meaning CLF, the front end point of the chain line) as 47.5 mm for bikes with a 68-mm-wide bottom bracket shell, and 50 mm for 73-mm shells (both of these specified dimensions are plus or minus 1 mm). CLR, the rear end point of the chain line, on the other hand, usually comes out around 44.5 mm. You can see that shifting is thus compromised to avoid chainring rub.

Since there is little or nothing you can do to change the rear cog position, the chain line is altered by: (a) using a different bottom bracket or bottom bracket spindle, or (b) moving the bottom bracket right or left. Bottom bracket installation, adjustment, and repositioning are covered in Chapter 8 of *Zinn and the Art of Mountain Bike Maintenance*.

Your bike will shift best and run most quietly if you can set CLF at around 45 mm without a chainring or two hitting the chainstay. You may have to set it wider than that, because at CLF=45 mm: (a) your front derailleur may bottom out on the seat tube before moving inward enough to shift to the inner chainring (this is particularly a problem with an oversized seat tube), and (b) when crossing from the inner chainring to the smallest cog, the chain may rub the middle ring (not a problem if you avoid that cross gear).

I recommend moving the right crank arm inward as far as it will go before the chainrings touch the chainstay or the front derailleur bottoms out on the seat tube.

Note **Don't assume that because you bought a complete bike at a shop that everything is perfect. Some brand-new bikes have terrible chain lines that can only be corrected by buying a narrower bottom bracket. To save 20 cents or a couple bucks per bike, a bean-counting product manager may have selected a cheap bottom bracket that does not match the cranks for that bike model. Product managers know that customers may pay attention to the quality and brand of the cranks on the bike, but very few pay attention to the bottom bracket.**

ANOTHER NOTE: The chain line can also be off if the frame is out of alignment. Checking frame alignment is covered in Chapter 14 of *Zinn and the Art of Mountain Bike Maintenance.*

FINAL NOTE: If your chain falls off to the inside, and you don't want to or can't improve the chain line, buy and install a Third Eye Chain Watcher (photo 3-24). It's an inexpensive plastic gizmo that clamps around the seat tube next to the inner chainring. Clamp it on and adjust the position so that it nudges the chain back on whenever it tries to fall off to the inside.

4.1B Moving the Bottom Bracket and Crank

If you need to move the crankset in or out to improve the chain line, you may be able to move the bottom bracket laterally, or you can get a new bottom bracket. Your other option, of course, is to get a whole new crankset.

Moving the bottom bracket inward is only possible if you have adjustable cups on both sides. In other words, each bottom bracket cup is secured with a lock ring.

***Moving the Bottom Bracket with Adjustable Cups on Both Ends* INWARD**

1. Loosen the lock rings.
2. Back the left cup out a turn or two.
3. Snug the right cup in.
4. Adjust the bottom bracket.
5. Tighten the lock rings down.

Correcting chain line on a mountain bike very rarely requires moving the crankset outward more. In the rare case that it might, any bottom bracket can be moved out somewhat. Another reason to move the crank outward, even though it throws off the chain line, is to provide clearance between the frame and the inner chainrings or to get the front derailleur to shift to the inner chainring.

***Moving a Shimano-Style Cartridge Bottom Bracket or Cup-and-Cone Bottom Bracket* OUTWARD**

1. Remove the fixed cup on the drive side.
2. Put a bottom bracket spacer (a large, thin washer obtainable at a bike shop) between the cup and the bottom bracket shell (photo 4-3).
3. Tighten the fixed cup down.
4. Tighten in and adjust the left-side cup.

***Moving a Bottom Bracket That Has Adjustable Cups on Both Ends* OUTWARD**

1. Loosen both lock rings.
2. Back the right cup out a turn or two.
3. Tighten the left cup in.
4. Adjust the bottom bracket.
5. Tighten the lock rings down.

Detailed instructions and illustrations about bottom bracket adjustment, repositioning, and installation are in Chapter 8 of *Zinn and the Art of Mountain Bike Maintenance.*

4.2 THE BOTTOM BRACKET

The bottom bracket should not only position the crank properly for ideal chain line, it should also be stiff and turn freely without play. Since it is a heavy part, it is nice if you can also have a low-weight bottom bracket without sacrificing any of the above features.

4.2A Bottom Bracket Adjustment and Free Rotation

Check Your Bottom Bracket for Side Play

Line the cranks up with the seat tube and pushing one arm back and forth toward the seat tube. If it clunks back and forth, it is too loose and needs to be adjusted. Bottom bracket adjustment is covered in Chapter 8 of *Zinn and the Art of Mountain Bike Maintenance*. If it feels tight laterally, please continue.

Check Your Bottom Bracket for Free and Easy Rotation

Flip the chain off to the inside so it is wrapped around the bottom bracket shell and does not touch the chainrings. Spin the crank (photo 4-4). It should go around a number of times, losing momentum slowly. It should rotate back the other direction a bit after it stops. Keep in mind that some bottom brackets have heavy-duty seals on the spindle that restrict rotation. Rotation should still feel smooth, however, even if the arms do not spin freely. If the bottom bracket comes to a halt rapidly or makes grinding noises, it needs to be overhauled or replaced. Bottom bracket overhaul and replacement are covered in Chapter 8 of *Zinn and the Art of Mountain Bike Maintenance.*

4.2B Upgrading Bottom Bracket

Is the allure of a titanium or other super-light bottom bracket too great to resist? Do you want a bottom bracket that turns more freely or is better sealed than yours? Well, go for it, then. Just make sure that the bottom bracket you get is compatible with your crank arms and will give you a good chain line.

Compatibility, in gross terms, means differentiating between cranks that accept traditional square-taper spindles (photo 4-5) and those that accept some other system, usually splined. For instance, Shimano XTR bottom brackets since 1996 have a large pipe-shaped splined steel spindle (photo 4-6), and other crank manufacturers (Coda is one example) offer crank models to fit Shimano pipe-spindle bottom brackets. The high-end Coda Magic crank (photo 4-7) has a different splined system, and Sweet Wings cranks have a splined stub welded to each arm which, when joined, make up the bottom bracket spindle (nice idea!).

The taper of the spindle varies on some square-taper bottom brackets, although this incompatibility is less of a problem than it used to be, since most companies now manufacture to Shimano specifications. You will still find that a crank arm goes farther onto some spindles than others. The spindle length, and more specifically, the distance from the face of the drive-side cup to the end of the

4-3
Putting a bottom bracket spacer between the fixed cup and the bottom bracket shell to move the chainrings outboard more.

4-4
Spinning the crank with the chain off to check the bottom bracket for freedom of rotation.

4-5
A standard Shimano cartridge bottom bracket with a traditional square-taper spindle.

4-6
A Shimano XTR bottom bracket, featuring a large pipe-shaped splined steel spindle.

4-7
Coda Magic splined bottom bracket and crank arms with bottom bracket cup installation tool.

axle on that end, will be the main variable in determining chain line.

Choose a bottom bracket either made specifically for your crank or one that has the same spindle length as that recommended by the crank manufacturer.

If your bottom bracket shell has not been tapped and faced (after welding and painting, that is), you will want to do that or have it done. The procedure for tapping and facing a bottom bracket shell is described in Chapter 13, section 13.1B. Tapping ensures that the threads on either end of the shell are lined up concentrically with each other. Facing ensures that the faces of the bottom bracket shell are cut parallel to each other and perpendicular to the threads. If you install an expensive bottom bracket into a shell that has not had these steps done to it, your bottom bracket will not turn as freely and is likely to wear out faster.

If you are on a bike-lightening kick, make sure that you *do not* install a titanium crank bolt into a titanium bottom bracket spindle. This also applies to threading *any* titanium bolt into any titanium part (stems, frames, etc.). The threads of the two titanium parts can gall and rip each other up. You will have to replace both of them. Besides costing you a bundle of money and the time to get the parts, removing the seized ones may cost you even more of both.

Install the new bottom bracket into your frame and the cranks onto your bottom bracket by following the instructions in Chapter 8 of *Zinn and the Art of Mountain Bike Maintenance*. Note the two installation tips below.

4.3 THE CRANK ARMS

Crank arms that are stiff and light and hold the chainrings in alignment without wobble definitely facilitate propelling the bike faster. If yours are lacking in these departments, upgrading the crank or spider could be a good idea.

4.3A Upgrade Crank

So you want stiffer, stronger, lighter cranks with straight chainrings—what do you pick? If you are *not* planning on upgrading your bottom bracket as well, then your crank options are limited. You need one that not only accepts the type of spindle you have, but also is designed for that length of spindle. It is easier if you upgrade both at the same time.

Some cranks only accept one specific bottom bracket. Recent (gray, 1996 and later) Shimano XTR cranks and 1999 Coda Tarantula cranks require a Shimano splined pipe-spindle bottom bracket (photo 4-6). I suppose soon enough there will be aftermarket bottom brackets from other manufacturers that fit it. Coda Magic (photo 4-7) and Sweet Wings are two other examples of cranks that only work with their own unique, splined bottom brackets. While lack of compatibility with other systems may be limiting, you cannot go too wrong with any of these three crank sets; they are all stiff, strong, and light. The bottom brackets all turn freely enough when new and are also very stiff. Expect to do fairly frequent overhauls of XTR pipe-spindle bottom brackets. Overhaul of this bottom bracket is not simple, either; there are lots of loose, tiny ball bearings and needle bearings (two sets of each) that can be tricky to get all lined up properly without losing any.

Coda's 1999 Tarantula cranks fit Shimano pipe-spindle bottom brackets (either XTR, Dura-Ace, Ultegra, or 105).

Installing the crankset, as well as overhauling an XTR bottom bracket, is covered in Chapter 8 of *Zinn and the Art of Mountain Bike Maintenance.*

4.3B Lighter Bolts

A complete set of lightweight inner and outer chainring bolts made out of titanium will cost you about $100 (!); made out of aluminum, maybe $25. A titanium crank bolt is around $25, and its aluminum counterpart about $12. Again, *do not* install a titanium crank bolt into a titanium bottom bracket spindle, or any titanium bolt into any titanium part (stems, frames, etc.). The threads of the two titanium parts can gall and rip each other up. Install the crank first to appropriate torque using a steel bolt. Remove it and tighten in the (greased) lightweight bolt.

4.4 THE CHAINRINGS AND SPIDER ARMS

Not all that long ago, replacing mountain-bike chainrings was fairly straightforward, and spider arms were not interchangeable. You had one standard bolt circle, and you only had to choose between round or BioPace rings (that's a choice?). Now, however, it's a whole new ball game.

CRANK TIGHTENING TIP

from Calvin Jones, Park Tool Master Mechanic

Thread-lock compound is almost always appropriate on the crank bolt . . . if it is the correct grade. It is critical to lubricate threads to achieve a proper preload on a bolt, and thread-lock compound will act as a lubricant when you tighten the bolt. You should still put a layer of anti-seize under the head of the bolt to keep it from galling.

Wipe off the threads inside the spindle and on the bolt. The threads do not have to be perfectly clean. Use thread-locker and put a few drops on the end of the bolt.

Clean the spindle and inside the crank arm with alcohol. Install the arm and secure with the torque wrench to the recommended torque setting. If you are racing, I would recommend you choose the high end of the torque range.

4.4A Chainring Compatibility: Drilling, Size, and Shape

Suntour started the reduced-size chainring revolution with Microdrive. Instead of relying on a 26-36-46 combination (or thereabouts), Microdrive rings were 22-32-42. Campagnolo copied Microdrive, and Shimano then followed with Hyperdrive-C compact rings, which used an entirely different bolt circle from Microdrive.

As if three bolt circles were not enough (at least BioPace had gone away by this time), shifting ramps and gates and varying tooth profiles also became common (photo 4-8). Simple round middle and outer chainrings with the correct bolt circle no longer cut it, as shifting is not as good as with ramped rings.

Shifting ramps complicated things in another way. Most rings were made for

Shimano's five-arm spiders, in which the crank arm is centered between two of the spider arms. Some cranks, like Ritchey, however, merged one spider arm with the crank arm. If you used an aftermarket chainring on these, not only was the pin that keeps the chain from falling down between the arm and the chainring in the wrong place, but the shifting ramps were also not where they were designed to be for effective shifting.

Some manufacturers also offer machined chainring sets that install as a unit (photo 4-9). Some of these accept a standard inner chainring (photo 4-14), but the outer two rings are a single piece of aluminum. The spider bolts on from the back side on some of these cranks (photo 4-10).

Since 1997, Shimano now offers removable chainring spiders. The cassette-style chainring sets come in two different bolt patterns: full-size on XTR and compact, Hyperdrive-C size on the rest of the

CRANK TIGHTENING TIP

from Jeff Cole, Former World Cup Team Mechanic

If you are using titanium crank bolts, first tighten the crank arms on with steel bolts. Remove the steel bolts and install the titanium bolts. You can get the cranks on tighter that way. You run less of a risk of losing a crank arm due to the titanium bolts stretching enough to allow the crank sufficient movement on the spindle to work the bolt loose. You also are less likely to damage the titanium bolt threads by overtightening.

Use Ti-Prep on titanium threads and avoid installing titanium bolts into titanium spindles.

4-8

The shifting ramps and varying tooth profiles on a Hyperdrive-C chainring.

4-9

Cook Bros. crank with snap-on one-piece double outer chainring pair.

4-10

Cook Bros. crank spider securing nut being removed with a 36-mm headset wrench.

line. Two chainring spider options are available: one that accepts standard five-hole chainrings, and one for a new four-bolt pattern (photo 4-11) that fit no aftermarket chainrings.

The back side of the new-style Shimano right crank arm has threads for a lock ring and splines to engage the chainring spider; it accepts spiders with either bolt pattern. The spider is installed and removed via a snap ring and the lock ring (photo 4-12). On XTR, a second tool threads onto the crank bolt and prevents the splined lock-ring remover from popping off (photo 4-13).

Single-ring four-bolt chainrings for downhill and dual slalom are also available from Shimano for XTR cassette cranks (photos 4-11, 4-12, and 4-13).

4.4B Interchanging Chainrings

Why replace chainrings? Well, they wear out, plus older, ramp-less chainrings will never shift as well as newer rings with shifting ramps. Sometimes a chainring will get notched from repeated shifting at the same place in the stroke. It will not release the chain easily, causing hesitation or even chain suck. Someone else who shifts at a different place in their stroke may not even notice a problem with a chainring you cannot get to shift. You will have to find and file away the notch or replace the ring.

If you have an aluminum inner chainring, durability will be improved with a stainless-steel or titanium inner ring (photo 4-14). These harder grannies will also help with shifting and reduce chain suck: being thinner, they will release the chain better, and being tougher, they will get less burred up and last longer.

Weight savings are also possible, by switching from steel to aluminum or titanium rings. I recommend *not* using an aluminum granny ring, though.

With a five-arm spider, changing chainrings is simply a matter of removing the chainring bolts, slapping another one on, and tightening the bolts. You only have to make sure that you get rings with the right diameter bolt circle. You can access the larger rings from the outside, but you must remove the crank arm to interchange the inner chainring.

Interchanging Shimano four-hole chainrings works in the standard way for the inner and middle ring. The outer ring, however, is integral with the spider and is replaced as a unit. The snap ring and lock ring are removed (photos 4-11, 4-12, 4-13) to take it off.

Ritchey and other systems with one spider arm merged into the crank arm require accessing that bolt from the back side, as it is tapped straight into the back of the crank arm.

4.4C Chain Suck

Chain suck is often caused by the chainring not releasing the chain from a tooth as the chain tries to exit at the bottom toward the rear derailleur. A worn chainring can cause this, as can a chainring that is too thick or a chain that is too narrow.

A chainring can get notched right where you shift every time. Most people shift at a specific point in the stroke. Ideally, you should shift with your feet at the top and bottom, as pedaling forces are lowest then. In any case, a chainring that may suck the chain for you every time may work fine for someone else who shifts at a different point in the stroke or with a different foot on top. You may be able to fix the problem by finding the spot and filing it away, or you should replace the chainring. A bent chainring or chainring tooth can also cause chain suck and mandate ring replacement.

Note **Any time you switch chainrings, even if it is the same size as the one it replaces, you need to check your front derailleur vertical adjustment. The teeth may be taller and will hit the derailleur. If you wait until you are on the trail before trying a shift to the big ring, you may be in for a surprise!**

Shimano offers a go/no-go tool for checking chain plate spacing. It is called the TL-CN24 and is listed in Chapter 1, photo 1-3. The tool is inserted into the chain to see if the link plates are far enough apart to release from Shimano-spec chainring teeth (photo 2-2). If the tool will not go in, the chain is too narrow (less than 2.38-mm inner link spacing), and chain suck may go away. If the chain is to Shimano specification, but you have a non-Shimano chainring, you ought to measure the width of the teeth at the base relative to Shimano ones. If it is thicker, try a chain with wider plate spacing or get a thinner chainring.

4.4D Interchanging Spiders

One of the great things about cranks that have removable spiders is that, if you bend or crack a spider arm, you can replace the spider without replacing the entire crank. Shimano four-arm spiders are integral with the outer chainring, while five-arm spiders accept standard, separate chainrings.

Shimano spider replacement requires removal of a snap ring and a lock ring (photos 4-11, 4-12, 4-13). The snap ring can be pried off with a screwdriver, and the lock ring is removed with a special Shimano tool. On XTR, the tool is held in place with a female-threaded knurled nut (also available from Shimano) that screws onto the crank bolt. This is all covered in Chapter 8 of *Zinn and the Art of Mountain Bike Maintenance*.

Cook Bros. crank spiders come off by turning a nut with a 36-mm headset wrench (for a 1-1/8 inch headset) (photo 4-10).

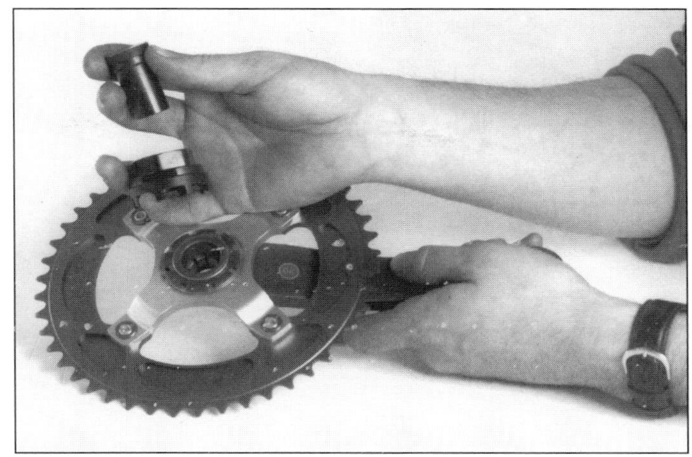

4-11
Shimano XTR crank showing four-arm spider, lock ring, and snap ring with splined lock-ring removal tool and tool-securing nut. The pictured crank has a single downhill chainring installed.

4-12
Splined lock-ring removal tool installed on Shimano XTR spider lock ring. The tool-securing nut threads onto the crank bolt.

4-13
Shimano XTR crank with splined lock-ring removal tool and tool-securing nut in place for lock-ring removal.

4-14
Installing a Cycle Dynamics titanium inner chainring on a Caramba crank with a torque wrench.

5

HUBS AND COGS

The spokes of the wheel are the rules of pure conduct; justice is the uniformity of their length; wisdom is the tire; modesty and thoughtfulness are the hub in which the immovable axle of truth is fixed.
—Buddha, *The Gospel (His Life and Teachings)*, 500 B.C.

This chapter completes our discussion of the mountain bike drivetrain. The cogs and freehub are the final components in that drive system, transferring your pedaling power into turning the rear wheel. Rigid, freely spinning hubs reduce parasitic dissipation of that power input. The cogs, freehub, and front hub are pictured in photo 5-1.

5.1 COGS

When I speak of cogs (a.k.a. "sprockets"), generally I mean freehub cogs (i.e., cogs on the rear cassette), rather than freewheel cogs. Freewheels,

5-1
Front hub and rear freehub with cogs installed.

which screw onto a threaded hub body, have become very rare on mountain bikes, and little or no freewheel development has happened in many years.

5.1A Cog Shape

The biggest improvement in cogs over the past 10 years has been in enhancing shifting by means of various ramps and gates on the cogs. Shimano started this revolution with the introduction of Hyperglide (HG). A Hyperglide cog features ramps on its outer face—to facilitate the chain shifting inward—and a few shorter teeth uniformly spaced about the cog—to allow the chain to easily step through the moving teeth (photo 5-2). The ramps are spaced so the chain can seat on both cogs simultaneously. Hyperglide chains have bowed-out link plates to exploit these cog features (photo 5-3).

Upon outward shifting, Hyperglide still lets the chain drop down with an abrupt "clunk" onto the next smaller cog, so Shimano introduced something called "Interactive Glide" (IG), which comes on the mid-level STX and Alivio groups. Additional shifting ramps are forged into the face of each cog (photo 5-4) to smooth the transition from a larger cog to a smaller one. The IG chain made to capitalize on these additional ramps has little nicks taken out of the opposite corners of each outer plate (photo 5-3).

Sachs has its own system for getting the chain to move from cog to cog with less shifting force. Teeth are removed at intervals about each cog to allow the chain to slip through (photo 5-5). The large entry gate is accompanied by taller

5-2
Hyperglide cogs have shifting ramps and varying tooth profiles.

5-3
Hyperglide (HG) chain has bowed-out outer link plates (bottom). Interactive Glide (IG) chain (top) has nicks out of opposing corners of each outer plate to facilitate outward shifting.

5-4
Interactive Glide (IG) upshifting ramps on the face of a cog.

5-5
Sachs teeth are removed at intervals about each cog to ease chain movement during shifting.

teeth elsewhere to hold the chain better, as the chain never needs to be shifted over them.

Ritchey makes a single cog to convert a Sachs or Shimano eight-speed cogset to nine speeds. The Ritchey cog has 33 teeth and is dish-shaped. It fits into the small space on the inner end of Shimano-compatible freehub bodies normally taken up with a spacer. The cog curvature moves the teeth inboard for standard eight-speed spacing from the teeth of the adjacent cog. The derailleur jockey wheels move one click further inboard to use the cog. On an ordinary wheel, the derailleur cage is likely to hook the spokes, so a special Off-Center Rear (OCR) rim is required. The OCR rim has the spoke holes drilled to the left (non-drive) side of center on the rim (photo 6-4). The spokes are directed toward the rim at a lower angle from the drive-side hub flange to avoid interference with the rear derailleur when the chain is on the 33-tooth cog.

For 1999 Shimano has nine-speed cog sets that fit on eight-speed freehubs and require a narrower chain.

5.1B Lightweight Cogs

There have been innumerable attempts over the years to make lighter cogs that wear well.

Aluminum has been tried many times over and usually ends up being abandoned eventually by the cog manufacturer. Even if alloyed and hardened, aluminum lacks the hardness or strength required to last on mountain bike cogs.

Shimano is successfully using aluminum in a different way to lighten up cog sets and increase their stiffness. Shimano's forged aluminum sprocket carriers are hollowed-out and cut-away cone-shaped parts with splines on the inside to fit onto the freehub body (photo 5-6). The cogs themselves are thin rings riveted or screwed to the aluminum carrier. The majority of the weight of most cogs is eliminated by only using the part of it that the chain runs on and eliminating the interior of the cog whose only purpose is to make it fit on the freehub body. The flex of each cog is reduced by rigidly fixing it near its outer diameter. The carrier also distributes the load on the freehub splines more evenly and protects freehubs made of softer materials, like titanium or aluminum.

Titanium cogs—at least larger ones—seem to offer acceptable durability for most riders. The cogs are usually CNC machined, rather than forged, so production and materials costs are both high. Most aftermarket manufacturers of titanium cogs machine Shimano-esque (or Shimano-licensed exact-spec) shift ramps and asymmetrical teeth into them for optimal shifting. Titanium is softer and more flexible than high-strength steel, but proper chain maintenance and good derailleur adjustment can yield good durability and shifting performance.

Shimano has upped the lightweight ante for its competitors by making titanium cogs combined with the alloy sprocket carrier. The largest three cogs on XTR cog sets are titanium. The aluminum is lighter yet than titanium, and by holding the cogs rigidly near the teeth (photo 5-6), flex is almost eliminated, enhancing shifting.

You can knock a tiny amount of weight off by replacing the steel cog lock ring with a colorful anodized aluminum version. It'll cost you $12 or so.

5.1C Freewheel Cogs

My recommendation on freewheels is: Don't use 'em. Few quality threaded hubs are available, hub axle rigidity and strength are lower, and a freewheel threaded onto a hub is heavier than a freehub. Tolerance stacking of the hub threads, freewheel threads, freewheel internals, cog/body interfaces and cog tooth cutting can result in lots of tooth wobble, reducing shifting performance and adjustablity. Freewheel cogs are not made with shifting ramps as effective as those of cassette cogs, and replacement cogs are essentially unavailable. If you insist on sticking with a freewheel system, buy up extra freewheels whenever you see them to replace yours when it wears out.

5.1D Checking for Cog Wear

Worn cogs have longer tooth valleys between adjacent teeth than they should. A good chain will not stay engaged as well, since it is only contacting one tooth at a

5-6
Shimano's forged aluminum sprocket carrier with cogs riveted to it.

5-8
Rohloff HG-check cog-wear indicator in use. The cog is shot if the last link on the measurement chain can be easily flipped in and out of the tooth pocket while tension is maintained on the tool arm.

5-9
Removing cassette lock ring with splined lock-ring remover and chain whip.

time. The expense of replacing worn cogs makes the case for immediately replacing a worn chain, since it will rapidly wear cogs. Cog wear can be detected visually, while riding, or with a wear-indicator tool.

Badly worn cogs are sometimes obvious to the eye, because the teeth become hook-shaped and bulged-out in the tooth valleys (photo 5-7). Do not confuse asymmetrical hook-shaped teeth designed for shifting enhancement with worn teeth.

You have worn cogs if you replace your chain, and, no matter how you adjust the rear derailleur, the chain skips under load on some of the cogs (assuming the chain does not have a stiff link, that is). Visual cog inspection can confirm the cog wear.

A cog-wear indicator tool can specifically reveal cog problems. The Rohloff "HG-check" indicator (photo 1-3) works by putting an attached length of chain under tension and seeing if the last half link can be flipped in and out of the tooth pocket (photo 5-8). It could be argued that the tool indicates replacement a bit prematurely; you can let the cog go a little longer. If the measurement chain itself can be lifted off any of the teeth while forward force is being applied to the handle, wear is excessive.

5.1E Upgrading and Replacing Cogs

When is cog upgrading useful? Certainly if your cogs are worn, any new cogs will constitute an upgrade. Upgrading from cogs with less-effective means of facilitating shifting to ones with better shifting ramps, etc., can also improve performance. Upgrading to lighter cogs can yield more weight benefit than a lot of bike-lightening upgrades, since cogs are relatively heavy compared to a lot of other bike parts.

My recommendation for cog upgrading is to get the best cogs you can afford. If you are willing to shell out for the lightest, I think that Shimano titanium cog sets on alloy sprocket carriers perform better than any other lightweight cog sets I have tried and will last about half as long as steel.

Remove the cogset (photo 5-9) and inspect all of the cogs once you have wiped

5-7
Worn teeth on a cog have become hook-shaped.

COG INSTALLATION TIP

from Paul Morningstar, Freehub Guru and Manufacturer of the Freehub Buddy Tool

The cogs do not fit tightly onto a freehub body, so they are free to move up and down a little bit. You can feel this vertical cog play when the lock ring is loose. The cogs usually start out off-center, and they certainly get pulled off-center by the chain. This results in the cogs' wobbling up and down as they turn, robbing some efficiency and shifting quickness and accuracy.

You can shim the cogs to get them firmly seated and more true on the freehub body. Cut some shims from a beer can 3/16x1-inch rectangular. Slip one shim into each of three freehub splines under the cogs, spaced equiangularly apart from each other (photo 5-10). If there is still room under other splines, space a few more shims evenly around the freehub.

them down. Except with old systems, you cannot usually replace single cogs anymore. Some older cog sets had three long bolts holding them together, which you could remove to replace individual cogs. You can install these cogs back on the freehub without replacing the bolts, if you like.

High-end Shimano cog sets on aluminum carriers are usually riveted to the carrier, so you need to replace the entire unit.

Many titanium aftermarket cog sets are separate cogs with spacers. These can be replaced individually. Replace the cogs with shift ramps and the number of teeth stamped on it facing outward. The asymmetrical large spline on the freehub body will prevent you from putting cogs on wrong.

5.2 FREEHUBS

A freehub is a complex, important part, but it is taken for granted by most riders. That is a mistake, because a tight and smoothly operating freehub is critical to your bike's operation. It must consistently lock up as soon as you pedal forward; it must run freely so you can coast quickly; it must not drag the chain forward while coasting; and it should not cause the cogs to wobble horizontally or vertically.

There are a lot of folks who just ride a freehub until it breaks and then replace it. Even though there are a lot of small moving parts inside and it is not usually sealed very well, riders often pay less attention to their freehub than to, say, their headset. I imagine this has to do with the perception that a freehub is a complex part with a ton of little parts that will jump out, skitter across the floor, be hard to find and even more difficult to reassemble. It just ain't so . . .

You can make a freehub spin more easily, lock up more quickly, turn truer, and wobble the cogs less. In fact, with a few changes, your old freehub can work much better than a new one . . . and you won't have to build a new wheel in the process!

The freehub body is attached to the rear hub and has at least two types of bearings

5-10
Slipping beer-can shims into freehub splines to the center the cogs.

5-11
Freehub cutaway showing bearings, pawl, and pawl spring. Freehub disassembly tool is on the right.

inside. In a Shimano freehub, two sets of 25 tiny balls on the core support the freehub body (photo 5-11). (Sometimes if you put an extra ball in each set, the freehub will run more smoothly with less wear.) A larger set of hub ball bearings at the outboard end reduces bending forces on the rear axle. A pawl and ratchet mechanism not only allows the freehub to spin backwards (i.e., to "freewheel" when the rider is coasting) with as little friction as possible, but also locks the freehub core to the hub shell when chain force pulls in the forward direction. This mechanism must be able to take very high peak loads from strong riders (even from two riders on a tandem!), yet it must spin freely when coasting. That is a lot to ask of a part that is subject to dirt and water from the trail and even high-pressure washing. And few riders ever even bother to lubricate it!

5.2A Freehub Lubrication

The freehub is susceptible to junk getting in it, primarily from the inboard side. A freehub without lubrication will deteriorate quickly, as hardened bearings and bearing surfaces oxidize (rust) rapidly. Also, a sticky freehub can cause chain suck by not freewheeling when you stop pedaling. The cogs will keep turning forward and push the chain forward where it can drop between the chainstay and the chainring.

Most freehubs come with very little lubricant in them. Lubrication, which one would normally think of as a maintenance procedure, actually constitutes an upgrade that protects your investment. Except on super-expensive sealed-bearing models, I recommend lubricating freehubs when new, before you ever go riding with them. Shimano freehubs come with very light lubricant in them of viscosity eight or so—equivalent to automatic transmission fluid. By lubricating the freehub with something heavier, you will increase the durability and sealing of the freehub. You may be amazed at how much more smoothly it turns.

Chain lubricant can be flowed into a freehub, as shown in Chapter 6 of *Zinn and the Art of Mountain Bike Maintenance*. To get heavier lubricant in there, you need a Morningstar Freehub Buddy tool. The Freehub Buddy allows you to force lubricant into a Shimano or Joy Tech freehub under pressure. It also allows you to force solvent through the freehub to flush grit out. The lubricant you use depends on the season, where you live, the kind of riding you do, and what grease you use on your hub bearings.

It is most efficient to service the freehub when you are overhauling the hub (see Chapter 6 of *Zinn and the Art of Mountain Bike Maintenance*). After removing the axle and the bearings (photo 5-12), you must remove the dust cap. Recent high-quality hubs have a thread-on dust cap, which you

5-12
Freehub with cogs off and axle and bearings removed.

5-13
Prying the dust cap out with a screwdriver.

5-14
Morningstar J tool hooked under the dust cap edge for removal. Pull up on the tool to pop the dust cap out.

5-15
Morningstar machined replacement dust cap seals hub-bearing race with an O-ring around the outside.

5-16
Flushing a freehub with solvent from a turkey baster through a Freehub Buddy tool.

unscrew. Older and cheaper hubs have pressed-in (or mashed-in!) dust caps. These can be carefully pried out with a screwdriver (photo 5-13) or, better yet, with Morningstar's hook-shaped "J" tool. The J tool hooks under the dust cap edge (photo 5-14). Pull up on the tool; you are using the head of the 10-mm fixing bolt that holds the freehub to the hub as a fulcrum. With either a screwdriver or the J tool, work around slowly, prying a bit at a time all of the way around. With the J tool, as the dust cap comes up higher, you can drop a short bolt into the head of the 10-mm freehub fixing bolt to lean the tool against as a taller fulcrum.

Put a little grease on the two rubber O-rings of the Freehub Buddy, and push it into the seat where the bearings were. If it does not fit, you may need to use the thinner O-ring that comes with the tool.

If you feel grit and hear crunching noises as you turn the freehub body, you may want to start by injecting solvent to flush the crud out. The lubricant alone, as it goes in under pressure, will push out some of the grit, but solvent will loosen things up to do a better job.

If you will be injecting solvent, use one that is compatible with the lubricant you intend to use. If you will be using a petroleum-based lubricant, inject diesel fuel. If you will be using a synthetic lubricant, inject a synthetic solvent.

FREEHUB LUBRICATION TIPS

from Paul Morningstar

Sticking pawls can be a problem with grease inside the freehub (especially old, dried grease), although not always. I have found greases that are as slick as anything, while there are oils formulated in such a way as to cause the pawls to stick. I know riders who have used Pedro's grease in midwinter without slippage problems.

I've found over the years that the operator's past lube experience and their desire to make their freehub work better is the key to success. The pawl's springs and their location on the individual pawls are the limiting factors. Not all freehubs have the same internal configuration. For example, if Shimano relieved the pocket under the pawl more, there would be more room for grease under each pawl. You can overcome sticky grease if you put greater spring tension on each pawl by the use of additional springs (see section 5.2D and the sidebar on page 65).

When finished, you can replace the stock dust cap with a machined Morningstar dust cap (photo 5-15) making subsequent lubrication and overhauls easier.

Put the solvent into a bulb-syringe turkey baster, and force-thread the tip of the baster into the center hole of the Freehub Buddy. Squirt solvent in as you slowly rotate the freehub (photo 5-16). Continue until the solvent runs clean, and the crunching sound goes away.

The O-rings on the Freehub Buddy surround the radial ports that distribute the solvent or lubricant. The inner O-ring prevents whatever you are injecting from going into the center of the hub and the outer O-ring keeps it from coming back out the front. These ensure that the solvent or lubricant coming out through the tool's two ports will be forced into the space between the shell of the freehub and the wheel bearing race. It will make its way to the freehub bearings and pawls and flush out the back, where the freehub body and the hub shell meet.

SELECTING THE RIGHT LUBRICANT

It is generally a good practice to opt for a thick lubricant in hot weather and a thinner one for cold. If you use petroleum-based grease in your hub bearings, use petroleum-based lubricant in the freehub. If you use synthetic grease in the hub bearings, use synthetic lubricant in the freehub.

Use chain lube for cold weather (silicone oil is a good choice in subzero temperatures), outboard-motor gear oil for medium temperatures, and even bicycle wheel bearing grease for very high temperatures. Lubricant that is too thin will not protect the mechanism as well, and one that is too thick will cause the pawls to stick.

(Important: Do not put grease in your freehub unless you replace it frequently and are prepared to forgo Shimano's warranty coverage. If grease dries out in there, it will cause the pawls to stick and risk chipped ratchet teeth and pawls from insufficient overlap.)

For most conditions the best choice is a petroleum grease in the wheel bearings and outboard-motor gear oil inside the freehub. The outboard-motor gear oil is sulfur-based, and adheres very well to parts. Alternatively, you can custom-mix compatible grease and oil and squirt it in with a 50-cc glue syringe.

Force lubricant into the tool as you turn the freehub, the same way as you would with solvent. The lube galley hole in the center of the Freehub Buddy will accept the tip of a bicycle grease gun (photo 5-17) or an oil can. You can also jam the wide, rounded tip of many bicycle chain-lube bottles to seal the wider, threaded part of the hole; chain lube is a bit thin for summer, but it is a whole lot better to put *something* in there than nothing! The tool also comes with a nylon threaded insert to accept the 2-mm plastic tube tip on some aerosol lubricants. Inject lubricant until it flows cleanly out the back of the freehub, where the inboard end of the freehub body meets the hub shell.

The Freehub Buddy also works with Shimano silent clutch freehubs. Make sure you use oil in these; a long roller can get stuck with grease more easily than a pawl can.

Without a Freehub Buddy tool, you can flow chain lube into the freehub between the hub bearing race and the wall of the freehub body. You will not be able to inject grease, but you can put thin chain lube in. Keep turning the freehub as you flow in lubricant (photo 5-18). Stop when clean lube is flowing out the inboard end of the freehub.

Important: Never submerge or rinse a freehub in a solvent bath, as the solvent will carry in grit from the freehub body/hub shell interface. The grit mixed with oil or solvent will make a great grinding compound that will wear away the freehub guts.

5.2B Overhaul Freehub Body

Sometimes it is worthwhile to overhaul the freehub body. This is indicated if it still runs roughly after repeated flushing with solvent and lubricant. There may be some broken parts inside, and if you are lucky, you may be able to find replacement parts for that particular model and year. Additionally, you can modify the internal configuration to make the freehub rotate without wobble (see section 5.2C and sidebar on page 65).

Freehub disassembly varies with the numerous types of freehubs on the market. Generally, you must remove the hub axle and then remove the freehub body, which usually comes off with a 10-mm hex key (photo 5-19).

After that, brands vary, and it may or may not be obvious what to do. I recommend reading an instruction manual for your particular freehub before ripping into it. Springs and pawls and ball bearings can fly every which way. Disassemble it in a clean, deep-sided tray or bucket to catch flying parts.

Many specialty freehubs use cartridge bearings instead of loose bearings and have titanium or aluminum freehub bodies. Hugi, DT, and some Mavic hubs have ratchet teeth and pawls on the facing surfaces of the freehub body and the hub shell, rather than radial pawls and cylindrical ratchet teeth inside the freehub. Cane Creek has produced

5-17
The center lube galley hole in the Freehub Buddy will accept the tip of a bicycle grease gun.

5-18
Lubricating a freehub without a Freehub Buddy tool: Flow chain lube between hub-bearing race and freehub shell as you turn it.

5-19
Removing the freehub body from the hub with a 10-mm hex key.

FREEHUB IMPROVEMENT TIPS

from Paul Morningstar

Almost all Shimano freehubs wobble a bit, which makes shifting less precise, wears the freehub faster, and creates friction. Get rid of the wobble by removing the thinnest internal shim (see section 5.2C) and/or sanding the back of the hub-bearing race.

Another upgrade is to put one or two additional springs on each pawl (see section 5.2D). With the extra spring tension, the freehub will always lock up, regardless of the lubricant. You can now lubricate your freehub with a grease that actually protects and helps seal it. The light oil that comes in a freehub offers little protection. Rather than replacing freehubs frequently, you can have a freehub that lasts a long time and works better than the stock one.

silent-clutch freehubs, and Chris King freehubs have precision-machined pawl systems with far finer and more numerous ratchet teeth for faster freehub lockup. Shimano makes both ratchet-type freehubs with radial pawls as well as silent clutch freehubs.

This book will only endeavor to illustrate disassembly of Shimano ratcheting freehubs, since Shimano sells so many of them, and since many hub manufacturers mount Shimano freehub bodies onto their hubs.

Shimano freehub disassembly:

Using Morningstar's disassembly tool, unscrew the hub-bearing race from the end of the freehub. The tool fits into the two notches (photo 5-20). *Important: the bearing race is left-hand-threaded!*

Once the bearing race is off to expose internal bearings, slide the body off the core (photo 5-21). You can now clean the bearings, races, pawls, and springs. Grease and reassemble.

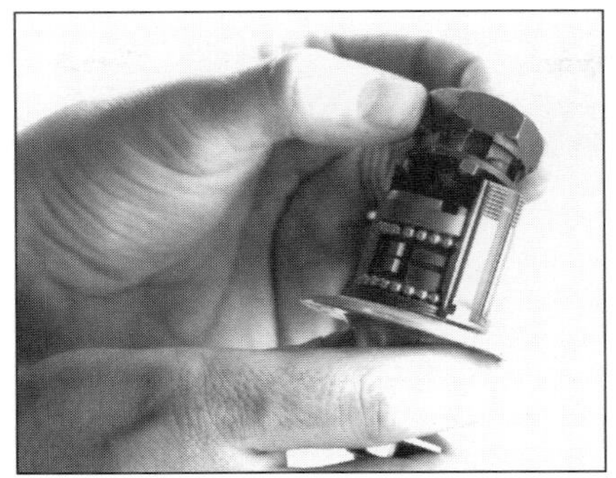

5-20
Freehub cutaway showing how the disassembly tool fits into the two notches in the hub-bearing race. Notice the groove with the thin C-shaped pawl return spring in the freehub core.

5-21
From left: the freehub shell, core, shims, dust cap, bearings, hub-bearing race, and Morningstar disassembly tool.

5.2C Tightening Up a Wobbly Freehub

Many freehubs wobble as they spin. You can see it when the bike is freewheeling. Grab your freehub and rock it to see how much play yours has. Eliminating the wobble will improve shifting and reduce freehub wear and friction.

You can practically eliminate the wobble in a Shimano freehub by removing one internal shim. The shims (photo 5-21) are inside to account for possible deviations in manufacturing tolerances. Since it is better to have a wobbly freehub than one that is too tight to turn, the shims are automatically installed in all freehubs to add a little play. Remove the thinnest shim, and reassemble the freehub, tightening the hub-bearing race down fully with the tool. The freehub should spin freely without rocking. The cogs will now stay in line and shift faster.

If removing the shim tightens the freehub too much, yet there is play in it with the shim installed (or if there is still play *after* removing the shim), you can eliminate the play with some sanding. Sand the bottom of the hub-bearing race (photo 5-21, second from right) by rubbing it on a piece of fine sandpaper held down on a flat surface. You are sanding the surface at the end of the threads. Reassemble the freehub with one or both shims installed, whatever works best.

5.2D Increasing Freehub Pawl Spring Tension

You can also put one or two additional springs on each pawl. Then the freehub will always lock up, regardless of the lubricant. The stock spring is a very thin semicircular ring fitting into a groove bisecting each pawl and circumscribing the freehub core (photo 5-20). The groove is many times the width of the spring; there is room for more springs in it. You may have to beg freehub pawl springs from bike shops throwing out old freehubs, since the springs are hard to get from Shimano.

5.2E Replacing Freehub Body

If the freehub body is shot, it can be replaced without replacing the entire hub. Usually, a 10-mm hex key removes it, once the hub axle has been removed (photo 5-19). (Removing the hub axle is covered in Chapter 6 of *Zinn and the Art of Mountain Bike Maintenance.*) Some freehubs require you to control the pawls and keep them from springing out as you insert the new freehub body into the hub shell. A twist tie can work for this, as can a bent piece of wire made for the task.

5.2F Freewheels

As I mentioned in section 5.1C, my recommendation of what to do with a thread-on freewheel is to throw it out (actually, recycle it or give it to a bike shop), and get a freehub and cogs. Shifting and rear-axle longevity will improve, worn cogs will now be replaceable, and bike weight will probably drop.

Again, if you insist on sticking with a freewheel system, buy up extra freewheels whenever you see them to replace yours when it wears out.

5.3 HUBS

Hubs are about as integral to a bicycle as it gets. If they did not spin, the wheels would not roll. Having well-adjusted, freely spinning hubs that are stiff enough for your application is important.

5.3A Fine-Tuning Hub Axle Adjustment

If the hub is loose, the wheel will flop back and forth between the brake pads and not track well. Check for looseness by grabbing the top of the rim or tire while the wheel is on the bike and pushing it side to side. If you can feel any play, you need to adjust it. Conversely, if the hub is tight laterally and feels really rough spinning, it could be too tight.

You can tighten a loose-bearing hub a bit by putting a wrench on the outer nut on either end of the hub. Holding one wrench, tighten the other one. If the hub is put together properly, it should only turn a fraction of a turn before coming to a stop. If it keeps turning, you need to tighten the outer locknut against the cone on either end of the hub before checking the adjustment with the wheel in the bike again.

If the hub is too tight, put a cone wrench on the cone on either side of the hub, and turn one counterclockwise while holding the other. You can do this while the wheel is still in the frame. If that is not enough, loosen the cone and locknut, and adjust as in Chapter 6 of *Zinn and the Art of Mountain Bike Maintenance.*

5.3B Overhauling Hubs

Hub overhaul is covered in detail in Chapter 6 of *Zinn and the Art of Mountain Bike Maintenance*. It is a good idea to overhaul your hubs as frequently as you can stand to. I know of no one who complains that they overhaul their hubs too often! Most people get to it rarely, and sometimes it is too late to save the bearings. Once you start doing it a bit, you can see how often it makes sense for you to do it with your kind of riding, based on what you find inside.

5.3C Upgrading Hubs

The reasons to upgrade hubs are 1). weight reduction; 2). stiffness, to keep suspension elements from moving independently; 3). friction reduction; 4). better seals; 5). simply putting on a better freehub; and 6). switching to disc brakes. When getting new hubs, unless you buy completely built wheels, you will be building some wheels. Consult Chapter 12 of *Zinn and the Art of Mountain Bike Maintenance* for wheel-building instructions, and Chapter 6 of this book for the finer points.

Stiffer hubs may be called for if you have trouble keeping your wheel going where you want it to, especially on technical descents. If the front rim is continually tapping back and forth against each brake pad, a stiffer hub could help. This symptom can also be caused by a wheel that is weak laterally, either because the spokes are too loose, or the rim is too weak. First assure yourself that the wheel is stiff enough by checking spoke tension and by installing it in a rigid fork and seeing if it behaves similarly. If the wheel is O.K., your hub may not be rigid enough to counteract the independent movement of the suspension fork legs.

Even though big hub shells look stiff, the main determining factor of a hub that is stiff enough for front suspension is the size of the end flange that clamps against the fork dropouts. Photo 5-22 shows a hub that not only has a large end flange but also a D-shaped axle to lock into the dropouts and help prevent fork twisting. After the end flange size, the main determinants of the hub's resistance to bending are the bearing size and the outer diameter of the axle at the point it passes through the bearing.

The older the suspension fork you have, the more you need a really stiff front hub, since the stanchions are skinnier and flexier, and so is the bolt-on fork brace. Recent forks have larger stanchions and a better interface between the fork brace and the outer legs. For example, a Rock Shox Judy or 1999 Manitou brace and post-1996 outer legs are cast as a single piece to build in rigidity. Manitou's 1995 to 1999 oversized outer legs are bonded into a cylindrical contact area molded into either end of the fork brace, providing similar rigidity. Here you thought you were only upgrading your hub, and you may be deciding to upgrade your fork, too!

BEARING SEAL TIP

from Wayne Stetina, Shimano North America R&D Manager

Better bearing seals mean more drag, which riders usually do not want. On the other hand, you do not want grit and water getting into your bearings. You can improve the sealing of your bearings by putting lots of grease behind the seal, as well as in front of it. This applies to bottom brackets as well as hubs.

If lubing and even overhauling your freehub does not result in the kind of performance you want, or if you just want a lighter freehub altogether, this can be a reason to upgrade the entire rear hub.

5.3D Internal-Gear Hubs

While internal-gear hubs have been a mainstay of city bikes for years, now they are starting to appear on high-performance bikes. The most obvious application is for downhill bikes, since eliminating the derailleur and the corresponding chain slack could reduce thrown chains. Rohloff has a 14-speed internal-gear hub that is starting to appear on downhill bikes, and Sachs has taken steps in that direction a few times.

5-22 Ringle's Super Duper Bubba oversized hub axle end flange with D-shaped axle end.

6
WHEELS

Rollin', rollin',
rollin', keep
those doggies
rollin'
—*Rawhide*
theme song

This chapter is devoted to two things: what to look for in wheels for your specific use, and wheel-building tips and special techniques for particular types of wheels.

This chapter does not have step-by-step wheel-building instructions, since I have an entire chapter (Chapter 12) in *Zinn and the Art of Mountain Bike Maintenance* describing in great detail every step in building front or rear three-cross wheels. That chapter also explains how to build a rear wheel using an off-center-drilled rim (photo 6-4). Nor is truing a standard wheel covered here. Chapters 3, 6, and 12 of *Zinn and the Art of Mountain Bike Maintenance* describe how to true a wobbly wheel.

This chapter does feature tips on how to make the wheels you build come out better, and it offers methods for building specific types of wheels. It also illustrates some methods of repairing nonstandard wheels, such as composite wheels and deep-section wheels.

6.1 RIMS

Obviously, the rim and spokes work together to form a wheel and give it structural strength. It may *not* be obvious, however, exactly what parts of that relationship are critical for the rim to play to make a strong, stiff wheel.

6.1A Rim Hoop Strength

The hoop strength of a rim, i.e., its strength without any spokes in it, plays a critical role in determining the strength of the finished product. Lateral stiffness and strength is also important. People are generally aware that higher-grade aluminum will make a stronger rim, but they may not be aware of the role rim section plays. Rim hoop strength and lateral stiffness, particularly of a light rim, is dependent on multiple walls and bigger sections. Generally, a stiffer rim has bigger air spaces inside.

A weak rim requires more spoke tension, because it takes less force to ovalize it to the point where the nipples on the top of the rim poke up enough that they lose contact with the rim, allowing them to unscrew. To stay tight, the nipples must maintain contact with the rim. A stronger rim makes it possible to accomplish this with lower spoke tension. A deeper, stiffer rim section with large air spaces inside spreads weight out over more spokes. You can get away with fewer spokes if you have high hoop strength.

6.1B Rim Roundness and Flatness

The wheel will build up with even spoke tension if the rim is perfectly round and flat. If the rim is misshapen, then some of the spokes will have to be tighter than others in order to pull it into roundness or trueness. This means that overall spoke tension will have to be higher, so that the least-tight spoke will still have enough tension not to unscrew. Each nipple must maintain contact with the rim at all times as the rim gets ovalized rolling across the ground. The problem will be exacerbated with a weaker rim. A weak rim will ovalize more and

RIM-CHECKING TIP

Prior to Wheel Building from Steve Hed, Founder, Designer, and Builder of Hed Wheels

Before lacing the wheel:

1. Lay the rim on a flat glass plate to determine whether it is flat. Get a flat rim.
2. Check the rim's roundness by putting two nails in a wall. Set the bottom of the rim on top of them. Rotate the rim, marking the high and low points of the top of the rim on the wall with a pencil. Choose a rim with which the pencil goes up and down the least.

A flat, round rim will build up much more easily and will have more even spoke tension, resulting in more longevity, fewer loose or broken spokes, and less truing.

6-1
The machined braking surface and ground-off weld bead of a Bontrager rim.

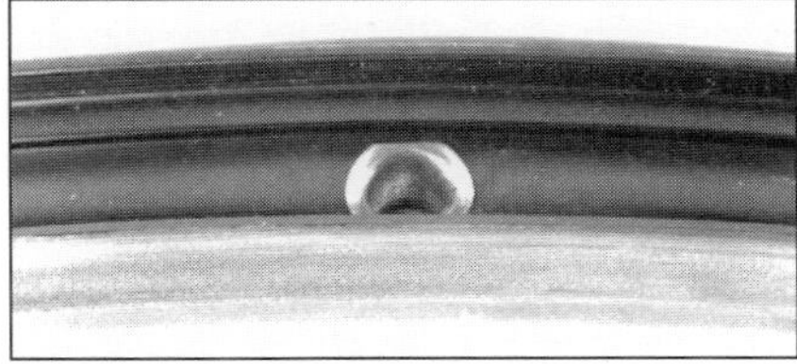

6-2
The ceramic braking surface of a Mavic Cross-Max rim.

require higher spoke tension, especially from those least-tight spokes on an imperfectly shaped rim, so that their nipples do not unscrew.

6.1C Machined Braking Surfaces

A rim will be much flatter, build up more easily, and not have uneven surging of the rim brakes if the braking surfaces are machined after manufacture. Mavic pioneered this machining method when it came out with welded rims in the mid-1990s. While a standard pinned rim seam always forms an irregularity in the braking surface resulting in uneven braking, a welded seam is simply too rough for anyone to tolerate. Thus, machining of braking surfaces was born.

Now many manufacturers offer machined braking surfaces on high-end welded rims (photo 6-1) as well as on pinned rims (photo 6-4). (Pinned rims are rims held together at the seam by forcing metal pins into each end as splints.) After machining, each side is uniform and parallel to the other side. While the braking surfaces start out smooth and parallel, overly high spoke tension or a weak rim can still result in the rim being bulged out at each spoke nipple, resulting in brake surging and vibration. Braking will be very smooth with most machined rims, though.

6.1D Ceramic Braking Surfaces

Coating the braking surfaces with a rough and super-hard ceramic (photo 6-2) results in greater braking-surface longevity and a higher coefficient of friction with the brake pads. The ceramic coating is usually sprayed onto the rim under heat and pressure to maintain a chip-free bond to the rim.

Brake pads grinding through the rim sides on wet and gritty descents is a virtual nonissue with a ceramic rim. Wearing away the brake pads could be an issue, however!

Drawbacks to ceramic rims (besides high cost) can be accelerated pad wear and brake squeal. If available for your brakes, use ceramic-specific brake pads when using ceramic rims. These will wear longer and squeal less.

Squealing can also be controlled with more brake pad toe-in and a brake stiffener arch. Brakes will squeal when they are grabbing the hardest, and they will generally grab better to the high-friction surface of a ceramic rim. The brake pads will be pulled forward by the rim, flexing the brake arms, pivots, and frame stays so that the heels of the pads are contacting the rims. The heels digging in this way results in chatter and squeal. Setting up the brakes with more toe-in will result in the pads ending up flat against the rim after being pulled forward under high braking. A brake stiffener arch will give the same result by reducing the flex in the seatstays or fork legs and brake posts.

6.1E Disc-Brake-Specific Rims

The advent of disc brakes has opened the door to many new rim and tire designs not possible before when the rim had to double as a braking surface and the tire and rim had to fit up between the pads. Rims and tires both had to fall into a narrow width range dictated by industrywide specifications on brake-post

6-3
Ultra-wide Hed disc-brake-specific rim laced to Rock Shox disc-brake hub. Tire is 3.0-inch Nokian DH.

6-4
Ritchey OCR off-center-drilled rear rim. This WCS model also has machined braking surfaces.

Tips on Disc-Brake Rims and Tires from Steve Hed

When riding cross-country with a disc brake:

If you use a really wide rim (40 mm or so), like the one in photo 6-3, you can run a 1.5-inch-wide tire and get the same ground contact profile as a 1.95- to 2.125-inch tire. (Note: Not all tire profiles work with a wide rim, especially square profiles.) The advantages to a thin tire with a wide rim over a narrow rim with a bigger tire are:

1. With a lighter tire, you have less rotating weight at the edge of the wheel where it matters the most, yet you make no traction sacrifices, because the ground-contact profile is the same as a bigger, heavier tire.
2. If the rim is as wide or wider than the tire, the tire sidewalls are vertical or beyond. This means that you cannot get a pinch flat, because the tire will compress within the width of the rim. (Pinch flats occur when you pinch the tube between the rim edge and the tire.)
3. Since pinch flats are not an issue, you can run the tire at lower pressure and have better cornering control and lower rolling resistance on rough trails.

When riding downhill with a disc brake:

If the rim is really wide, you can use a really wide tire (photo 6-3) and have far more cornering and braking control in a downhill. The swing-arm of the bike will have to be built to accommodate the huge tire. It will be worth it.

placement, and rim sidewalls had to be smooth and vertical.

The rim for use with a disc brake can be built strictly with weight and strength considerations in mind; width and sidewall shape play much less of a role. The evolution of disc-brake-specific rims, particularly for downhill, is toward wider and wider rims (photo 6-3). Advantages to a wider rim are that the tire is opened out to increase the radius of curvature of the tread and get more tread on the ground. Sidewalls are also closer to vertical, giving them more lateral stiffness, so they can be run at lower pressures and not fold over when cornering or suffer pinch flats.

6.1F Off-Center-Rear (OCR) Rims

A rim drilled off-center (photo 6-4) can reduce the spoke dish on the rear wheel. It makes a lower spoke angle from the drive side and a higher spoke angle from the left side to meet the rim off-center to the left. OCR is a Ritchey acronym for "Off-Center Rear" rim. This type of rim is a necessity when using the dished ninth cog on a Ritchey 2x9 system to provide enough spoke clearance for the rear derailleur.

6.1G Wheel Size

When it comes to wheel size, there is not a lot of choice for most people, since the industry has pretty much settled on 26 inches as the way to go. Smaller riders may benefit from smaller wheels (say, 24 inches), however.

Advantages to a Smaller Wheel Size for a Small Rider Are:

1. The smaller wheel and shorter fork will put the rider's headset less high above the ground, allowing a lower stem height. A small rider can then have a handlebar-to-saddle height relationship proportional to that of a big rider, rather than being forced to have a handlebar higher than the saddle.

2. The bike's top tube can be shorter without the rider's toe hitting the front tire in a low-speed turn. This allows the small rider to have a reach from the saddle to the bar proportional to that of a big rider. With big wheels, the small rider, if he or she can be fit at all, must use a super-short stem, which throws off the weight distribution over the wheels.
3. Smaller wheels are lighter and can be started up from a stop and hauled up hills more easily. It is illogical for a small rider with correspondingly low power output to lug the same amount of bike weight around as a big rider.

Disadvantages to Small Wheel Size Are:

1. A smaller wheel falls into holes that a big wheel would roll over.
2. The smaller wheel is less stable. It has less angular momentum and thus provides the bike with less stability from gyroscopic action. Watch a kid riding on 12-inch wheels to see this.
3. Smaller wheels get less traction in sand and gravel.
4. A smaller contact patch results in higher rolling resistance due to higher stress concentration in a smaller area.

6.2 SPOKES

Defining characteristics of spokes are length, thickness (gauge), the material they are made of, the finish they have been given, and whether they have chromed brass nipples or aluminum nipples. All spokes are threaded on at least one end. Most spokes have a nail-head with a bend (the elbow) adjacent to it (and threads on the opposite end). Some "straight-pull" spokes have a nail head with no elbow. Some spokes are flattened (bladed) in the midsection and round only at the ends. Some spokes are threaded at both ends (double-threaded) and fit into nipples at the hub and at the rim (photo 6-5).

6-6 Checking spoke tension by squeezing two spokes with your hand.

Be aware that the thread inside the nipples is different depending on spoke gauge. Fourteen-gauge nipples will thread onto 15-gauge spokes, but the spokes will soon be yanking out of them, and the wheel will rapidly fall apart.

6.2A Spoke Check

Check your spoke tension periodically on your wheels by squeezing pairs of spokes together (photo 6-6). You can avoid having a wheel fall apart on a ride if you notice in advance when a spoke or two is loosening up.

Check spokes on the drive side (behind the largest cog) frequently for nicks from overshifting, resulting in weakened spokes that break easily. Whenever you *do* shift into your spokes, check the spokes right away for damage. Replace

6-5 Ringle's Super-Bubba radial hub laced radially with bladed titanium double-threaded spokes to Sun CR17 rim.

6-7 Hed Cross-Country radial deep-section composite-rim wheel. Spokes are titanium blades.

the external drive-side spokes if they are nicked or bent from the chain jamming into them. The very high torque in low gear on a mountain bike can break spokes that have been chewed into by the chain. A plastic spoke guard is not a stupid thing to use, particularly if you have a problem with overshifting your large cog. Some straight-pull hub designs have a fragile drive-side flange that can be costly to replace if you overshift into it. Mavic CrossMax hubs come with a plastic spoke protector for this reason.

6.2B Choosing Spoke Type and Gauge

Unless you are getting titanium spokes, get stainless steel, not galvanized, ones. You spend too much time and money building a wheel to save a few bucks with galvanized spokes. You would end up regretting the choice after they rust, look terrible, and become hard to true.

Your choice will be between straight-gauge and double-butted spokes. Straight-gauge spokes have uniform thickness end to end. Double-butted spokes are thicker on the ends and thinner in the middle to save weight.

If you are a heavy person, using a disc brake, or racing downhill, get straight-gauge spokes at least 2.0 mm (14 gauge) thick. The more the better, too. Use chromed brass nipples (they are shiny silver) rather than alloy nipples.

Lighter riders riding cross-country with rim brakes can choose along the spoke strength continuum from double-butted 14/15 gauge (2.0/1.8 mm) for heavier use to straight 15-gauge (1.8 mm) and even double-butted 15/16 or 15/17 gauge for lighter use. Choose double-butted spokes with gradual thickness transitions, as they tend to break at the butt if the transition is abrupt. Lighter riders can save some weight at the rim with aluminum nipples.

Bladed (i.e., aero-shaped) spokes used to be limited to trick time-trial road wheels, but they can now be found on mountain bikes as well. Bladed spokes either must be double-threaded and laced radially to a radially drilled hub (photos 6-5, 6-7), or the hub holes must be slotted to allow bladed spokes with an elbow to fit through.

Titanium spokes are also getting wider use on mountain wheels. Expect more stretch and breakage with them than with stainless-steel spokes. Titanium spokes are stronger if they have been cold-worked by hammering them into a bladed shape (photos 6-5, 6-7).

6.2C Choosing Spoke Length

The simplest way to get the right length spokes is to let a shop be responsible for it. Go to a bike shop and request the proper-length spokes for the rim and hub and spoke pattern you are using. If they screw up and give you the wrong length, they will have to exchange these for the right length. Problem is, you will have to build the wheel before you will know if they are the right length or not.

You can also depend on a spoke table in a shop reference book, like *Sutherland's Manual* or *Barnett's Manual*. The manual may not have the exact hub and rim you are using, though, since things change quickly in the mountain-bike industry. It is hard for a manual to keep up.

You can also use a spoke length calculator. Wheelsmith makes a manual spoke calculator with which you take measurements of your rim and hub.

Wheel Wizard is a $20 computer software spoke length calculator for Windows 3.x or 95. It calculates the correct spoke lengths for any combination of hub and rim. It is very easy to use, and has hundreds of hubs and rims already measured and entered into a database. All you have to do is select the correct hub and rim you are using, and the needed measurements are entered automatically.

Wheel Wizard comes on one 3.5-inch floppy and takes up about 1MB of hard-drive space depending on the operating system. It includes a Vernier caliper, free updates to the program, and help and tech support via e-mail.

Finally, you may need spokes of an unobtainable length for some special wheel you are making. This is particularly common with fathers building trick little wheels for their kids; fancy hubs will not have the same flange size as cheap coaster-brake hubs. You need not completely despair, though. Some shops have a Phil Wood spoke threader, which can make spokes with rolled threads as nice as ones you buy. There are also cheap spoke-thread cutters, but the thread quality is lacking.

6.3 WHEELBUILDING (BEYOND THREE-CROSS)

In *Zinn and the Art of Mountain Bike Maintenance,* Chapter 12 shows step by step how to lace up and true three-cross wheels, front or rear, including for off-center-drilled rear rims. Three-cross is the most common spoking pattern. It's name refers to the fact that each spoke crosses over three others from the same side of the hub.

Sometimes, you may wish to use another spoking pattern. Generally, the more crosses in a pattern, the more vertical compliance the wheel has. If you want a really soft wheel, you can build it four-cross. If you want a really stiff wheel, you can spoke it radially.

With any spoked wheel, remember that too much tension will be its death. The spoke nipples will get rounded off the rim, will bulge at each spoke hole, and the spokes will pull the ferrules out of the rim, deforming and possibly cracking the rim around each hole. If you start with lower tension, you can always retrue and tension the wheel more as needed.

6.3A Radial Spoking

Radially laced spokes go straight out to the rim, taking the shortest possible route to get there (photos 6-5, 6-7, and 6-8). Radial spoking makes for very stiff wheels because the spokes are directed along the same direction as impact forces on the wheel. Crossing patterns allow some give by meeting the impact forces at an angle.

Radially spoking a wheel will also make it lighter, since the spokes are shorter.

If the rim is not strong enough, radial wheels can loosen up easily. As the rim ovalizes and shortens vertically, the top and bottom spokes poke through out from the rim, and the nipples lose contact with their seats in the rim. The spokes will rapidly loosen up under these conditions.

6-8
Mavic CrossMax radially spoked wheel with ceramic braking surfaces.

6-9
Three-cross wheel with Rock Shox rotor mounted. The rotor is on the left side of the bike.

Even with a rim of high hoop strength, radial spokes need to have high tension to counteract this, whereas normal crossing spokes do not lose contact quite as much, not meeting the rim at the radial 90 degree angle.

Mavic CrossMax wheels (photo 6-8) are some of the first lightweight radial mountain-bike wheels that seem to really stand up to the rigors of racing. The large box section of the CrossMax rim, combined with a stronger aluminum alloy, gives it high enough hoop strength to hold its shape and keep the spokes tight enough. Do not expect this kind of result if you take a common mountain bike rim and lace it radially.

A radial pattern is easy to lace up. You simply take each spoke straight out to each hole. This only applies on the front wheel and left side of the rear wheel. The drive side needs to be laced at least two-cross, and preferably three-cross, to counteract the chain-induced twist on the hub.

It is also easy to measure spoke length for a radial wheel. You can simply have someone hold a hub in the center of the rim and measure straight out to the rim. You will need to average a few lengths, since the hub will likely not be held exactly in the center. You can also easily calculate the length from the hub and rim diameters.

A radial pattern is the only pattern in which you can use radially drilled hubs with straight-pull spokes. Any other pattern requires that the spokes be able to exit the hub at an angle.

6.3B Disc-Brake Wheels

The considerations for building a front wheel for a disc brake are quite different from a normal front wheel. The wheel first of all must be dished on the left side to make room for the disc. It must also be built in such a way as to oppose the twisting force at the hub generated by the disc brake. No radial spoking or aluminum nipples here!

Use stainless-steel spokes of at least 2.0-mm spoke thickness (preferably thicker for downhill) and brass nipples. Use at least a three-cross pattern (photo 6-9). The higher the number of crosses, the lower the angle of the spokes and hence the more they resist twisting forces on the hub. Spoke tension must be even and high. Spokes on the disc side of a front wheel often are 1 mm shorter than on the right side.

To make the strongest front disc-brake wheel, you want to have the spokes that are coming *outward* from the hub holes point forward (photo 6-9). This means that the spokes that oppose the braking forces are also the ones that have the widest angle to the rim, coming from the outside of the hub flange. Photo 8-22 in Chapter 8 shows a close-up of this. It is the same thing as you do to build a strong standard rear wheel; you make the "pulling" spokes come to the outside (except that the pulling spokes opposing chain forces on a rear wheel point backward, not forward).

When building a front disc wheel using the instructions in Chapter 12 of *Zinn and the Art of Mountain Bike Maintenance*, you must make one change right at the beginning. In step 3, wherever it says the "right side" of the hub, use the disc-brake side. In the illustrations in that chapter, the side with the skewer *nut* on it (i.e., the side opposite the skewer *lever* side) will be the side of the hub with the rotor-mounting holes on it. Follow all of the rest of the instructions as is, and you will end up with a three-cross front disc-brake wheel whose outermost spokes point forward to oppose the disc-brake forces.

For a rear disc-brake wheel, the spokes on the drive side counteract the chain forces, and spokes on the left side counteract the braking forces. Ideally, the spokes coming outward from the hub flange should point forward on the disc side and backward on the drive side. Otherwise, the same considerations hold. You want lots of crosses, thick spokes, brass nipples, and high and even tension.

6.3C Two-Cross Wheels

Two-cross spoking makes a slightly stiffer and lighter wheel than a three-cross wheel, while not being as stiff or light as a radial wheel. Each spoke crosses over two other spokes from the same flange. Obviously, you need to specify two-cross when buying spokes so that you get the right length.

Lacing a two-cross wheel is very similar to lacing a three-cross one. Instead of crossing each spoke with another from five hub holes away, you cross each spoke with one from three holes away. Using Chapter 12 of *Zinn and the Art of Mountain Bike Maintenance*, you will notice the change comes in section C, when you lace the third set of spokes. In steps 21 and 22, pick a spoke three holes away instead of five, and otherwise follow the same procedure. Do likewise in steps 28 and 29. Otherwise, the lacing and truing procedures are the same.

6.3D Four-Cross Wheels

Four-cross spoking makes a slightly softer and heavier wheel than a three-cross wheel. Each spoke crosses over four other spokes from the same flange. Specify four-cross when buying spokes so that you get the right length.

Lacing a four-cross wheel is very similar to lacing a three-cross one. Instead of crossing each spoke with a spoke from five hub holes away, you cross each spoke with one from seven holes away. Using Chapter 12 of *Zinn and the Art of Mountain Bike Maintenance*, you will see that the change comes in section C, when you lace the third set of spokes. In steps 21 and 22, pick a spoke seven holes away instead of five, and otherwise follow the same procedure. Do likewise in steps 28 and 29. Otherwise, the lacing and truing procedures are unchanged.

6.3E Building Downhill Wheels

Generally, building downhill wheels means building wheels for disc brakes. Everything in section 6.3B on disc-brake wheels holds true for downhill, and then some. More spokes, thicker spokes, more crosses, and higher tension are where it's at. The rim should be wide, strong, and stiff (photo 6-3).

If you want a downhill wheel for rim brakes, you want to get the widest, strongest rim that will fit into your brakes, coupled to the stiffest hub you can find (photo 6-10). You still want heavy-gauge spokes in a cross-three or so spoking pattern. Spoke tension should generally be high.

6.3F Tying and Soldering

While not a completely lost art, tying and soldering is close to it. Tying and soldering is a method used to stiffen and strengthen a wheel by tying spokes together where they cross each other. It was very popular on road-racing wheels from the 1950s through the 1970s when aluminum rims were much softer than modern ones. Now it is hardly necessary, since there are lightweight rims strong enough to build radial wheels with, something that would have been impossible with the weak rims of a few decades ago.

To tie and solder a wheel, you tightly wrap a number of turns of thin copper wire around each spoke-cross intersection. You use a soldering iron to flow normal electrical solder into the copper-wire wrappings to hold them in place.

6.4 COMPOSITE AND DEEP-SECTION WHEELS

Carbon-composite wheels and deep-section wheels have dramatically changed road and triathlon racing. Their impact has been smaller with mountain bikes.

A deep-section composite rim for a mountain bike will offer the same benefits as a similar rim for the road, namely greater hoop strength and improved aerodynamics. Zipp and Hed (photos 6-7, 6-11) both make deep-section composite mountain rims. Wind-tunnel tests have shown that wheel fairings for downhill wheels similar to those in photo 6-7 will cut aerodynamic drag by one pound at 30 miles per hour, or 6–8 percent of total wind drag of the bike and rider, depending on rider size. (Incidentally, baggy clothes versus a skinsuit on a 5-foot-8-inch rider adds 2.5 pounds of drag, well over 10 percent of total drag!)

A complete composite wheel with composite spokes falls into two categories—one rigid and one compliant.

The rigid category includes the three-spoke Spin wheel. Each spoke is a hollow rigid beam, making the wheel vertically stiff. The Spin wheel has a modular splined hub that tightens into the wheel with lock rings. One primary benefit of this wheel is that, being quite narrow at the center, it is a dishless wheel, even when used with a disc brake.

The other category, of which the eight-spoke Spinergy is an example, offers vertical and lateral compliance. Rather than being a rigid beam, each Spinergy spoke is a flat, flexible composite sheet under tension.

6.4A Truing Deep-Section Composite-Rim Wheels

Truing deep-section wheels whose spoke nipples extend out of the rim is no different than truing any other wheel. (Wheel truing is covered in Chapters 3, 6, and 12 of *Zinn and the Art of Mountain Bike Maintenance*.)

Truing a deep-section wheel whose nipples do not extend below the rim is a bit different. For instance, a Hed wheel can be trued at the hub, due to the double-threaded spokes (photo 6-11). It can also be trued at the rim like a deep-section road wheel by removing the tire and rim strip and grabbing the spoke nipple heads with a deep-wall 5.5-mm socket wrench.

6.4B Composite Wheel Repair

The rim on a Spin wheel can be replaced. You need to send it back to the factory for this service.

6-10
Ringle's Super Duper Bubba suspension hub laced to a wide Sun Rhyno rim.

6-11
Truing deep-section Hed spoked wheel at the hub.

7

TIRES

The appearance . . . is peculiar. It is as knobby with countless little domes as a prison door is with bolt heads.
—Mark Twain, *The Innocents Abroad,* 1869

This chapter is where the rubber hits the road (or the off-road). How do you choose which tires and pressure to use under what conditions?

7.1 TIRE OVERVIEW

There is always a tire that is the current rage. It changes quickly, too. Keep in mind before following the latest rage that tire preference depends on riding style; some riders will love a tire on a course, and others won't.

7.1A Tread Pattern

What knob will do the job?

The ideal knob only has as much size and weight as is needed to grab the ground at the optimal traction angle. The angle at which different blocks on each particular line on the tire can most effectively grab the ground differs. Hence straight blocks are in the center of the tire and the more curved blocks are on the sides. On a front tire, each block has a working edge, and the rest of the knob is only there to support that edge. Each rear block may have two working edges, one used in braking and one in propulsion. Block support comes from the breadth of the block, buttresses built into the block, the stiffness of the rubber, and how well the block adheres to the casing.

The base layer of rubber forms a transition up into the block, and it must be thick enough to hold the block onto the casing. Problem is, the base layer is something tire designers often try to thin down as much as possible, since it is one of the heaviest parts of the tire. The bigger the lugs, the thicker the base layer you need to support it. If you have tall, narrow lugs with a thin base layer, you will tear the lugs right off on hard ground.

The lower or wider the lugs, the thinner the base layer can be, and the more the weight is reduced.

7.1B Semi-Slicks

The latest hot cross-country tire is a semi-slick (photos 7-1 to 7-3). The 1996 Olympics and 1997 World Championships were won on semi-slicks.

A semi-slick usually has a fine tread, like a file pattern, with side knobs. Some also have shallow, broad cross bars or paddles. Tire durability is low with these tires (you don't have to wear through knobs first; you start out riding on the base rubber), but rolling resistance and weight are low, too.

Semi-slicks get surprisingly good traction as long as you don't have to stop when going down a really steep hill. If the course is not very rocky or muddy, try these tires. World Cup riders are using semi-slicks, but World Cup courses are usually not very rocky.

Most World Cup and NORBA National cross-country races are won on the uphills; more than five times as much time is usually spent on the climbs than on the descents. Racing the downhills flat-out on any lap other than the final one often takes so much energy for not enough time gain to be worth the risk of running out of steam, not to mention the risk of punctures and crashes. The lighter, lower rolling resistance tire will be an advantage on dry climbs without loose sharp rocks. Climbing and descending with these tires requires smoother climbing technique and better downhill control (often at a bit lower speed).

With a full-suspension bike, these tires work incredibly well in loose traction,

7-1
Ritchey SpeedMax semi-slick.

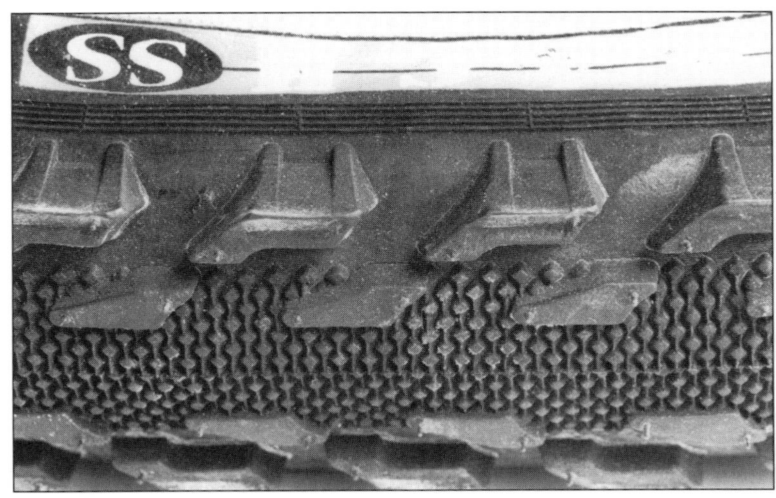

7-2
Panaracer SS semi-slick.

7-3
Continental Double Fighter semi-slick, gray silica compound.

even in deep sand. On a hardtail with these tires, you practically need to be a World Cup rider to climb in loose traction; you must pedal very smoothly in the saddle.

If the traction is insufficient for good downhill control but enough for climbing traction, you can just run one on the rear. On a climb, the majority of rolling resistance benefit to be had from semi-slicks will be on the rear tire, since probably 80 percent of the rider's weight is concentrated there. Thus, a knobby on the front will not slow you down much, and it will be a big help on loose or rocky descents.

7.1C Front versus Rear

The front and rear tires are performing different tasks, so it makes sense that they should be different. The rear tire's major function is generating traction for propulsion, while the front tire's job is to get braking and cornering traction. The rear tire will tend to have crosswise center paddles and transition knobs and shoulder knobs arranged in a parabolic or chevron shape open toward the rear. A front tire's biting edges may also be arranged in a parabolic or chevron shape, but open to the front for braking grab. You also want beefy side knobs that are well supported on the front to prevent tire washout.

You can determine the mounting orientation of a tire not labeled for rotation direction by holding it above your head and viewing it as the ground sees it. Consider which way the tire is turning and what happens during braking and driving. The way to orient the tread will be obvious (except on symmetrical, square-knobbed tires, where rotation direction is irrelevant).

7.1D Cross-Country versus Downhill

For cross-country, you want flexible casings like a radial car tire. You want them to give for control and suspension. With a downhill tire, though, you want stiff casings so you can still ride them if they go flat. They are slower, due to the extra half-pound those stiff casings add, but they are much faster than a lighter tire that is flat!

In cross-country, weight is at a premium. This encourages a reduction in tire size and the amount of rubber on top. Downhill is largely gravity-driven, so weight is not as much of a determining factor, although, all things being equal, you could go faster on a lighter bike. All things are not equal, though, and getting better control and making it to the finish line on a cushion of air sometimes require paying a weight penalty. A bigger tire definitely has handling and flat-resistance benefit in downhill. Tubeless tires and pinch-resistant or sealant-filled tubes also add weight but increase peace of mind.

7.1E Tire Profile

Tire profile (a.k.a., tread radius) refers to the tire's cross-sectional shape. The casing takes a round shape when inflated, and if the knobs are all equally tall, they form a rounded shape as well. A square-profile (or large tread-radius) tire is formed by making the knobs progressively taller farther out on the shoulders. Rounded-profile tires are preferred for hard conditions and are favored in soft conditions as well by those with road and cyclo-cross backgrounds, as they roll over and lean nicely. Square-profile tires are favored by those with a moto-cross background who like to stuff it into the corner and put the tire up on the sharp edge.

7.1F Tire Pressure

World Cup cross-country riders often use very high pressure. The courses do not have a lot of sharp, sidewall-cutting obstacles and thorns or cactus spines. It requires a great amount of nimbleness to use a hard tire like this, but World Cup riders have that and are more concerned about avoiding pinch flats than about the better control they could have with a softer tire. Regular mortals running 55–60 pounds in a tire will get beaten up since they do not have the finesse of the World Cup riders.

Since a lot of suspension is in the tires, you want to look at it similarly to the discussion in the suspension fork section. For improved traction, comfort, and control, you want to run the lowest pressure you can without getting pinch flats. Even using heavier, thicker anti-pinch-flat tubes at low pressure (30 psi or so) will result in a faster bike on a rough course. As with soft suspension, the soft tire will be faster over big rocks, because the tire will compress at each rock, instead of wasting much of your energy by having each rock lift you and the entire bike. On a smooth surface, of course, the mushy tire will not be faster. It will be sucking up your pedaling energy, just like mushy suspension would be.

7.1G Tire Weight

A Kevlar tire bead (rather than steel) saves you weight. So does a smaller tire, thinner casing, smaller knobs, no knobs, or thinner base rubber. Rotational weight at the edge of the wheel costs you more energy than static weight or weight at the center of the hub. Furthermore, the more you can cut down on unsprung weight (weight that is *not* held up by the suspension), especially rotational unsprung weight, the better your suspension will work.

7.1H Tread Compound

The tread compound will either be based on natural rubber or synthetic rubber. To strengthen it, it will either be compounded with carbon black (hence a black tire) or, in the case of colored tread, silica or clay. (Clay is used in cheap colored tires, silica in good ones.) Generally, colored compounds from bike tire companies that do not also make car tires will not be as durable as black compounds, since the investment in the special, much larger mixers to get bonding as good between rubber and silica as between rubber and carbon black is cost-prohibitive for a bike-tire-only company.

Natural rubber is susceptible to ozone and UV decay, just like a rubber band that gets stiff and brittle. Even though anti-ozonants are added to tread compounds, it is better to store tires out of the sun as much as possible.

7.1I Tubeless Tires

Many companies are working on tubeless tires. These may become commercially viable and popular for the same reasons they did on cars and motorcycles.

TIRE PRESSURE TIP

from Dave Wiens, Former NORBA National Champion

Kirk Molday, Rishi Grewal, Paola Pezzo, and I raced a lot in 1997 with Hutchinson Pythons (photo 7-4) at low pressure with Hutchinson green, pinch-resistant tubes inside. The traction on side hills with such soft tires is incredible. For example, at the Snoqualmie Pass, Washington NCS race, there were slanted slabs to ride across, and the soft tires held great across those slopes, while you had to slow way down or run with a hard tire. (Molday won, Wiens was second, and Grewal third at Snoqualmie.)

The green tubes prevent pinch flats at these low pressures. I was running 35 psi, even with my 180-pound weight, and I understand that Molday usually used 30 psi and Pezzo 25 psi. I slammed into sharp-edged Moab-like sandstone tabletops with these tires and tubes at 35 psi near Fruita, Colorado, so hard that I dented my rim twice, but I did not pinch-flat! The tubes add 50 extra grams each.

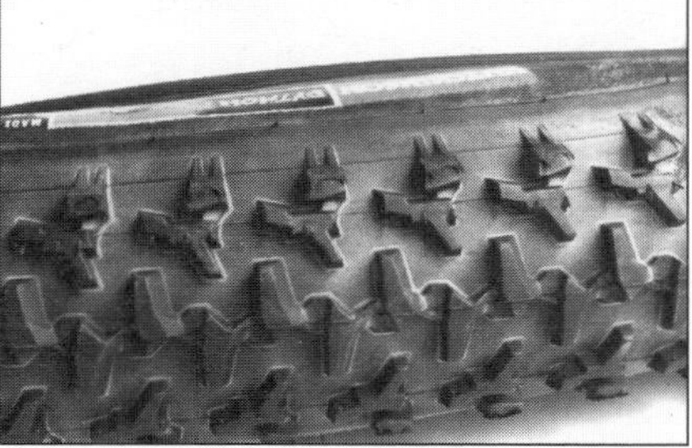

7-4
Hutchinson Python.

7-5
Ritchey MudMax.

Instead of having a tube, the inside of the tire is coated with enough rubber to be airtight. The tire bead seals against a special rim that will not leak. Pinch flats do not happen, because there is no tube to pinch. Punctures leak only slowly out through the hole, often sealing around the thorn, rather than losing air rapidly between the tire and tube. The tire's extra rubber adds casing stiffness that allows it to be ridden when flat with more control than a standard flat tire would.

7.2 TIRES FOR SPECIFIC CONDITIONS

This section includes not only tire choice for various conditions, but also air pressure guidelines. Often, you will be encountering a variety of conditions on a given ride, so a compromise will be necessary. Aim the tire choice for the section of the course where you have the most trouble.

7.2A Mud or Loose Dirt

Lightweight, rounded, skinny tires with tall and thin knobs do the trick in mud or loose dirt or fine dust (photo 7-5).

A thin tire can dig down and get traction, while a wide tire will float on top of soft, slippery stuff. (This is one reason why you see the ditches of a snowy road full of four-wheel-drive SUVs with big, wide, macho tires; they've slid off.) Since it is harder to move through mud, you want as little wheel weight as you can get away with. The thin tire will be lighter and have less surface area to pick up mud and drag it around.

Self-cleaning capacity is at a premium, since you do not want to be dragging around a lot of heavy mud on the tire, nor do you want the tread clogged when you need traction. A rounded tire shape will naturally push dirt and mud to the outside as it sinks in. Small tread blocks with larger spaces between them are less likely to clog and will allow movement of mud to the outside (photo 7-8). You do not want large side fins, which would impede clearing of mud to the outside. You can't lean over very far without slipping anyway, so you don't need 'em.

Tall, thin knobs will go deep into the soft ground, like your little snowshoeless feet do in deep snow. The radius where the tread blocks meet the base rubber can be very small to keep weight down and improve grip. This is only a problem if you use these tires on hard ground, since weakly supported knobs are not likely to get torn off in mud.

Pump these thin tires up to high pressure (65 psi or so) for mud and loose dirt. The soft ground is forgiving, so the harder tire won't necessarily be harder on your body. The pressure will also protect the thin tire from pinch-flatting on the hidden roots and sharp rocks.

7.2B Hard Surfaces

The tire for hardpack, slickrock, and pavement should first of all be rounded in cross-section. Square-edge tires are scary on hard surfaces, since once you lean over the square edge, that's it. The square edge also tends to bend over when you need it to be stiff. If you have a long ride on pavement to get to your trail ride, pick a round tire, and have the tread pattern and tire size be determined by the trail.

TIRE PRESSURE TIP

for Mud Riding from Tom Ritchey, Mountain Bike Pioneer and Tire Designer

High psi is where it's at in mud. Under any conditions, you always want to direct as much force (pounds) into the ground as you can. Since you have fewer square inches of contact area with a skinny mud tire than you would with a bigger tire, you need more psi to get as many pounds of force into the ground as possible.

A hardpack tire can be big with shallow, well-supported knobs (photos 7-4 or 7-6), or it can be a semi-slick (photos 7-1, 7-2, 7-3). A larger tire with low knobs can keep more edges biting into the ground at a variety of lean angles. Tall knobs without broad support structures can get easily torn off, or at least flexed over by the high pace and hard surface.

A semi-slick with a file tread and side knobs can give good traction and low rolling resistance and weight on hardpack. If it is really hard and smooth, traction will not be a problem with a slick (photo 7-7), and rolling resistance and weight will be optimized.

7.2C Loose Rock

A large tire at medium pressure will grab enough rocks to give some traction but not pinch-flat easily. The knobs should be well supported and of medium height to grab rocks and be less vulnerable to being torn and flexed (photo 7-6).

At high speeds over big rocks, avoid pinch flats with a). higher pressure, b). tires with soft strips above the bead to

7-6
Specialized Ground Master.

7-7
Upper right: Continental Avenue slick with sipes.

7-8
Michelin Wild Gripper Lite, green silica compound.

cushion rim impacts, or c). pinch-flat-resistant tubes.

7.2D Sand

For deep, dry sand, you want flotation (i.e., large size) and deep tread. Shallower sand is best traversed on thinner knobbies that can bite down through it to something more substantial. In wet sand, whether you want wide or thin is dictated by how slick the wet sand is: The slicker the sand, the thinner the tire.

7.2E Snow and Ice

These are actually two completely different kinds of concerns.

For deep snow, you want deep knobs and wide tires, since there is no substantial surface for a thin tire to dig down to. You want to keep as much snow under the tire as you can and pack it down in order to grab onto it. In the Iditabike race in Alaska, riders use double-wide rims and super-wide, deeply knobbed tires at low pressure. Pinch flats are not usually a problem in snow!

In some slushy conditions, semi-slicks sometimes work well.

Ice requires metal studs to get any kind of decent grip. Without them, the best you can do is a tire with lots of small, closely spaced knobs. You want as many edges contacting the ice at a time as you can get, and big, widely separated knobs don't cut it.

7.2F Downhill

All of the above about specific conditions applies to downhill, with the addition that the tires should be large and have lots

7-9
Tioga Factory DH downhill tire.

7-10
Serfas downhill tire.

of knobs to maintain knob contact at all angles at all times. Photos 7-9 and 7-10 show two methods for accomplishing that. Downhill tire sidewalls often are very stiff so that they can be ridden if they go flat.

7.3 TIRE PRESSURE

Section 7.2 has tire pressure guidelines for specific conditions. These are more general recommendations.

7.3A Suspension

Without suspension, your tires are your only suspension besides your elbows and knees. Bigger, softer tires will save your butt on rough ground.

With effective suspension, the function of your tires as a suspension member is less important. You can run higher pressures and smaller tires without its costing you in efficiency and comfort.

7.3B Downhill and Dual-Slalom Racing

Slamming into hard, sharp things without pinch-flatting requires high pressure, but you do not want it to be at the expense of control. Downhill often requires pushing the balance more toward pinch-flat resistance. The berming and soft earth of most slalom courses makes tire pressure of 35–40 psi quite reasonable; pinch flats are not much of an issue, and the control is better than with rock-hard tires.

7.4 TIRE SEALANTS

Slime and True Goo are examples of sealants you can squirt into tubes, though they usually will only go into Schrader valves (this procedure is described in Chapter 6 of *Zinn and the Art of Mountain Bike Maintenance*, Second Edition). Many companies sell Presta-valve tubes with sealant already inside. Kits and methods to get sealants into Presta tubes do exist.

The benefit of sealant is very little loss of pressure with small punctures. (Pinch flats are usually not sealed, since the sealant is thrown to the outside of the tube, and the snake bites are on the inner diameter of the pinched tube.) The negatives are 1) weight, and 2) rolling resistance. The amount that these increase depends on how much sealant is inside. Also, if you are not careful, sealant can get into the valve, which makes it difficult to top up the pressure in the tire.

The intermediate position is to carry sealant with your patch kit. If you pick up a thorn, put in the sealant and reinflate. If it works, you've saved the hassle of remounting a tire.

8

BRAKES

Hydraulics are a big part of mountain biking now . . . get comfortable with it.
—Bob Gregorio, John Tomac's mechanic

Whoa, slow down, pardner! Stopping for braking information is a good idea. Even if you want to go fast, your speed is actually dependent on having good brakes. Reliable braking allows you to push the limits further, because you can always slow down at the last minute when you need to.

The look of premium brakes has changed radically the last couple of years and is following two divergent paths. The traditional cantilever is being driven out by V-brakes and disc brakes (and, to a very small extent, by hydraulic rim brakes). Most brakes are still cable-actuated, requiring smooth cable movement.

8.1 CABLES AND HOUSINGS

Sticky cables wreck your brake performance. It takes more effort to apply the brakes, and the brakes do not return immediately. Why is that a problem? Can't you just apply more force to overcome it and live with a little brake pad rub? Don't you go faster if you cannot apply your brakes very well?

Actually, sticky cables lead to overbraking and slower overall speed. If your cables are sticky, you cannot feel precisely when the pad contacts the rim, so you cannot add a little more or less pressure as needed to control your speed accurately. Instead, you must pull hard to overcome the cable resistance, and the lack of modulation will slow you down more than you need to. When you release the pressure on the lever, the pads will not immediately snap back away from the rim, delaying your acceleration.

8.1A Cable-Friction Reduction

If your cables and housings are not kinked, frayed, or split, the best place to start is with cleaning and lubrication. Pull the cable housing sections out of the cable stops after releasing the brake. Wipe the cable down and lubricate the areas that run inside the housing (photo 8-1). Use a lubricant that will not get dry or gummy inside the housing. A good lube for this is the molybdenum disulfide grease that comes with some shifters from Shimano; many chain lubes work well, too. If the cable still sticks, replace it along with the cable housings.

Some frames have the brake cable stops on the right side (drive side) of the frame, which requires a lot of cable bending to work with sidepull cantilevers (e.g., V-brakes), which usually have a left-side cable entry. Hurricane (photo 8-10) and OnZa (photo 8-2) make V-brakes in which the cable link and cable-fixing bolt sides can be reversed. Smoothing the cable routing will reduce friction considerably and improve braking.

8.1B Cable and Cable Housing Replacement

You will be amazed at how much improvement you get in your braking by installing new cables and housings. Brake cable installation is covered in detail in Chapter 7 of *Zinn and the Art of Mountain Bike Maintenance*.

Reducing friction is a combination of good cable routing and low-friction cables and housings. Avoid sharp bends and restriction of the housing against the frame. Housing that is too short can restrict the rear brake caliper's movement or cause your rear brake to come on when you turn the bars sharply. Excessively long housing also diminishes performance: There is more cable to stretch and housing to compress; the cable bends are tighter, and there is more cable/housing contact length to cause friction.

8.1C Low-Friction Cables

The housing must be spiral-wound lined brake cable housing, which can oppose burst pressure from high braking force. Coaxial shift cable housing cannot, because it is *only* held together from bursting by the plastic sheath. The plastic sheath is sufficient for shifting forces, but not for emergency braking!

Cables are smoother if they are "die-drawn" (that is, the cable is pulled through a small hole in a hardened "die" to flatten the outer cable strands).

Coated cables, like Gore-Tex RideOn, will move more freely yet and stay better sealed. Care must be taken when installing them, however, or you will have some very expensive cables that will not move because of wadded-up Gore-Tex inside the housing. The Gore-Tex coating must be removed from the cable at either end wherever it is running inside the lever and where it is clamped at the brake cable-fixing bolt. The Gore-Tex can be scraped off with a razor blade.

The RideOn cable slides inside a continuous plastic tube that runs the full length from the lever to an inch before the brake cable-fixing bolt. A little rubber accordion-shaped seal called a "Grub" (photo 8-3) is required to cover the single exposed end of the plastic tube to prevent entry of water or dirt. On a V-brake, the Grub replaces the stock rubber accordion seal. Rather than sealing over the end of the guide pipe nipple like the stock accordion seal (and requiring removal and replacement every time the brakes are

CABLE ROUTING TIP

from Wayne Stetina, Shimano North America R&D manager

Run your cables short to avoid the big loop that would hit your leg. On V-brakes, you can bend the guide pipe (i.e., the "noodle"—the curved metal tube that brings the cable into the brake) a little to get it to not hit your leg. This will also make the brake work better. The cable lies down close to the frame and is shorter to reduce stretch and compression in the cable and housing.

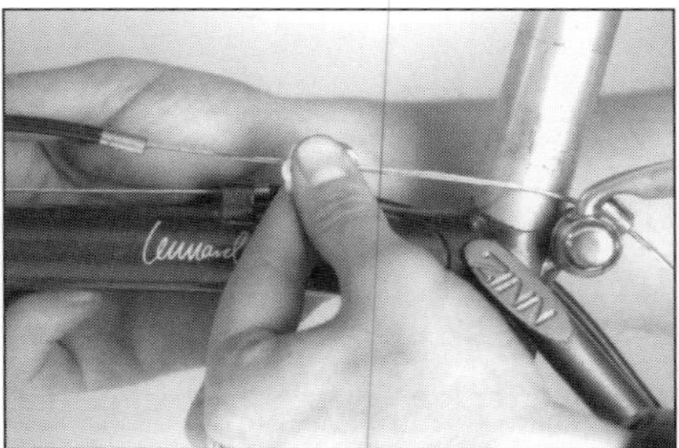

8-1
Lubricating a section of cable that runs inside housing.

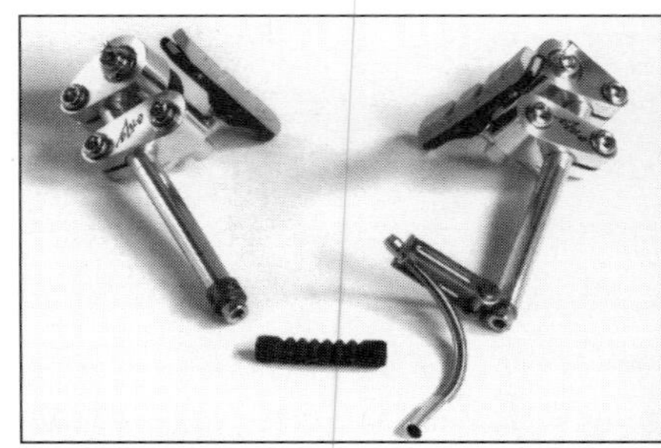

8-2
OnZa sidepull cantilever brake. Note that both the cable link securing the guide pipe (right) and the cable-fixing bolt (left) bolt straight into the top of the brake arm and can be reversed to route the cable in from either the right or the left.

opened!), the grub simply fits over the end of the plastic cable sheath, which ends halfway between the end of the guide pipe and the cable-fixing bolt. Opening the brake is a snap, since you need only pop the end of the noodle out of the cable link, and you do not need to mess with moving a seal. The down side is that the end of the cable link can cut through the Gore plastic sheath after a number of wheel changes.

8.2 V-BRAKES

Even straight out of the box, V-brakes offer a number of advantages over traditional cantilevers. With longer arms, they apply greater leverage; their sidepull cable actuation is far more efficient than the yoke on a cantilever; and with simplified cable routing and no need for a cable stop, V-brakes work on even the most complicated full-suspension bikes. Of course, the near disappearance of traditional cantilevers proves that most consumers already know the advantages. But there are a number of tricks that can milk even more performance out of the now-popular V-brake—and most of them aren't in the owner's manual.

"V-brake" is a Shimano-trademarked name referring to a tall, sidepull cantilever brake. Since many people refer to other sidepull cantilever brands as V-brakes (and since it takes less space to write than "sidepull cantilever"), for simplicity, I will refer to sidepull cantilevers in general as V-brakes.

A guide pipe attached to a hinged cable link on one V-brake arm stops the housing and guides the cable to the fixing bolt, eliminating the need for the straddle wire of a cantilever. The cable ties the two arms together (photo 8-3). V-brakes are more efficient than cantilevers (or U-brakes), since pulling the arms from the side is more efficient than pulling straight up on a cable yoke.

A V-brake must be tall for the cable to clear the tire. The tall arms provide more leverage than a cantilever, so it takes less cable-pulling force to stop the bike. It also takes more cable pull to move the pads to the rim. This requires a lever whose cable attachment point is farther from the lever pivot than a standard cantilever brake lever, resulting in more cable pull and less leverage.

A really nice feature of some top-end V-brakes is parallel pad movement. Instead of the pads swinging on an arc, as with a cantilever, a linkage moves the pads straight inward and outward. Pad linkages can be seen in photos 8-4, 8-7, and 8-10. The arc movement of standard cantilevers causes the pads to vary their contact height and angle

8-3
OnZa sidepull cantilever brake setup with Gore RideOn cables. The accordion-shaped tube (called a "Grub") covers the exposed end of the Gore cable sheath, which terminates midway between the end of the noodle (left) and the cable-fixing bolt (right). Since the sheath runs all the way to the brake lever, the cable is now completely sealed from dirt and water entry.

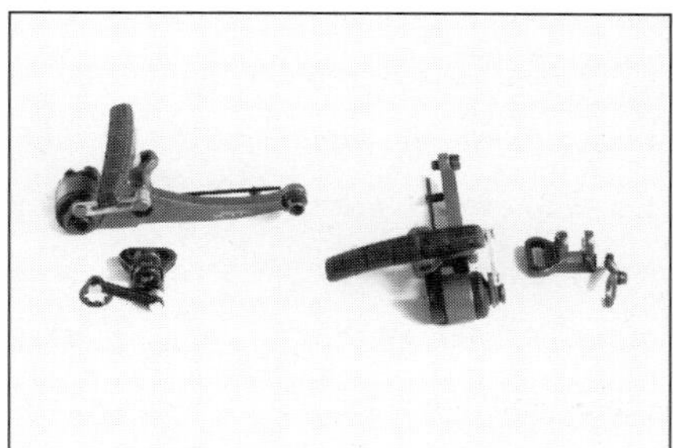

8-4
Shimano replacement pad linkage parts next to an XTR V-brake. Replacing the linkages tightens rattling V-brake pads up again.

on the rim with differing rim width and with reduced pad thickness after wear. The "parallel-push" (or "horizontal-push") design eliminates the need for pad position readjustment with pad wear or wheel changes. As long as each rim has vertical (i.e., parallel) braking surfaces, changing to wider or narrower rims requires only adjustment of cable length. Incidentally, this makes the case for only using rims that have parallel braking surfaces.

When you *do* have to adjust the brake pads, the threaded pad posts and nesting washers on most top-end V-brakes make pad adjustment far quicker, easier, and more accurate than most cantilever pad adjustment systems.

8.2A V-Brake Caliper Setup Details

This is not a "how to set up V-brakes" section. *That* section is in Chapter 7 of the second edition of *Zinn and the Art of Mountain Bike Maintenance. This* section is filled with the fine details that make for exceptional braking.

TOE-IN: You want to adjust your V-brake with some toe-in, even though the early Shimano setup recommendations said just to set the pads flat to the rim. This is because, in practice, there is enough play and flex in the system that a flat pad, when pulled forward by the rim, ends up being effectively toed out. This squeals. The squealing will occur when it is stopping you the fastest, as light braking will not pull the pad forward so much. Even when wet, Shimano's "multi-condition pads" will still stop so fast that you can lock up the wheel, and, if toed-out under braking, will squeal.

You can also tell if you have a setup problem by the wear pattern on the pad. If the heel of the pad wears out faster than the toe, it is not toed in enough.

Add some toe-in if you have squeal or pad heel wear. As more play develops in the system, you will need to add more toe-in.

PAD LOCATION: Center the pad vertically on the rim. Set the pad flat to the rim, so it will not try to climb up into the tire or down into the spokes. Pad wear will be uneven and linkage wear will be rapid if the pad is not set flat to the rim. How to make pad adjustments is in Chapter 7 of *Zinn and the Art of Mountain Bike Maintenance.*

LINKAGE PLAY: Linkage play in Shimano XT and XTR V-brakes can allow them to rattle noisily. It does affect pad rigidity, but the play is not an issue until it is so great that the pad keeps going up or down off the rim. The play will increase over time, so monitor it. Shimano makes a linkage guts replacement kit to tighten 'em up again (photo 8-4).

BRAKE PIVOTS: Check often for free rotation on each brake pivot. If the pivot is too tight, the brake will stick and be next to impossible to keep centered. Some brakes (XTR, Avid Arch Supreme, and others) have a bearing that pivots the arms on the frame boss, not a bushing. The post needs to be long enough that it prevents the bolt from pinching the bearing when tightened. If the bearing gets sticky, you can remove it (photo 8-5) and replace it or overhaul it.

Brakes without pivot cartridge bearings or their own independent internal bushings are dependent on the brake post not being bulged by overtightening.

8-5
Replacing the brake pivot cartridge bearing on an Avid Arch Supreme brake using Avid's special tool.

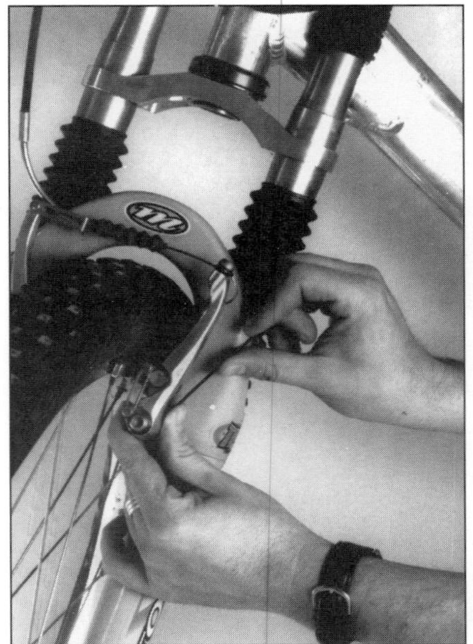

8-6
Bending outward on an XT vertical return spring to increase spring tension. Support the spring at the bottom while bending to avoid cracking the plastic spring housing.

Replace the post if it is enlarged (or sand it if it is not a replaceable post). Keep the post well greased.

SPRINGS: Increase the tension on the springs, so the brake returns faster and centers better. While a light brake touch with a weak spring is easy to squeeze, a stronger spring can overcome a little stickiness in the system (as mud builds up) and keep the brake centered. You can quickly increase spring tension on a Shimano V-brake by bending the vertical spring slightly outward rather than using the tension-adjust screw (photo 8-6). This will also allow you to avoid stripping the head of the little adjustment screw. Support the spring at the bottom while bending to avoid breaking the plastic housing.

The vertical springs on Shimano V-brakes are notorious for not holding their adjustment. They get weaker over time, and you have to bend them outward again. A running change in new XT and XTR brakes has replaced the round-cross-section springs with square springs, which hold their tension better.

CENTERING: Keeping the brakes centered is often an issue with parallel-push V-brakes. One little bit of grit in any of the pivots involved with moving the pads straight in and out can throw off the centering. Also, as I said above, the vertical return spring on XT/XTR V-brakes also may not hold its adjustment, and increasing spring tension by just bending out the spring a bit on the side that is dragging (photo 8-6) will take care of the problem for a while. Obviously, keeping the pivots lubricated and clean will also help.

Avid Arch Supreme brakes are centered by squeezing the brake lever while loosening and retightening the knob at the top of the arch. The W-shaped return spring passes through the knob (photo 8-7) and can relocate to its balance point that way. You may need to lube where the spring passes through the knob or tap the spring with your finger while the knob is loose so it moves to where it needs to be for centering.

Centering of all the various spring types found on V-brakes (and cantilevers; the same return spring systems will work on either) is in Chapter 7 of *Zinn and the Art of Mountain Bike Maintenance*.

RIMS: If you are having thump-thump-thump brake problems, check your rim. If it is out of true, bulged at the spoke holes, or split at the seam, you have found the problem. Rim replacement may be in order.

You can get some loud squealing and rapid wear due to *not* using ceramic-specific pads on ceramic rims.

Finally, a non-ceramic rim that is too polished can also cause brake squeal. If you rough up the rim a bit, it may go away.

HOT TIP TO TEXTURE THE RIM AND REDUCE BRAKE SQUEAL: Place two brake-pad-sized pieces cut from a green Scotchbrite dish scrubbing pad between the rim and the pads. Ride slowly with the brakes on lightly. Shimano mechanics do this at races with some squeal-silencing success.

BACK-AND-FORTH BRAKE FLEX: Your pads will tap the rims when you pedal out of the saddle due to side-to-side flex in the suspension fork. It can happen on the rear, too, with flexy stays. It should

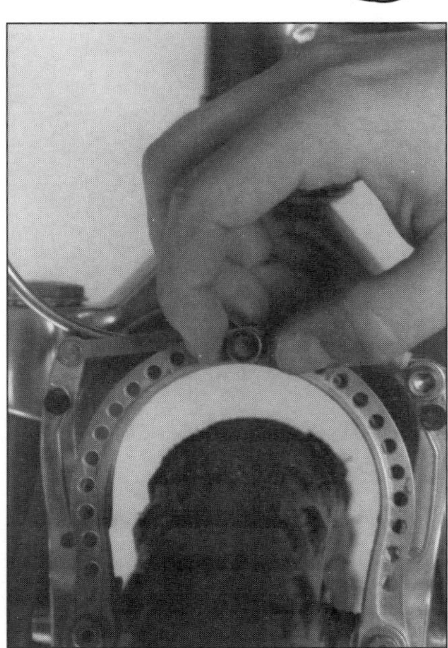

8-7
Close-up of Avid Arch Supreme spring balance adjustment knob. The W-shaped spring is hidden behind the arch and the top of the W passes through a hole in the knob bolt. Loosening the bolt allows the spring to move back and forth to balance the brakes.

not be slowing you down significantly. You can loosen the brake some to get more pad clearance, but do not sacrifice brake performance for this problem. A stiff suspension hub can make a difference in fork flex (see Chapter 5, section 5.3C).

PAD OPTIONS: Experiment with pads to find out which ones work best for you. When you are getting new pads, why not get good ones? There are lots of good aftermarket brands out there.

Shimano has an aftermarket "severe-condition" pad that is 25 percent (1 mm) thicker than the stock pad. It is not supplied with the brakes, since some frames have so little seat-stay clearance that you can rip the pad out of the pad holder when removing or replacing the wheel. If your frame has room for it, you can get more pad longevity by using the thicker pads.

8.2B V-Brake Booster Plate

A brake booster is a U-shaped brake stiffener designed to reduce flex in the system (photo 8-8). It is useful because V-brakes can overpower the frame and flex the stays on the stiffest frames. This is only a minor problem with occasional braking, since a light touch will still stop the bike. On a long, extended downhill, however, the pads will heat up, and the power will drop off. You will keep applying more and more force, and all you will be doing is flexing the frame more (and tiring your hands out), rather than slowing the bike. Adding a brake booster gives a more linear response to your braking force.

On the front, even though the fork legs cannot twist much, the brake bosses themselves will flex outward as the rim pulls the pad forward. Tying the bosses together with a brake booster will dramatically increase braking power under heavy loads or when the pads are hot.

For riders heavier than 180 pounds, a brake booster can make as much difference in power and modulation control as switching from a cantilever to a V-brake in the first place.

Brake booster plates are nothing new. They have been around a long time for U-brakes, cantilevers, hydraulic rim brakes, roller-cams, and now for V-brakes. A cantilever booster plate will fit most V-brakes.

BRAKE BOOSTER TIP

from Wayne Stetina

I recommend a using a carbon-fiber brake booster as opposed to an aluminum one, because it damps brake-chatter resonance, much like a carbon-fiber frame can. It will prevent most brake squeal. A composite booster is particularly important with titanium frames and ultralight aluminum frames. The flexy stays in these frames really resonate, and the brakes will squeal when set up for high power.

V-BRAKE HEEL CLEARANCE TIP

from Jeff Cole, Former World Cup Team Mechanic

The different-thickness washers on V-brake pad posts allow you to adjust how much the V-brake arms stick out for heel clearance. Reverse the thin and thick washers from inside to outside, having thinner washers on the inside if you need more heel clearance. Make sure you install the washers with the concave and convex washer faces nesting into each other.

8.2C V-Brake Lever Setup Details

A major point to address in getting the most out of a V-brake is to increase the power in the lever. As the pickup point for the cable head gets closer to the brake lever's pivot, more leverage is obtained and less force is required to produce a given braking force at the rim. Less cable is pulled for a given lever movement, though.

Now then, if you turn the brake lever up to maximum power and pull with two fingers, you will stop too fast in panic-braking circumstances. You can soft-touch the brakes consciously under controlled conditions, but not if you get startled. You *can* safely run the brake at high power if you pull the brake with one finger (see sidebar on page 92). That leaves three more fingers to hold the grip and give you better control. One-finger braking never was possible before with cantilevers, because it took too much hand pull to manage it. V-brakes make that possible.

As I mentioned above in regard to cables and housings, modulation is better with a powerful, freely moving brake, because your touch is lighter. If you are pulling hard, you cannot feel for modulation control. Powerful brakes that you can modulate well allow you to relax on the bike and work the bike more with your arms and legs over bumps. A relaxed rider without suspension can go over bumps better than a tight rider with suspension!

Many brake levers offer adjustability of the cable pickup point relative to the lever pivot. Some lever designs sim-

8-8
A Shimano carbon-fiber brake booster. This U-shaped brake stiffener is designed to reduce flex in the brake pads and frame seatstays or fork legs.

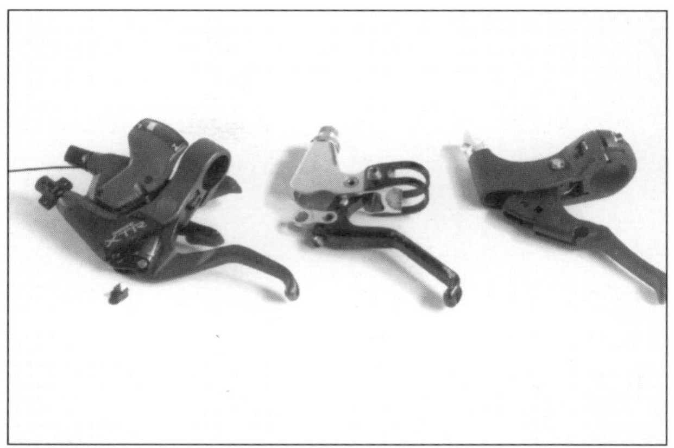

8-9
Different V-brake levers showing leverage-adjustment designs. Left: Shimano XTR lever, center: Avid lever, right: SRAM lever. Note the leverage adjustment screws in XTR and Avid and the square holes that hold movable plastic plugs in the SRAM lever.

ply move the cable hook or cable leverage point toward or away from the pivot, which has the effect of reducing the cable pull over the entire stroke when you increase the leverage.

Shimano V-brake levers have a cable hook that slides up and down in a slot in the lever, allowing you to get more leverage without sacrificing much cable pull. For example, in an XTR lever, you can turn down the knurled adjustment screw that fills the space in the slot to allow the cable-hook pivot to slide inward toward the lever pivot point (photo 8-9, left). (You first must remove the plastic piece that will not allow tightening the screw. That piece is there to prevent the naive from cranking up their lever power, squeezing it with their whole hand, landing on their nose, and suing Shimano.) On an XT lever, there is no leverage adjustment screw, but you can remove one or both of two spacers that fill the inboard end of the slot.

At the beginning part of the lever stroke, the slot in the Shimano lever is angled toward the cable direction, and the cable hook pivot stays out at the outboard end of the slot. The cable hook pivot slides inward toward the bottom of the slot as the lever is pulled to the point that the slot angles away from the cable direction. Thus, the lever pulls cable through the majority of the stroke the same as on the low-power setting, and it only increases the leverage at the end. This design allows the pad offset from the rim to be set almost the same as on the low-power setting. Increasing power in many non-Shimano levers requires adjusting the pads closer to the rim or the lever hits the bar before the bike stops.

Avid's design (photo 8-9, center) also has a pivoting cable hook, although the pivot is fixed on the adjustment bolt and moves up and down as the screw is turned. Avid's philosophy is that a linear feel is better and that lever power should *not* ramp up (by the cable hook sliding in) when you put the power to the rim.

The cable inside SRAM's lever (photo 8-9, right) runs from the cable hook halfway out on the lever over a

V-BRAKE LEVER SETUP TIPS

from Wayne Lumpkin, Founder and El Presidenté of Avid

There are two important things to do with your sidepull cantilever levers. One has to do with leverage and the other with lever position, and they are interconnected.

1. Even though a lot of people want a hard feel to the brakes, you should know that the harder the brakes feel, the less power you have. The hard feel indicates that you have less mechanical advantage. It is like climbing a hill in the big ring; it feels hard because you are doing all of the work!

A softer feel to the brakes means that you have more leverage. You will do less work and stop the bike more easily.

Set your brake levers up for high leverage, even though you may lose some pad travel. Then position the levers as I describe below.

2. Move your levers inboard so that the tip of the lever is under your index finger. The lever will bypass your second finger and let you pull it to the bars, rather than losing some range by hitting your finger(s). Hold the bars with three fingers and pull with one. Make sure you pull on the end of the lever, since that is where the most leverage is.

AUTHOR NOTE: The above tip seems to work fine with twist shifters and with Rapidfire integral brake/shift levers, but not so well with Rapidfire levers on a separate band clamp. The band clamp goes inboard of the brake lever, and it prevents the lever from moving inward enough for a rider with large hands to get unimpeded one-finger braking. The band clamp hits the bulged section of the handlebar and stops. The brake lever cannot move inward enough to clear the second finger of a big hand.

plastic guide. The guide can be snapped out of its square hole and into another one closer to the lever pivot or removed completely to maximize leverage.

Booster plates also allow the pads to be set farther from the rims on high power, as less cable pull will be used up in flexing the stays or brake pivots. Running brake cable casings with short lengths and small loops to minimize housing compression has a similar effect as well. With a V-brake, a booster plate, short cables, and the lever set on high power, you will come close to the power of a disc brake!

8.2D V-Brake Upgrades

A V-brake with a horizontal-push linkage on each pad (photos, 8-5, 8-6, 8-10) will make wheel changes easier than a brake with the pad fixed to the arm (photo 8-2).

A V-brake with a roller instead of a noodle (photo 8-10) should have less cable friction than one with a noodle. Replacing the guide pipe with an aftermarket pulley thingamajig can reduce cable friction at the entry into the brake cable link.

Leverage-reduction and leverage-enhancement devices can make it possible to get the leverage you need out of a cantilever lever or a nonadjustable V-brake lever. A cable roller with an offset pivot hole (photo 8-11) and a cable clamp can increase cable pull of a short-pull lever with its cam action. An alternative design for leverage alteration uses two cables attached to an inline enhancing lever (photo 8-12). By hooking the cable segment attached to the lever and the segment attached to the caliper at varying points on the enhancer's lever, you can change the leverage and cable pull. For instance, if you hook the segment from the lever close to the pivot on the enhancer and the segment from the caliper farther outboard on it, you increase cable pull and decrease leverage. You can invert them for the opposite effect.

For about 90 bucks, you can get a 14-piece kit of lightweight brake bolts and hardware for a pair of XT or XTR V-brakes and save yourself some grams.

Upgrading your pads to ones that are less mushy or designed more with your application in mind will improve your braking. For instance, use ceramic-specific pads with ceramic-coated rims, or use Shimano "severe-condition" pads or another wet-weather pad if you live in the Pacific Northwest or similar wet clime.

Replace the pivot studs on your frame or fork if they get bent, bulged, or scored. On brakes that have cartridge bearings, replace the bearings when they need it (photo 8-5).

8.3 CANTILEVERS

While Shimano started a revolution with the V-brake, cantilevers are still tried-and-true brakes and can be made to work decently. If you choose to simply improve your cantilevers rather than upgrading your cantilever brake to a V-brake or a Magura hydraulic rim brake, there is a lot that you can do.

8.3A Getting More out of Your Cantilevers

STRADDLE CABLE: Make the straddle wire as flat and short as possible (photo 8-13). Yanking upward on a yoke to pull two brake arms toward each other is not the greatest way to apply a brake, so you have to help it by adjusting the wire for optimal performance. The flatter wire pulls on the arms at an angle closer to 90 degrees.

If you run a tall straddle wire it may feel strong when the bike is standing still, but it will not stop the bike because you have to squeeze so hard. To generate enough force at the rim to control your speed on a long descent, your hands and forearms will complain.

While squeezing the lever of a stopped bike is something we all do, a static test of brake feel is misleading. It is like putting on the brakes in your car with the engine off and making a determination about how the brakes would work if the car were moving. When squeezing the levers of a stopped bike, a really strong brake will be flexing the stays and mashing the pads. The brake may feel very spongy, even though you may actually be generating five times as much force as would be required to stop the bike.

INCREASE CALIPER LEVERAGE: Loosen the pad post bolts and push the pads inward to make the arms stick out

Note **Important safety note: On any cantilever brake, it is a good idea to have a bracket bolted between the straddle cable and the tire (like the reflector bracket on a shop-floor bike). If you do not have the bracket and you break your brake cable, your straddle cable will drop down onto your tire knobs and stop you dead (and that may literally happen—the dead part!).**

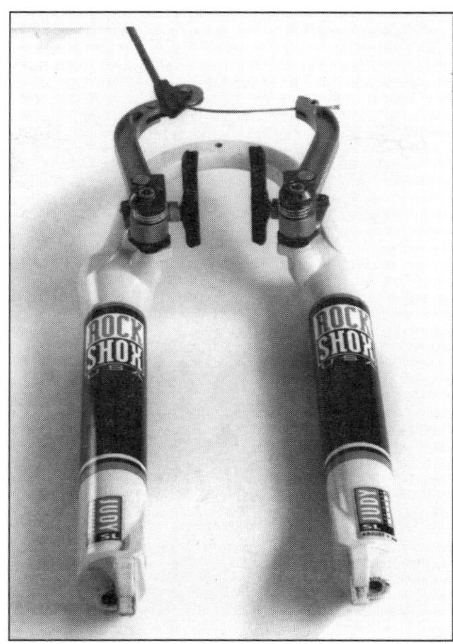

8-10
Hurricane sidepull cantilever brake. Notice the cable pulley instead of a noodle and cable link and the horizontal-push pad mechanisms. The arms of this brake are reversible to change cable routing side by switching the pad-linkage hardware. The pad linkages come off by means of circlips. The spring tension is adjusted on the front of each pivot with a cone wrench.

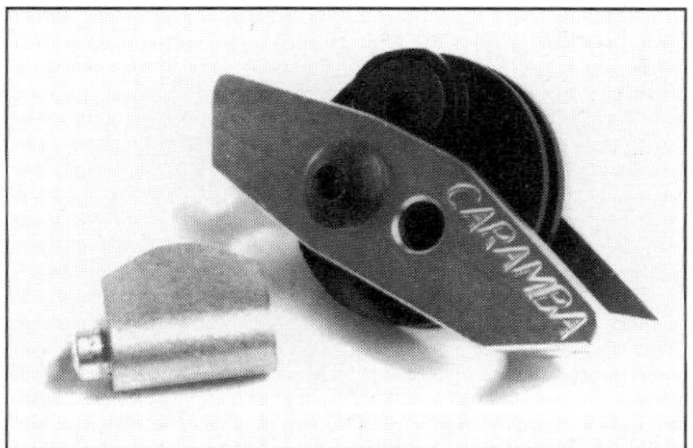

8-11
Caramba leverage-changing offset cam cable roller.

8-12
Sidetrak brake cable leverage variation device. Note the three cable hook points in the lever for cable heads.

8-13
To get maximum leverage, the straddle wire on a cantilever should be as flat and short as possible without interfering with the tire.

farther. (Retighten the bolts, of course. Set the pad adjustment as in Chapter 7 of *Zinn and the Art of Mountain Bike Maintenance.*) Since the brake cable is pulling upward rather than inward on the brake arms, if the arms stick outward farther, you will have more leverage. Make sure you still have heel clearance.

PAD ADJUSTMENT: Set the pad height centered top to bottom on the rim and recheck it frequently as the pads wear. Set each pad flat to the rim in the vertical plane, (it needs toe-in in the horizontal plane), so it will not try to climb up into the tire or down into the spokes. If the bottom edge is hitting, it will try to slide down, and vice versa. An angled pad also puts excessive wear in the linkages and loosens the brake up faster.

BRAKE BOOSTER PLATE: Your brakes will work much better if you are not flexing your stays or flexing your fork's brake posts whenever you apply them. The same as it does with V-brakes, a horseshoe-shaped cantilever brake booster (photo 8-8) attaches to both brake pivot bolts and reduces that flex.

WEIGHT REDUCTION: Another cantilever upgrade is to replace the bolts with titanium ones. If you are going so far as to upgrade old equipment like cantilevers, you could consider a lightweight bolt kit for the entire component group. It will cost you about $300. You will save some weight and your old parts will look cooler. Whether that is cost-effective is another question entirely.

8.4 HYDRAULIC RIM BRAKES

Magura hydraulic rim brake setup is covered thoroughly in the second edition of *Zinn and the Art of Mountain Bike Maintenance* (Chapter 7). This section holds extra details and tips from the pros.

Magura rim brakes (photo 8-14) offer lots of power, simple pad replacement, and abundant pad-to-rim clearance.

8.4A Bleeding

Bleeding is the process of pushing the old brake fluid out with new fluid from the low point to the high point of the system. Bleeding is covered in detail in Chapter 7 of *Zinn and the Art of Mountain Bike Maintenance.* Although Magura claims its brakes never need bleeding, do not believe it, at least if you ride a lot in muddy or gritty conditions.

Use only Magura brake fluid in Maguras; *never* use automotive (DOT) brake fluid!

ELIMINATING AIR: Air in a hydraulic brake system reduces power. The reason that hydraulics work is that liquids are virtually noncompressible. If there is air in the system, your pull on the lever is compressing air, rather than moving brake pads. Whenever the brakes get spongy, or the pads do not begin to move as soon as you begin pulling the lever, there is air in the system. Bleeding can drive the air out.

ELIMINATING CONTAMINATION: Even though Magura rim brakes are supposedly completely closed and impervious to contamination, the realities of mountain bike riding violate the seals. The slave cylinders that push the pads to the rim are located right behind the pads where the tires regularly drag gunk past. Grit and water get on the slave pistons as they extend. When they retract, they draw the grit and water back in with them. If the grit is fine enough, it can get past the seals. Periodically bleed the system to purge it of the contamination, especially if you are riding in either really muddy or dry, finely abrasive conditions.

MAGURA RIM BRAKE TIP

from Bob Gregorio, John Tomac's Mechanic

I bleed the brakes on John's race bike weekly. When I push the old fluid through, it comes out black after only a week of racing and race training. A "normal guy" will not have to bleed the brakes weekly; a couple of times a season should do it. It is hard to say how often you will need to, because it is dependent on the amount of contamination you expose the brake to.

You can prolong the life of the system and improve its performance with frequent bleeding. If you get out the old fluid when it is only mildly contaminated, you can save the seals. Leaving really contaminated fluid in there will tear everything up, though.

8.4B Pads

Replace the pads whenever they need it. Magura's pop-in, pop-out pads (photo 8-14) could not make this job any less time-consuming for you.

Adjust the pads to meet the rims flat, without toe-in, with about 2 mm of rim clearance. It is a pain in the neck (and unnecessary) to adjust Maguras with toe-in. Rather than improving braking, you even run the risk of ruining it. Too much toe-in can conceivably allow the rim to twist the pads out of their sockets.

Black pads are the standard pad for anodized or polished rims. The red pads are softer and are meant for non-ceramic rims

8-14
One side of a Magura hydraulic rim brake.

8-15
John Tomac's race-winning bike from the 1997 Cactus Cup criterium. Notice the Magura hydraulic rim brakes and ceramic rims.

and dry conditions. Green pads are meant for wet conditions. Gray pads are for ceramic and black-anodized rims. Experiment.

CASE HISTORY: John Tomac used gray Magura pads in almost all conditions, wet or dry, on ceramic rims (photo 8-15). Tomac also used brake booster arches front and rear.

8.4C Levers

ADJUSTMENT SET SCREWS: Dial in the brake lever reach and rim-to-pad clearance you want with the set screws in the lever (photo 8-16). The brake reach adjustment takes a 2-mm hex key, and the piston travel adjustment is a finger-knob or a 2-mm hex bolt, depending on model.

LUBE PIVOT: Take the lever pivot out and clean and grease it to make the lever work more smoothly and extend the life of the bushing. Do not over-tighten the pivot pin so it binds up the lever. Adjust the pivot and grease it. Put a little blue threadlock on the pivot bolt threads when you replace it.

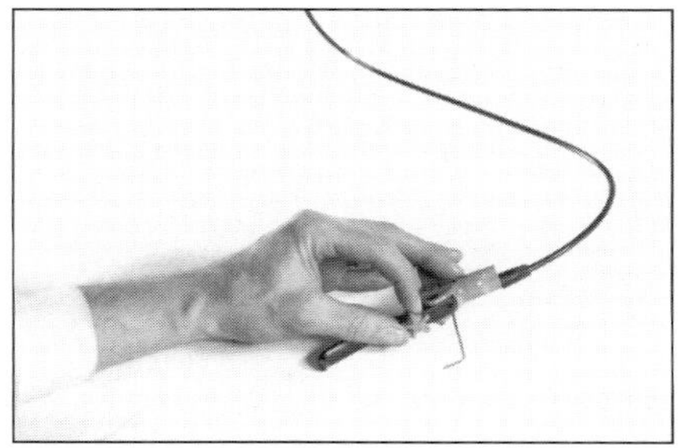

8-16
Adjusting lever reach and rim-to-pad clearance with set screws in a Magura lever.

8.4D Upgrades

BRAKE BOOSTER PLATE: As with V-brakes and cantilevers, your brakes will work much better if you are not flexing your stays or flexing your fork's brake posts whenever you apply them. The Magura stiffener arch attaches to one brake housing clamp bolt and pops over the head of the opposite one.

QUICK RELEASE: If you do not have the quick-release lever on your Maguras, you can buy them and retrofit them to your brakes. Magura has graciously not changed its rim-brake castings for years, so all new parts fit on old brakes.

8.5 DISC BRAKES

Disc brakes offer some advantages over rim brakes. Being at the center of the wheel, they get less contaminated. The tire does not splatter mud all over them. They can offer great modulation and power. Disc brakes allow the use of upside-down fork designs, which rim brakes do not.

Disc brakes for mountain bikes have improved enormously in weight, durability, and performance in the past couple of years, and mounting systems have become simpler and stronger. Most suspension fork manufacturers offer standardized mounting tabs as an option on the left fork leg (photo 8-17). Most current disc brakes mount to these tabs. Almost all brakes have some sort of separate brake mounting adapter bracket to attach the caliper to the mounting tabs (photo 8-18).

Manitou offers two mounting-tab options on its forks. In addition to the standard tabs, you can get a Hayes-brake-only mounting with forward-drilled mounting holes, as opposed to the transverse drilling in the standard mounts. Hayes also makes adapters that work with standard mounts.

8.5A How Disc Brakes Work

Disc brakes work by hydraulic pressure pushing the pads against a hub-mounted disc. Some brakes, like Magura Gustav M (photo 8-19), Hayes, Formula, and Coda, are hydraulic all the way from the lever to the pads. Others, like Rock Shox (photo 8-20), Amp, Hope, and Mountain Cycle, are hydraulic/cable actuated. A cable

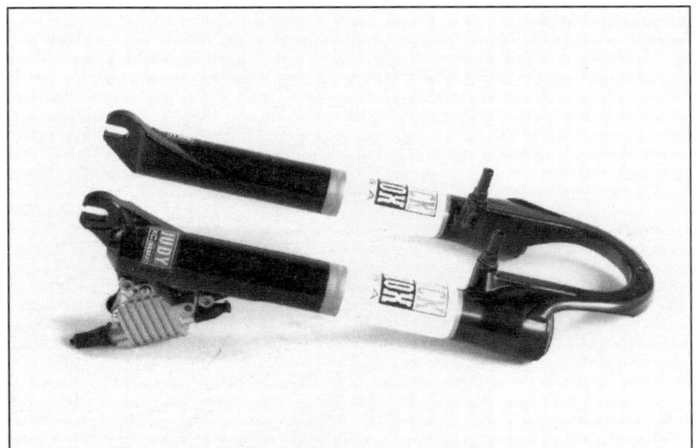

8-17 Rock Shox Judy lower legs with standardized disc-brake mounting tabs.

8-18 Magura Gustav M brake mounting adapter bracket separated from the caliper.

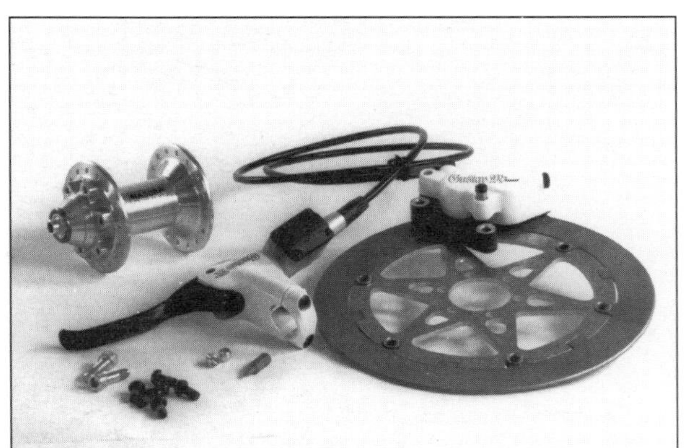

8-19 Complete Magura Gustav M disc brake with rotor, mounting screws, and extra "olives"—brake line fitting seals. The Torx bit is for opening the reservoir cover on the lever.

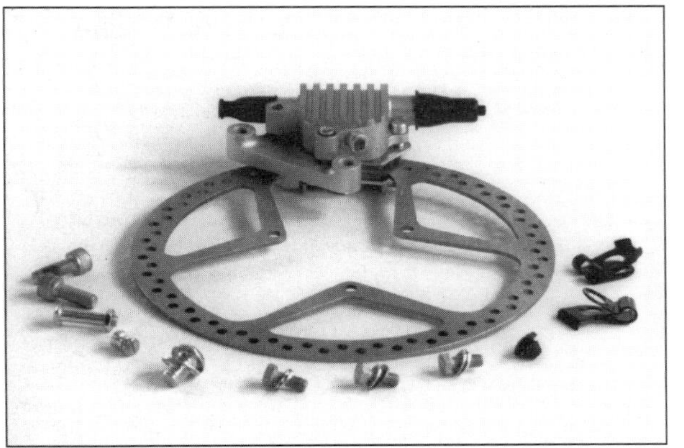

8-20 Complete Rock Shox Disc brake set with rotor, mounting screws, and fork cable brackets.

runs from the lever to the caliper, which is entirely hydraulic inside. A new low-priced Formula brake model is completely mechanical as is the new Dia Tech brake.

A hydraulic brake uses hydraulic fluid to transmit a force applied to a piston inside a master cylinder to one or more pistons inside slave cylinders. Each slave piston presses a pad against the wheel rotor. Some brakes have two adjacent sets of pads and pistons to increase the surface area of contact.

Many bicycle disc brakes have a "floating caliper," meaning that the housing containing the slave cylinders is free to move in and out to follow the disc. On a floating caliper, the slave pistons move the outboard pads, while the inboard pads are fixed to the caliper (photo 8-21). The outboard pads push inward against the rotor, pulling the entire brake caliper outward to force the inboard pads against the rotor equally hard. A floating caliper brake usually takes up less room inboard of the rotor, and the wheel requires less dish (and is thus stronger).

This floating feature means that the pads will drag on the rotor when released, since at least one set of pads cannot retract. There is no mechanism other than the rotor itself to recenter the brake. Pad rub, anathema to most bike mechanics, is unavoidable (and slight, with good alignment). Pad-to-rotor clearance is around 0.010–0.020 inch, and the drag can resonate and drive you nuts. Putting Ti-prep on mounting pins, adjusting cable routing, fully retracting the pads, flattening the backside of the pads, sanding their faces, and truing the rotor may help.

Notable exceptions to the floating caliper trend are the Hayes, Hope, and high-end Formula disc brakes, which are "fixed mount" with opposing pistons on either side of the rotor. Both brake pads can retract and eliminate "free running drag."

Fixed-mount disc brake calipers must be very accurately centered around the rotor.

Hayes brakes on Hayes fork mounts can be centered easily. Fixed mount disc brakes on standard mounts require shims for centering.

Obviously, any disc brake is sensitive to good alignment of the hub, rotor-mounting flange on the hub, dropouts, and mounting tabs so that the disc runs parallel with the slot in the caliper.

Eyeball the rotor between the pads as it spins to see if it wobbles back and forth. You may be able to true it a little with your thumbs or an adjustable wrench on one of the rotor's spider arms.

8.5B Wheels for Disc Brakes

Obviously, wheels are dished to make room for the rotor, resulting in some wheel weakening due to the difference in spoke tension from side to side. Just as with a rear wheel, this tension difference requires a bit more beef in the rim and spokes to compensate. The wheel must be built to take high twisting forces at its center when the rotor tries to stop turning while all of your mass and velocity are devoted to keeping the wheel turning very fast.

The spokes should not be radially laced, as there would otherwise be no component of the spoke angle to counteract the pull by the disc. Do not use aluminum nipples, as the spokes could yank out of them. Don't use lightweight thin steel or titanium spokes.

Three-cross wheel lacing works well. It is best if the pulling spokes go to the out-

8-21
Rock Shox caliper, showing the floating caliper design. Outboard pads are pushed by slave pistons; the inboard pads are fixed to caliper.

side, same as with a good rear wheel. This means that the spokes opposing the windup in the hub come out to the outside of the hub flange (their heads face inward) to have the widest angle to the rim (photo 8-22). In the case of a disc, the pulling spokes are facing forward to oppose the backward brake pull on the rotor. On a rear disc brake wheel, have the drive-side exterior spokes directed backward and the left-side exterior spokes directed forward. (Chain-tension-opposing pulling spokes point backward.)

Use at least 14-gauge (2.0-mm) spokes and brass nipples. Spoke tension should be high.

8.5C Heat Buildup Compensation

As I mentioned before, hydraulic power works on the principle that, unlike air, liquids are not compressible. By maintaining constant volume, fluid that is constrained within a system can be pushed at one end and move something on the other end the same distance. Well, there is a caveat to that: liquids can expand in volume when heated! While the expansion is modest compared to what a gas will do, expansion in a brake can be as much as the spacing from the pads to the rotor, meaning that the brake is applied even when you are not pulling the lever. This is a bad deal. Fortunately, mountain bike disc brake technology has advanced to the point where most brakes have methods for dealing with this problem.

Thermal compensation approaches vary widely. Some fully hydraulic systems have a hole in the wall of the master cylinder that allows excess fluid to move back up into the reservoir when the lever is released. Others use hydraulic fluid formulated to control missile fins and resist expansion

DISC BRAKE TIPS

from Bob Gregorio

Note: John Tomac uses Magura disc brakes, but many of these tips apply to other disc brakes as well.

PAD/ROTOR ALIGNMENT: You may need a file and/or some shims to ensure good alignment of the brake and rotor, which is dependent on the straightness of the frame and mounting bracket. To accommodate misalignments, file and/or shim the brake mounting adapter bracket until the brake lines up with the rotor. It's the bracket that should be shimmed or filed, since a bracket is more easily replaceable than a frame! Alignment is usually less of a problem with the front brake, but sometimes filing or shimming of the bracket is needed there, too.

BLEEDING FULLY HYDRAULIC BRAKES: A disc brake does not get as contaminated as a hydraulic rim brake, since it is away from the tire. You should still bleed a Gustav M periodically, since some dirt does get past the seals and into the fluid. I bleed Johnny's disc brakes weekly, just as I do with his rim brakes, but I could get away with doing it less often. After a week under Johnny, the fluid still comes out with visible contamination.

Make sure you do not drip any brake fluid on the rotor. Here are two tricks to prevent it.

TRICK #1: Rubber-band an old water bottle or can with its top cut off under the master cylinder to catch any fluid that might overflow the reservoir, despite using trick #2. Author's note: with Hayes, run a hose from the lever bleeder into the bottle or can.

TRICK #2: Use two syringes. Insert fluid at the slave cylinder with one syringe and extract it at the reservoir with another. As the fluid level at the reservoir rises, suck it down with the second syringe, so it does not overflow. Initially, you can empty the reservoir, fill it from the syringe at the wheel cylinder, empty it, fill it, etc., until the fluid is coming out clean.

BRAKE LINE CONNECTIONS: Unless they are damaged, there is no need to mess with your brake lines once you have set them up for length. On the Gustav M, do not overtighten the master cylinder fitting (i.e., "sleeve nut"). You can expand the "olive" (brass compression washer) so it will never come out again. Tighten the fitting gently (Magura's recommended tightening torque is 4 N-m). Check the fitting frequently for leakage.

8-22
The center of a wheel for a Rock Shox Disc. The wheel is laced three-cross with the pulling spokes (which point forward) exiting from the outside of the hub flange. You are looking at the hub's left side.

under intense launch temperatures. Some cable-actuated systems have a compensator in the caliper that allows the excess fluid to flow into another chamber.

8.5D Care and Feeding of Disc Brakes

WHEEL REMOVAL: On a floating-caliper-type brake, push the caliper inward to retract the pads before removing the wheel. This moves the pads away from disc.

TRAVEL PROTECTION: Do not pull the brake lever without the pads in place and either a disc or a travel plate (photo 8-23) in between the pads. At minimum, pulling the lever without a plate in between would bring the pads together and prevent you from being able to insert the disc between them. More insidious yet, the pistons can pop completely out of the slave cylinders, which can require you to return the brake to the manufacturer.

PROTECT ROTOR: Do not let any lubricants, brake fluid, or soap get on the pads or the rotor, assuming you are planning on being able to stop your bike.

Protect the rotor from impact during shipping/travel. A bent rotor will give you lots of braking problems.

BLEEDING: On hydraulic/cable-actuated disc brakes, do not monkey with the bleed screw. There is so little fluid in the system, being completely contained within the caliper, that letting any air into it would be disastrous. Bleeding a hydraulic/cable-actuated brake is usually a factory service.

A little air bubble in a fully hydraulic brake is usually not such a big deal. There is often a fluid reservoir above the master cylinder that allows air bubbles to rise to the top without being pumped back into the lines. Fully hydraulic brakes can usually be bled by an adept consumer.

Bleed a fully hydraulic brake with the purge kit and correct fluid that came with the brake. Remove the cap covering the master cylinder (lever) reservoir, insert new fluid with a syringe at the slave cylinder, and purge it out of the reservoir at the lever (and see 'Disc Brake Tips' sidebar). Remember that air bubbles always find their way to the top of the system (i.e., the lever), so *never* try to pump new fluid down from the lever toward the wheel cylinder with any type of hydraulic system! Make sure that there is no air in the syringe and the filler tube. (Get air out the same way a nurse about to stick you in the butt does: hold the syringe vertically, tap it with your finger, and push some liquid out of the top. Another way is to squeeze the fluid bottle a few times while the hose is connected to the bleeder valve on the caliper with the bleeder closed. This will force air back up and out the hose.)

Be careful when replacing the screws holding the reservoir cover on; they are small and should not be overtightened. The cover can crack, among other things. The Magura Gustav M has T-7 Torx screws on the cover to avoid overtightening with a hex key; it comes with the Torx wrench.

8.5E Fine-Tune Adjustment

There are enough different types of disc brakes on the market that it is not feasible to go into adjustment details for each

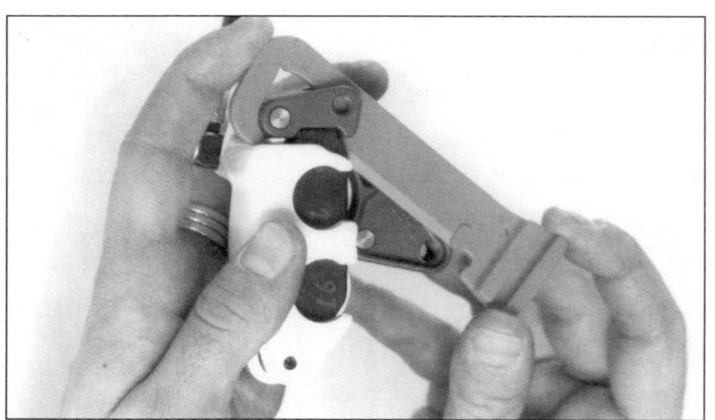

8-23
Installing a travel plate in between Magura Gustav M pads.

8-24
The two-piece Magura Gustav M front rotor. Rolling rivets separate the outer braking surface ring from the inner spider.

8-25
Shimano HRB hub roller brake.

one. You will have to read your owners manual. I know—I hate doing that, too.

In general, however, hydraulic systems share some features. One really cool characteristic is that they are often self-adjusting. Rather than messing with adjustments for pad spacing, you can often pump the lever until you get a firm feel.

Fine-tuning of brake pad spacing can often be done at the lever with both fully hydraulic and hydraulic/cable actuated systems. A barrel adjuster can be turned just like with a cantilever, or a set screw in some levers makes the adjustment. A flaw in some fully hydraulic brakes is that the system lacks sufficient adjustment. The set screw in some levers is too limited, and you can't adjust pad-to-rotor spacing and range of motion of the brake lever enough. Maybe by the time you are reading this book that problem will have been addressed. We can always hope that the design engineers ride their bikes hard.

8.5F Periodic Check of the System

Check the rotors for scoring, looseness, warping, and cracks. This is particularly important with rear rotors, which are usually smaller and less able to handle the heat. Replace the disc before it breaks or ruins the pads.

Check that the caliper-mounting bolts and rotor-mounting bolts are tight. If necessary, apply threadlock compound. Tighten to recommended torque.

Check pad wear frequently. Some brakes come with a gauge to check pad thickness. Replacement is usually simple.

Check that the caliper can move in and out easily. If it cannot, remove it, and clean and lubricate the pins and bushings.

Check levers for proper function and adjustment.

Check cable connections. Clean and lube or replace sticky cables and housings. Replace frayed cables.

Check hydraulic fittings and calipers for leakage.

Apply the brake. Release it and check that the wheel spins freely.

CASE HISTORY: John Tomac's rear rotors warp and crack regularly, whereas a new front rotor design seems to hold up well for him. On the Magura Gustav M, the rear rotor is smaller and made in one piece. The new front rotor has been improved from a similar one-piece design to a two-piece setup. Rolling rivets separate the outer braking surface ring from the inner spider (photo 8-24). The rivets isolate the two sections, reduce stress on the spider, and allow each part to be designed for its very different application.

This case history is not meant to point out strengths and weaknesses in a particular brand but rather to illuminate how a rider like this helps make better parts available for the rest of us. Tomac's ability is always at very edge of current mechanical possibility. He is riding at the absolute limit of every piece of his equipment, and he breaks a lot of it. By having a great mechanic (Bob Gregorio), who notices weaknesses in components and brings them to the attention of the manufacturers, designs improve, and we are the better off for it.

8.6 SHIMANO HUB ROLLER BRAKES

Shimano HRB hub roller brakes (photo 8-25) are an alternative to disc brakes. Shimano engineers strongly believe in them, but they have yet to hit the market. One argument for them is that they can be sealed against the elements better than discs (which already stay much cleaner than rim brakes). Shimano also claims that an HRB's ultimate braking power and modulation will exceed that of a disc and that shoe replacement will be less frequent. Arguments against them are that, relative to discs, they are heavier and more cumbersome to make wheel changes with.

9

PEDALS (AND SHOES)

He put every ounce of energy he possessed on to the pedals. He was flying like a racer.
—Sir Arthur Conan Doyle, *Sherlock Holmes: The Adventure of the Solitary Cyclist*

An ideal pedal spins without friction, supports the foot effectively, attaches to and detaches from the foot immediately when you want it to (under any conditions), and is extremely light. This chapter deals with what to do (and how often) to come closer to attaining this pedal Nirvana. We are talking here about clip-in pedals (and, peripherally, shoes). Cage-type (non clip-in) pedals ain't in this here book. This information *does* apply, however, to the Shimano DX-style platform pedals with pivoting SPD-style clip-in systems so popular now for downhill and BMX.

This chapter is devoted to making pedal clip-in and clip-out as smooth and quick as possible, keeping the pedals spinning freely, and reducing pedal weight. Shoes are included because great performance from your pedals will be obscured by crappy shoes or sore feet. You will also find a section on cleat positioning for optimal efficiency. If you want information on pedal installation, overhauling (including exploded views of numerous pedal brands), retention adjustment, and cleat positioning and mounting, look in Chapter 9 of *Zinn and the Art of Mountain Bike Maintenance*, Second Edition.

Another nice feature of this chapter is a table illustrating which pedals work with which cleats of various brands. If you have several bikes and/or like to try out other people's bikes, this is handy to know. You may not need to constantly switch pedals from bike to bike. You can also avoid getting locked into a pedal that you think might work with your cleat.

9.1 ENHANCING ENTRY/EXIT AND RETENTION OF CLIP-IN PEDALS

If your foot pops out on a gnarly downhill, you want to be able to get it back in as quickly as possible. The conditions are not favorable, as you are bouncing around and too busy to look down at your feet. You want the cleat to pop in as soon as you can hit the pedal. If your pedal normally requires standing up and twisting and shoving to clip in, you will be in a world of hurt as you bounce around on the saddle trying to get your foot in.

Similarly, if you suddenly run out of steam on a steep, bumpy climb, you want to be able to clip out fast before tipping over, yet you don't want to clip out unintentionally.

9.1A Lubrication of Pedal Mechanism

Every pedal will be improved by lubricating the pedal clip-in contact points with a chain wax like White Lightning (photo 9-1). This applies to SPD-style pedals as well as to Time (photo 9-3, 9-7), Look (photo 9-8), Speedplay, and others. The dry lubricant allows your cleat to slip in and out easily without attracting dirt to the pedal or the shoe. You can also walk into the house without making as much of a mess as you would with oil on your cleats.

While wax on the contact points will make a huge difference, you also want the spring mechanisms on SPD-style pedals to work smoothly so those contacts will open and close easily. For that, you want something more rust-protective than chain wax. Lube the springs and pivots with grease or chain oil (photo 9-2). Even without chain wax on the cleat contact points, you will clip in and out more easily with well-lubricated pivots. Oiling pivots does not apply to Look or onZa H.O. (elastomer spring systems without pivots), or to Speedplay (no moving clip parts). On a Time A.T.A.C., oiling the spring coils would probably have little or no effect. The clips are loops of the springs themselves, and there are no pivots (photo 9-3).

Every time you lube your chain, lubricate your pedal contact points and springs and pivots as above. If you ride in wet conditions in which daily chain lubrication is advisable, then so is daily pedal lubrication.

9.1B Cleat Maintenance

The condition of the shoe cleats is integral to easy exit from the pedals, especially with SPD-style pedals. If the cleat is overly worn, it will not be able to push the pedal clip open far enough to release. At the same time, it will rattle around a bit and cost you some pedaling efficiency. Whenever your pedal is hard to get out of, despite lubrication of the contact points, springs, and pivots, it is time to look at your cleat. Put a new one on, and see if it improves. Betcha it will.

9.1C What If Your Cleat Bolt Heads Are Stripped?

If you cannot remove your cleats because the 4-mm hex-key hole in a bolt or two (or four) is stripped, despair not. First, try hammering a new hex key with sharp edges on the end into the bolt head. If that does not give you enough purchase to remove the bolt, *do not* do what some riders try, namely drilling out the bolt. That is a great way to completely

9-1
Lubricating the clip-in contact points on a Shimano 737 SPD pedal with White Lightning dry chain wax.

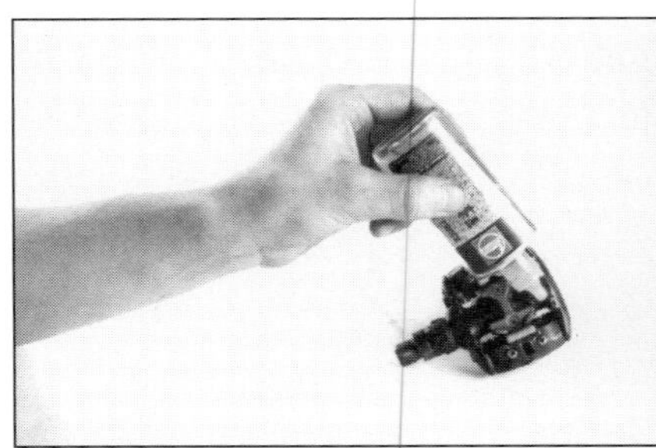

9-2
Lubricating the springs and pivots in a Shimano 737 SPD pedal with chain oil.

9-3
Time A.T.A.C. pedal with plastic top cover open to reveal spring loops.

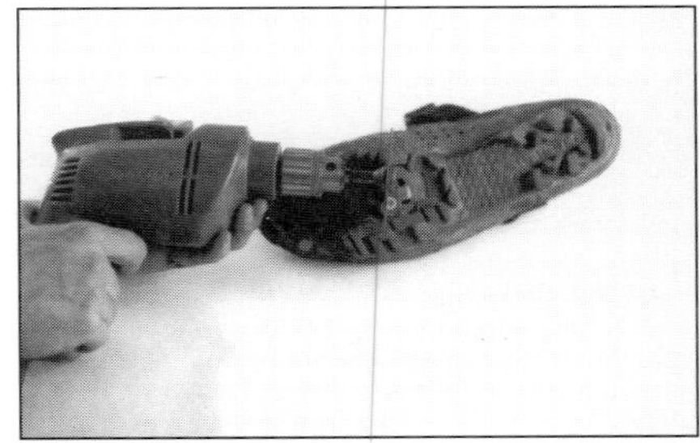

9-4
Slotting a rusted-in cleat bolt head with a rotary disc in a drill. The screw can be removed with a screwdriver after slotting.

ruin the threads in your shoe sole and send you on a trip to buy new shoes.

What *does* work is slotting each bolt head for a screwdriver. The best way I have found is with a rotary fiber cutting disc in a drill (photo 9-4). Hold the shoe in a vise, and wear safety glasses. You can also slot the screw with a hacksaw, if you flex the sole enough that you are not hacking up its tread excessively.

Make the slot deep enough that you will be able to unscrew the bolt on the first try without galling the slot, yet do not chop all the way through the bolt head. Make either mistake, and you will have even less bolt head to work with.

Make this a lesson for you to replace your cleats, or at least the bolts, more frequently.

9.1D Bent or Loose Pedal Contact Points

Smashing your pedals on rocks can affect their operation, so it is best to avoid that. If you do not heed this advice, and the clips that hold the cleats get bent, you will have all kinds of trouble entering and exiting. Similarly, the tabs on the little hourglass-shaped guide plate in the center of the pedal that guides your cleat into position can get bent. The guide plates themselves can get loose or fall off, especially if the screws holding them on were not properly thread-locked.

Check the clips and guide-plate tabs for bending and the guide-plate screws for tightness periodically. Replacement parts are available for some pedals.

9.1E Dialing in Release Tension

If your cleats and your pedal contact points and guide tabs are all in good condition, you can now look at the spring tension adjustment. (Note that there is no tension adjustment on Time or Speedplay pedals.)

On most pedals you must make a compromise between entry, release, and retention, as these adjustments are linked with a single adjustment screw (photo 9-5). Some pedals (some Ritchey, many Wellgo, for instance) reduce the rotational free float available for the foot as the spring tension is increased. Even with a tighter spring, retention may be lacking, since free-float range helps protect against twisting prerelease. The cleat position must be set more accurately as the pedal is tightened, since the reduction in float range removes some latitude for the foot to find its preferred pedaling position.

Ideally, you want entry tension very low so that you can clip in with almost no effort. You also want low release tension so that you can get out easily whenever you want, yet you want high retention so that you never pop out unexpectedly on bumpy descents or when using "body English" on corners or rough climbs. With most pedals, you cannot have your cake and eat it, too, as these requirements are contradictory. On an SPD-style pedal, you will simply need to monkey with the tension setting until you find the best compromise possible. Keeping the springs and clip edges lubricated, as in section 9.1A above, will allow you to get in and out easier while running a higher tension to protect against prerelease.

Time A.T.A.C. pedals (photo 9-3) avoid this compromise and offer great mud-clearing ability. With Time pedals, entry force, release force, and retention

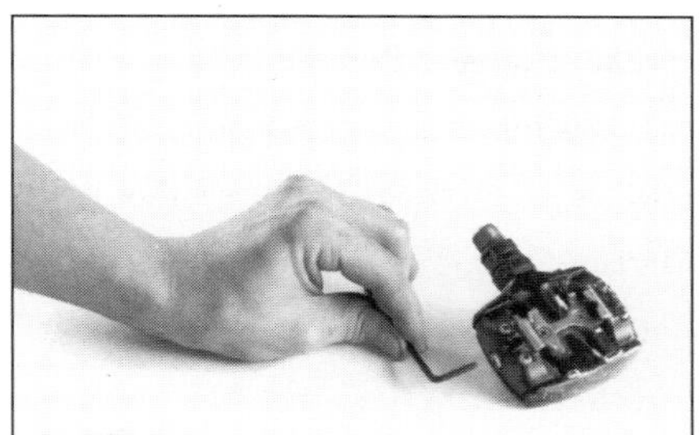

9-5
Entry, release, and retention adjustment screw on a Shimano 737 SPD pedal.

force are less interrelated than they are on SPD-style pedals. The Time cleat, if pushed *forward* rather than straight down, slips in with very low force; it can even be pushed in easily by hand. Release requires a twist beyond the wide float range. Upward prerelease takes an unrealistic amount of force.

Speedplay Frogs, which have no springs, also separate the entry force, release force, and retention force. A very wide float range keeps the foot from twisting out unexpectedly and interlocking steel tabs keep the foot from pulling straight up and out.

9.2 CLEAT POSITIONING

The details of how to set your cleat position initially are gone over in detail in Chapter 9 of *Zinn and the Art of Mountain Bike Maintenance*. This discussion goes a step further.

9.2A Fore-Aft Cleat Position

The neutral position is with the ball of the foot over the pedal spindle. If you have the cleat farther back, it enhances big-gear pedal stomping. Placing the cleat farther forward enhances low-gear spinning. Adjust according to your predominant style.

9.2B Rotational Cleat Position

Set it so that you have some float range either side of your most comfortable pedaling foot alignment.

9.3 KEEPING THOSE BABIES SPINNING FREELY

No sense wasting any of your energy turning resistant pedals. Overhaul them frequently, an operation that is explained and illustrated in detail in *Zinn and the Art of Mountain Bike Maintenance,* Second Edition. Note that "sealed bearing" pedals still need to be overhauled. Some pedals, like Look and Time, require less axle-bearing maintenance than most, but you want to pull them apart periodically and see if they need to be cleaned and lubricated (photos 9-6, 9-7, 9-8, 9-9). Pedals with bushings on the inboard side, which is most of them, need frequent overhaul, especially if they do not have a big rubber lip seal where the axle protrudes from the pedal.

9.4 REDUCING WEIGHT OF CLIP-IN PEDALS

A popular rule of thumb bandied about among bike tech types is that any additional rotational weight out at the edge of the wheel causes 1.7 times more resistance to acceleration than does static weight on a nonmoving bike part. Pedals, also being rotating mass, are more important to keep light than nonmoving parts.

9.4A Lightening up the Pedal Spindle Assembly

The only realistic place to reduce weight in a pedal is in the axle assembly, unless you are a holdout from the 1970s road-bike era who drilled holes in parts to make them lighter. That is probably not a good idea to try with mountain bike parts.

Many pedals are available with either steel or titanium spindles. The spindle is easy to take out and switch on most pedals (photos 9-6, 9-7, 9-8, 9-9). Time (and others) offers lighter spindles for its own pedals, and aftermarket titanium spindle assemblies are available for popular pedals, especially Shimano. SPD-style spindle assemblies are often interchanged as a unit with the bearings incorporated (photo 9-9), although some are available as a spindle only. Replacing the spindle is performed identically to pedal overhaul, which is illustrated in Chapter 9 of *Zinn and the Art of Mountain Bike Maintenance,* Second Edition.

9.5 COMPATIBILITY OF CLEATS AND PEDALS OF DIFFERENT BRANDS

Many SPD-style pedals have cleats that look different yet work well in pedals from other manufacturers. In some cases they work even better than the cleats that came with the pedals! On the other hand, some similar-looking pedals and cleats will not work together at all. Some will allow you to step in but then will not clip out without your having to take your foot out of the shoe and pry open the pedal clips with a screwdriver (for example, Ritchey pedals with Shimano cleats).

Since you may want to trade bikes with friends or ride demo bikes at mountain bike events, it is good to know whether your cleats work with other pedals. You may also want to have different pedals on some of your own bikes without having to invest in specific shoes for each bike. The table on page 106 shows what you can expect when interchanging various pedals. I tried 'em all myself, and I know the chart is accurate.

It is obvious from the table that I highly favor free-floating operation, as it makes cleat setup easier and can save your knees. I also like high retention against unexpected release, and easy entry and intentional release.

9-6
Shimano 737 SPD pedal with splined spindle removal tool in place for spindle assembly removal.

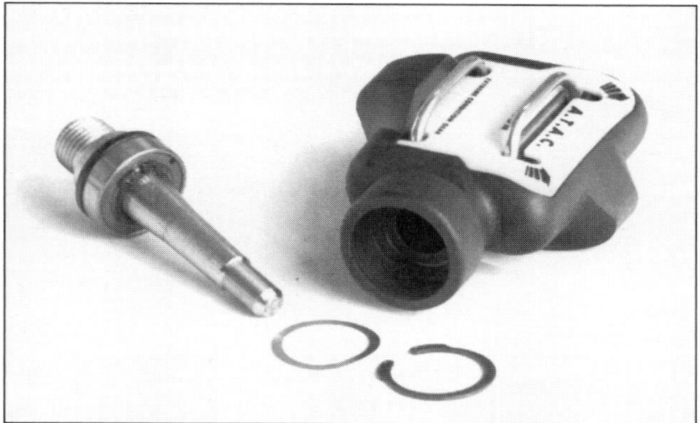

9-7
Time A.T.A.C. pedal with axle assembly removed. Notice the large-diameter spindle and cartridge bearing. Needle bearings are inside the pedal body. The spindle is accessed by removing the circlip at the lower right.

9-8
Look pedal with axle assembly removed. Notice the large-diameter spindle and cartridge bearing. Needle bearings are inside the pedal body. The spindle is removed in the standard way with a special Look splined tool.

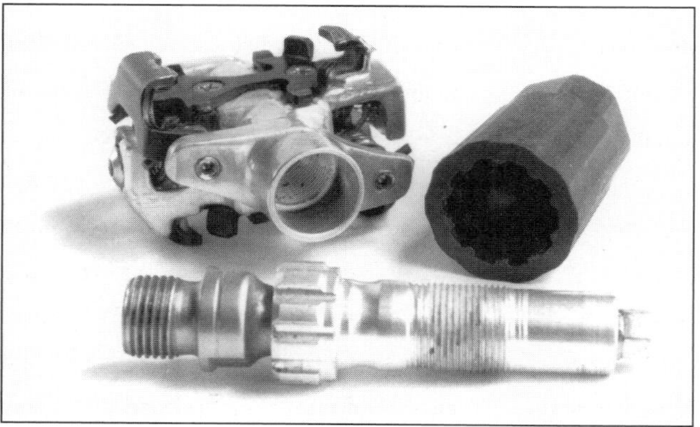

9-9
Exus E-M2 SPD-style pedal with spindle assembly removed. Disassembly tool is to the right rear. The spindle runs on a bushing on the inboard end and a bearing on the outboard end.

PEDAL

CLEAT	VP 103	VP 104	ONZA H.O.	TIME A.T.A.C.	WELLGO WPD-800/ ONZA H.O.X.	SHIMANO 747	SHIMANO 737	SHIMANO 636	RITCHEY LOGIC	CODA CO	SCOTT TWIN CAM '97	SCOTT TWIN CAM '96	TIOGA CLIPMAN	LOOK SL3	EXUS E-M2	SPEEDPLAY FROG
Shimano 747 (SM-SH-51)	B	C	F	F	C	A	A-	A	D	C	C	B-	F	F	B+	F
Shimano 737 (SM-SH-50)	B	C	F	F	C	A	A-	A	D	C	C	B-	F	F	B+	F
Scott '96 (WP-98A)	B	C	F	F	C	A	A-	B	B-	C	C	B	F	F	B+	F
Scott '97/Wellgo/Coda (WP-97A)	B	C	F	F	C	A	A	B	A	C	C	C	F	F	B+	F
Look SL3	F	F	F	F	F	F	F	F	F	F	F	F	F	A	F	F
onZa H. O. (pre-1998)	C	—	B+	F	C	D	D	D	C	C	C	C	F	F	—	F
Ritchey Logic	D	—	F	F	C	B+	B+	B+	A	A	A	A-	F	F	—	F
Tioga Clipman	F	F	F	F	F	F	F	F	F	F	F	F	B+	F	F	F
Time A.T.A.C.	F	F	F	A+	F	F	F	F	F	F	F	F	F	F	F	F
VP (E-C01)	B	C	F	F	C	A	B	B	D+	C	C	C	F	F	B+	F
Speedplay Frog	F	F	F	F	F	F	F	F	F	F	F	F	F	F	F	A
onZa H.O.X. (1998–)	A	A	F	F	A	A	A-	A	—	A-	A	—	F	F	A	F

The grading scale is as follows:

A+ = very easy entry and release, abundant float, and very high retention

A = good entry, good release, good retention, good float

A- = good entry, good release, good retention, small float range

B+ = good entry, retention, and float; hard or intermittent release (or break-in required)

B = good entry, retention, and release; no float

B- = same as B with hard or intermittent release (or requiring break-in)

C = good entry, release, and float; poor retention (foot can be pulled straight up and out)

C- = same as C, and pedal is fixed (no float)

D+ = can clip in, but foot can only be released by twisting inward (won't release outward)

D = can clip in but cannot release

F = cleat will not clip in

— = I have not tried this combination

NOTE: COMBINATIONS GRADED D+, D, OR F ARE NOT SAFE TO RIDE!

9.6 SHOES

It is through the shoes that your energy to propel the bike is transmitted.

9.6A What to Look for in a Shoe

The first thing to find in a mountain bike shoe is good fit. That goes without saying, perhaps, but it is always amazing to me how many people ride with foot discomfort from poor fit. Different brands fit different foot types better, so shop around.

9-10
Thread-on spikes with a Nike shoe.

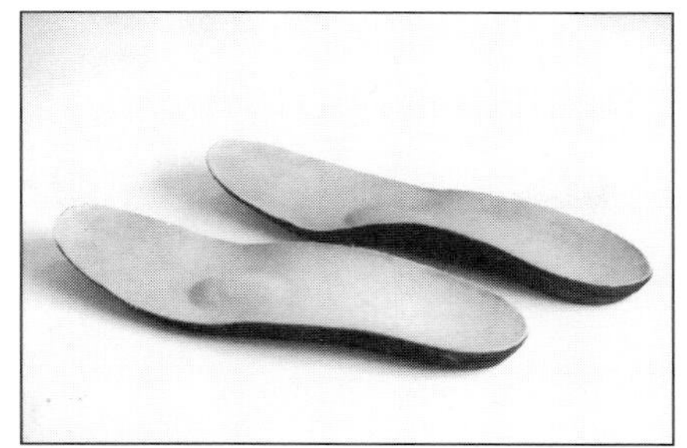

9-12
Custom footbeds shaped to the foot with additional metatarsal-arch pads in the forefoot.

You want the lace/strap system to hold the foot securely. There is no need to fit them so tightly that your toes are wedged against the end, contrary to some popular beliefs. Quick ways to adjust shoe tightness while riding, like buckle systems or Velcro straps, are nice.

The second thing to look for is a stiff, well-fitting sole to distribute pedaling pressure away from the spot directly over the pedal. A completely rigid sole hampers running and walking somewhat, but you want as little sole flex as you can get away with and still be able to do the non-riding things you want to with your shoes. Some racers use completely rigid road shoes with some tread glued to the bottom (see Case History below). If the shoe fits well, the rigidity is less of a problem for ambulation than you might think. If you have a high arch and a very flat, stiff shoe sole, however, expect discomfort. That is *not* a way to distribute pedaling pressure over the whole foot!

The third thing to look for is light weight. Running and pedaling both involve lifting the feet a lot, and the less weight attached to them, the better.

The shoe should also have decent traction for running. If you race cyclo-cross or run in mud or on other slick, soft surfaces a lot, having the option of thread-on spikes is nice (photo 9-10). The tread design should also facilitate the cleat clipping into the pedal. Sometimes really tall knobs prevent the shoe from clipping in and must be cut down.

Finally, all these features are negated if the shoe will not mount your cleat where you need it. Most shoes now have two sets of threaded holes and long slots for them to move in, so this is rarely a problem anymore. Still, if the holes will not move to where your cleat needs to be for you, the shoe is not for you.

CASE HISTORY: Shimano has built custom cross-country shoes for top North American pro Kirk Molday. He won the 1997 NORBA NCS series on a used a top-of-the-line Shimano carbon road shoe to which Shimano had bonded the standard rubber tread from the bottom of its top-of-the-line mountain bike shoe (photo 9-11). It was an extremely light cross-country shoe with a completely rigid sole.

9.6B Custom Footbeds for Shoes

Custom footbeds (photo 9-12), also called orthotics, are a way to transmit more pedaling force with less discomfort. While I think everyone would benefit somewhat from footbeds shaped precisely to fit their feet, some people have specific foot problems that, if not

9-11

Kirk Molday winning the 1997 Park City NORBA National Finals on custom-modified Shimano road shoes.

addressed with custom footbeds, will result in pedaling agony.

Custom footbeds can either be made of rigid plastic (this used to be the *only* style of orthotic available) or of molded closed-cell foam. Either type is molded to your foot when warm. They can then be shaped on the bottom to fit your shoe soles. The footbed allows the sole to support the foot uniformly over its entire length. Coupled with a rigid shoe sole, instead of having a hot spot under the ball of your foot where the pedal is, the load is distributed over your entire foot. The total load on any given part of your foot is substantially lower.

A custom-molded footbed can also be further customized to address a certain problem. It can have additional pads added to it to support a specific part of your foot, or ground away in spots to let part of your foot drop (see following Case History).

Some shoe companies make custom shoes for their top pro riders, since they understand how critical good foot support and comfort is to performance. For example, I have been to the SiDi shoe factory in Monte Belluno, Italy, and seen racks of shoe lasts labeled with top pro riders' names. The lasts are formed to be identical to the riders' feet, and their shoes are built over them for a perfect fit.

CASE HISTORY: I know the value of custom footbeds from personal experience, as I have a condition called "Morton's neuroma," an inflammation of the nerves between the metatarsal heads. Without custom footbeds, the pain under the ball of my foot when pedaling hard or when skiing or skating is intense.

I have a "Morton's foot type," in which my second toe is longer than my big toe. This results from a short first metatarsal, which reduces my ability to bear weight on my foot. Most people bear most of their weight when walking on the head of their first metatarsal, the big knob at the base of the big toe. Since my first metatarsal is shorter than my second one, I am not able to carry as much weight on it. To compensate, I tend to curl my toes to take some of the load that the first metatarsal is not.

A "metatarsal pad" on top of my custom-molded footbed (photo 9-12) lifts my metatarsal arch (Did you know there's an arch there?). The metatarsal arch pad separates and supports the metatarsals and keeps them from impinging on the nerves in between them, causing inflammation and pain. The pad also allows my first metatarsal to support more weight. Grinding away some of the footbed under my big toe so that it drops more also lets the first metatarsal do more work.

10

HEADSETS, STEMS, AND HANDLEBARS

I had to watch the steering and circumvent those snags.
—Joseph Conrad, *Heart of Darkness*

You gotta have something good and sturdy to hold onto that steers well when screaming down a rough trail or when yanking on the grips when climbing. A good, freely rotating headset and a strong and stiff handlebar and stem give you that (photo 10-1).

10.1 HEADSETS

If the headset is not turning smoothly and in good adjustment, you cannot hope to control your bike the way you would want to. You want to know how to check it, adjust it, and maintain it.

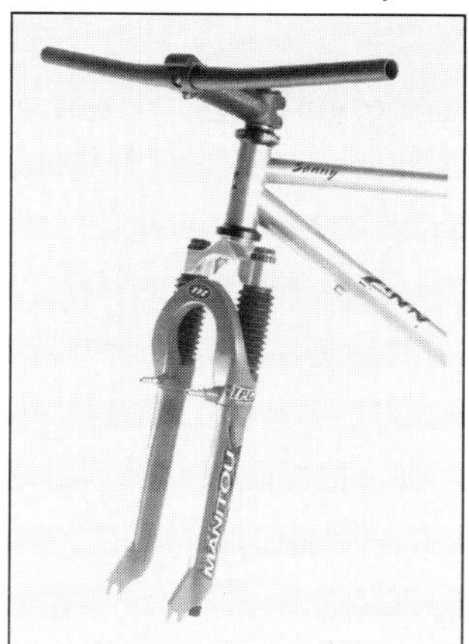

10-1
The stem, bar, and headset.

10.1A Check Headset

Grab the bars and swing them slowly back and forth with the front wheel off the ground. The rotation should feel smooth and resistance-free, except for flexing of the control cables that must happen as you turn the bars. If you feel distinct clicks, notches, or pits in the rotation, you probably need a new headset. Headset removal, replacement, overhaul, and adjustment are covered in Chapter 11 of *Zinn and the Art of Mountain Bike Maintenance*. If the rotation just feels slow and sticky, then the headset is probably too tight. See sections 10.1B and 10.1C below.

Now squeeze the front brake lever as you rock the bike forward and back. Turn the bars at 90 degrees to the bike and rock it back and forth some more with the brake on (photo 10-2). As you do these steps, grab each headset cup with your free hand. Feel and listen for any back-and-forth movement of the fork steering tube inside the head tube.

You can also lift the front end and drop it, listening for any rattling, and you can ride the bike and feel if the fork feels loose, especially at slow speeds on rough downhills. Looseness in the headset is a little tricky to separate from play in the suspension fork. If you feel for it with enough different methods, you should be able to distinguish headset movement from fork movement. If the headset is loose, see sections 10.1B and 10.1C below.

10.1B Fine-Tune Adjustment of Threadless Headset

Loosen the bolts that clamp the stem to the steering tube. If the headset is loose, tighten the top cap bolt 1/4 turn (photo 10-3), retighten the stem clamp bolts, and recheck adjustment as in 10.1A above. Repeat as needed.

If the headset is too tight, loosen the top cap bolt 1/4 turn, retighten the stem clamp bolts, and recheck adjustment as in 10.1A above. Repeat as needed.

10.1C Fine-Tune Adjustment of Threaded Headset

As in Chapter 11 of *Zinn and the Art of Mountain Bike Maintenance*, loosen the headset top nut with a headset wrench while holding the stem. If the nut is too tight for that, you will need to hold the adjustable cup with a headset wrench.

If the headset is loose, tighten the cup 1/4 turn while holding the stem (photo 10-4). Still holding the stem, tighten the top nut down against it. Tighten the cup and the nut against each other with the headset wrenches.

If the headset is tight, loosen the cup 1/4 turn while holding the stem. Still holding the stem, tighten the top nut down against it. Tighten the cup and the nut against each other with the headset wrenches.

10.1D Wear Indicators

A headset needs to be replaced if the bearing surfaces are rough, pitted, uneven, or rusted. Headset cups can crack sometimes, so look for that as well.

10.1E Upgrade Headset

All headsets are not created equal. As you travel up the continuum of improving headsets, besides becoming more expensive, they have better bearing surfaces, better bearings, better seals, and, usually, lighter and more durable materi-

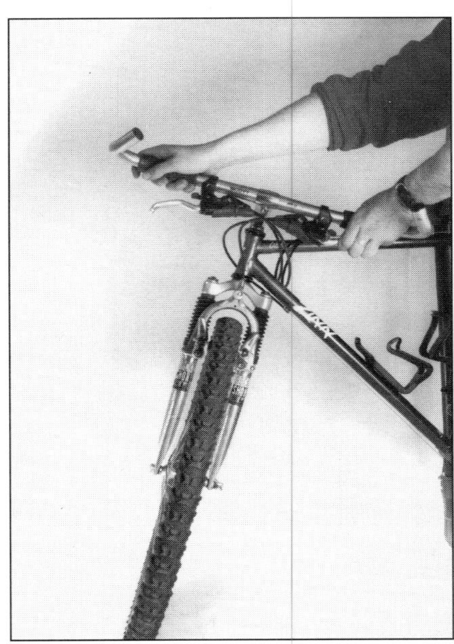

10-2
Check for headset play by turning the bars at 90 degrees and rocking bike back and forth with the brake on.

10-3
Turning threadless headset top cap bolt to adjust headset.

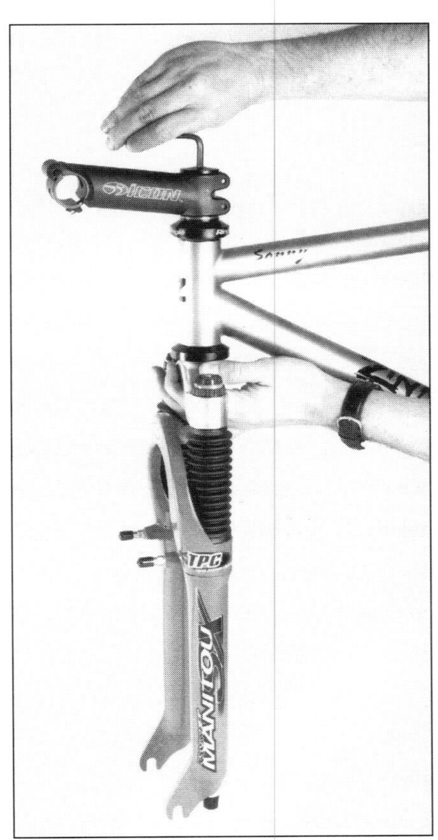

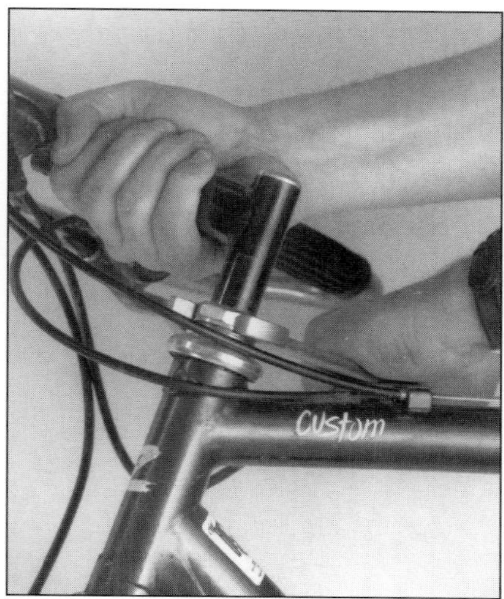

10-4
Turning threaded headset cup with headset wrench while holding stem.

10-5
An inexpensive threadless headset.

10-6
Inexpensive headsets have steel cups pressed out of a single piece with no machining or polishing of the bearing races. There are relatively few ball bearings with a lot of space between them.

10-7
XTR high-quality ball-bearing headset with numerous seals.

als. If your headsets wear out quickly or get full of grit rapidly, you could benefit from a better headset.

The cheapest kind of headset has steel cups and cones, sometimes with plastic covers, and widely spaced ball bearings held into steel retainer cages (photo 10-5). You can see how the cups are simply pressed out of a single piece of steel with no machining or polishing of the bearing races (i.e., the surfaces on which the bearings roll), and there are relatively few ball bearings with a lot of space between them (photo 10-6). There may be no seals to keep dirt out (or only thin, loosely fitting, hard plastic ones).

Better headsets have precision ground and polished hardened-steel bearing surfaces, which are pressed into aluminum cups and cones. They have more ball bearings of better quality that are closely spaced and held into steel or plastic retainer cages. The harder bearings and bearing surfaces resist denting on hard impacts, as does the distribution of the load over more bearings. Pressing each steel bearing race into an aluminum cup reduces weight and provides a little more shock absorption (and hence protection of the bearings and bearing races) than a solid steel cup could. The dirt seals fit well and may consist of a combination of separate interlocking rubber seals (photo 10-7) requiring grit to take a labyrinthine path in order to get to the bearings.

Other good headsets have needle bearings held into plastic retainers that run on conical steel bearing surfaces sitting in/on aluminum cups and cones. The needle bearings distribute the load over more surface area than ball bearings, since each cylindrical needle bearing contacts each bearing surface along its entire edge, rather than at a single point, as a ball does. The Ritchey needle-bearing headset (photo 10-8) has a small top cup and cone to reduce weight. The idea is that the lower bearing takes the majority of the impact, and the top bearing does not need to be as big. Note the rubber O-ring seal.

More recent headset designs have "angular-contact" cartridge bearings. Angular-contact bearings differ from standard cartridge bearings (like you might find in hubs, bottom brackets, and derailleur jockey wheels) in that angular-contact bearing walls are angled (that is, the walls are shaped like concentric chopped-off cones), rather than straight (that is, the walls are shaped like concentric cylindrical rings) as in standard cartridge bearings. In photo 10-9, the angular-contact bearings are the two black rings in the center. Angular-contact bearings are designed to take side loads, while standard cartridge bearings are only designed to take radial loads. The angled sides of the rings oppose the side forces that would otherwise be forcing the bearings sideways out of a standard cartridge bearing and breaking it apart. As in any cartridge bearing, the balls are trapped within the cartridge unit (photo 10-10). Steel or plastic seals usually protect the ball bearings inside the cartridge (photo 10-11).

As with standard ball-bearing headsets, better angular-contact cartridge-bearing headsets have more higher-quality ball bearings in each cartridge (photo 10-10), and the cartridges are in lighter aluminum cups (photos 10-10 to 10-12), rather than in stamped steel ones (photo 10-9).

10-8
Ritchey needle-bearing headset has a small top cup and cone to reduce weight. The lower needle bearings carry the majority of the load.

10-9
STX headset. The angular-contact bearings are the two black rings in the center. The cups are stamped steel.

10-10
Ball bearings in an angular-contact cartridge unit are trapped. Better angular-contact cartridge-bearing headsets have many high-quality ball bearings in each cartridge, and the cartridges are in light aluminum cups.

10-11
Ringle's headset lower cup (second from left) and the top cone with the large cover (second from right) hang over the bearing below to allow water to drip off. Steel covers protect the ball bearings inside the cartridge. The cartridges are in light aluminum cups.

10-12
King headset (exploded). Cartridges are in light aluminum symmetrical top and bottom head tube cups.

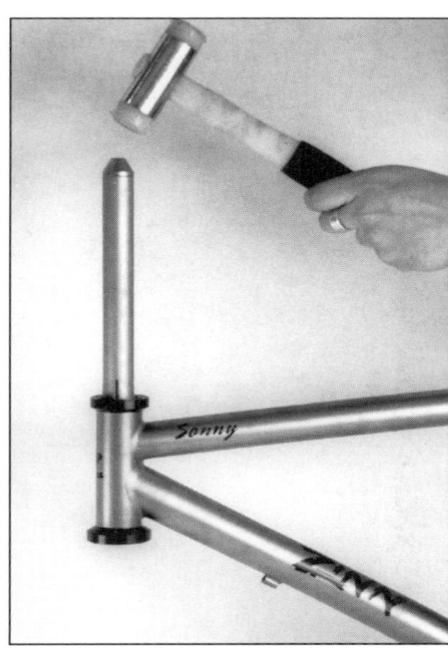

10-13
Knocking headset cups out of the head tube.

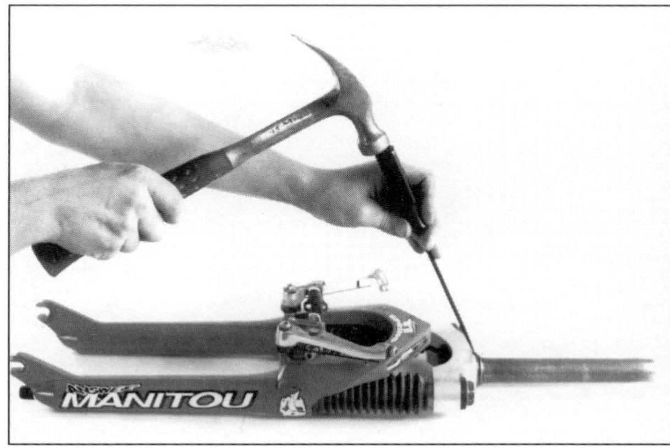

10-14
Removing fork crown race from suspension fork by tapping it with a screwdriver and a hammer. Alternate doing this from either side.

The seals are also better in premium angular-contact cartridge-bearing headsets than in cheaper ones. Sealing methods differ, however. The King headset (photo 10-12) has symmetrical top and bottom head tube cups. The seal on the top cup, then, must be very good, since the cup is open to the top. The top cone is sealed around its inner edge (against the steering tube) and its outer edge with O-rings. The Ringle headset (photo 10-11) uses a water-sealing method approved by plumbers for centuries. Both the lower cup (second from left) and the top cone with the large cover (second from right) hang over the bearing below to allow moisture to drip off. There are rubber seals inside as well, especially around the bottom cup, where dirt and water are thrown up at the cup by the tire.

A partial headset upgrade consists of replacing the top cap and bolt with lighter (or cooler looking) ones. For about 15 bucks, you can get a colorful anodized aluminum top cap and a titanium adjuster bolt.

10.1F Remove Headset

The old headset cups are knocked out of the head tube with a tool that looks like a tube that has been split open on the end (photo 10-13). The old fork crown race often has to be removed from a suspension fork by tapping it off from either side with a screwdriver and a hammer (photo 10-14). You may need to get it started by tapping a razor blade in the gap between the crown and the crown race (with safety glasses on, of course!). A fork crown race remover tool or a vise works for removing the crown race from rigid unicrown forks. This process is illustrated in Chapter 11 of *Zinn and the Art of Mountain Bike Maintenance.*

10.1G Preparing the Frame for a New Headset

When you install a new headset, especially an expensive one, you want to make sure that the top and bottom bearings are precisely parallel to each other and perpendicular to the steering axis. If the bearing surfaces are not parallel, the

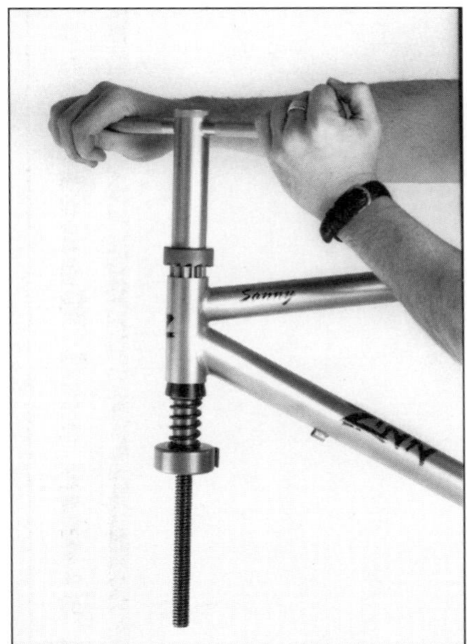

10-15
Reaming and facing the head tube.

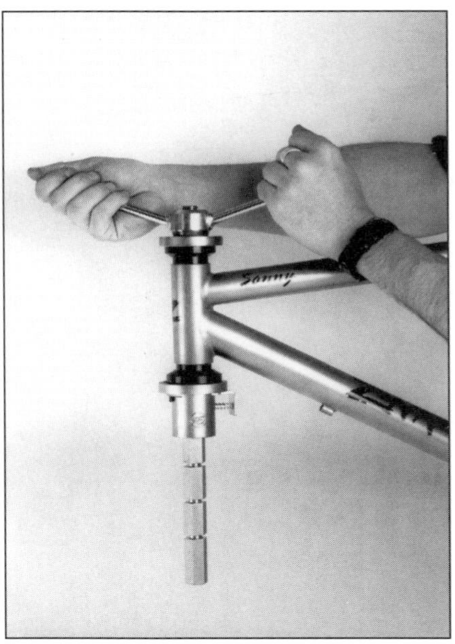

10-16
Pressing headset cups into either end of the head tube with a headset press.

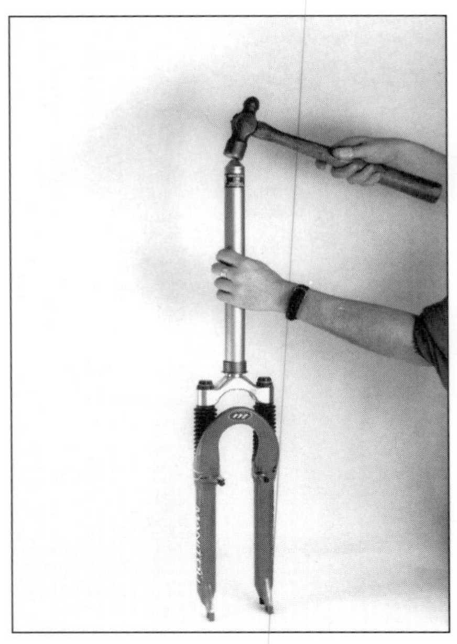

10-17
Pounding a headset bottom cone onto a fork crown with a crown-race setting tool.

headset will be impossible to adjust so that it turns smoothly without either being too loose or having tight spots. It also will wear out quickly.

You ensure that the headset will last as long as possible and turn as smoothly as possible by reaming and facing the head tube ends. Reaming the inside of the head tube at the ends ensures that the headset cups press in straight in line with each other and parallel to the steering tube. Facing cuts the ends of the head tube parallel with each other and perpendicular to the steering axis. When the headset cups are pressed against the ends of the head tube, the bearings in either end will run true with each other.

The head tube is reamed and faced with a head tube reamer/facer. (Duh!) The tool has a cylindrical reaming cutter and a disc-shaped facing cutter attached to a handle with a long shaft running through the center of the reamer. The shaft passes through a pilot plug on the opposite end of the head tube that centers the tool shaft. Put cutting fluid on the cutters. Turn the tool handles until you have cut a clean, new surface on either end of the head tube (photo 10-15).

10.1H Installing a New Headset

You press the headset cups into either end of the head tube with a headset press (photo 10-16). The headset bottom cone is pounded onto the fork crown with a headset slide hammer or crown-race setter (photo 10-17). Put a little grease on the surfaces of the headset, frame, and fork that contact each other before pressing them together.

Assemble a threadless headset with the fork and stem. Mark the top edge of the stem on the fork steerer (photo 10-18). You will cut the steering tube off 3 mm below this line, if you will be using no headset spacers. You will cut at the line, if you will use a single 3-mm spacer. You will cut above the line by the thickness of any additional spacers beyond 3 mm, if you plan to use more spacing. Remove the stem and, using a cutting guide, cut the steering tube off to length (photo 10-19). Pound in the star nut to 12–15 mm below the top edge of the steerer with a star-nut-setting tool (photo 10-20).

HOT TIP: If you are using a thick-walled aluminum fork steerer, the stock headset star nut may be too wide to insert without getting mangled. If so, bend each pair of opposite tabs of the nut inward a bit with channel-lock pliers before insertion. This tip, and all assembly and adjustment of threaded and threadless headsets, are described in detail in Chapter 11 of *Zinn and the Art of Mountain Bike Maintenance.*

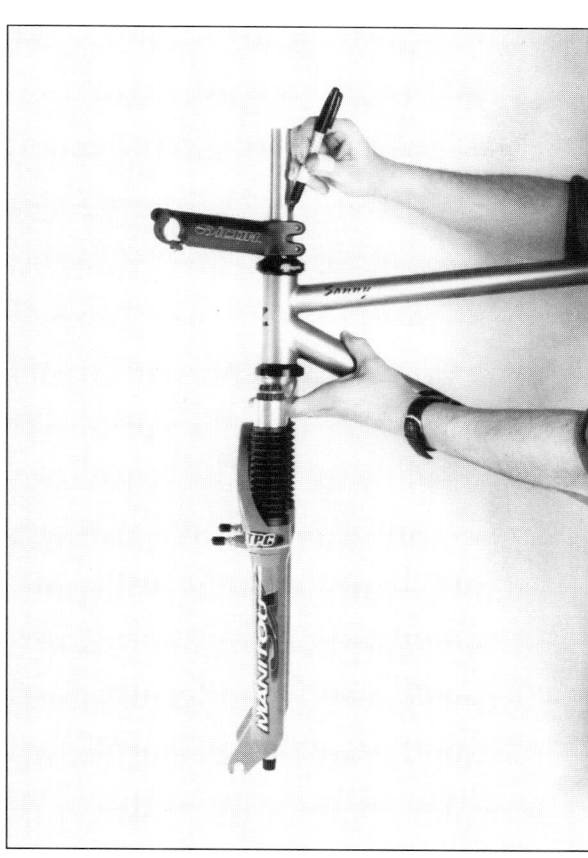

10-18
Marking the top edge of the stem on the fork steering tube.

10-19
Bottom left: Using a cutting guide to cut the steering tube off to length.

10-20
Pound in the star nut to 12–15 mm below the top edge of the steerer with a star-nut-setting tool.

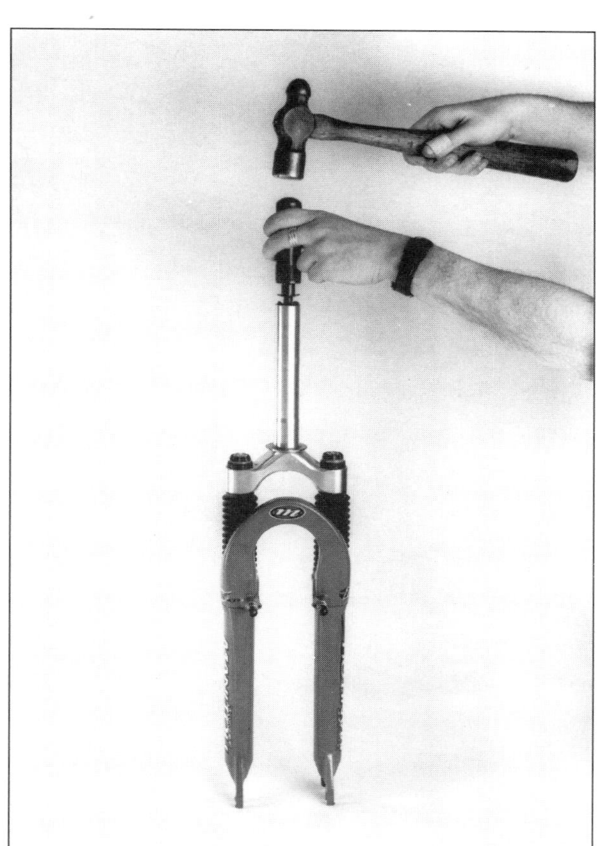

10.2 STEMS

The main purpose of a stem is to rigidly attach the handlebars to the steering tube. Suspension stems are designed to connect those two parts less rigidly. With the vast improvements in suspension fork technology in the past couple of years, the interest in (and development of) suspension stems has fallen off dramatically, so I won't bother to address them here. I do have a section on suspension stems in Chapter 11 of *Zinn and the Art of Mountain Bike Maintenance*, if you are interested.

10.2A Stem Upgrades

The stem is more rigidly connected to the steering tube with less weight by using a threadless headset and clamp-on stem, rather than a threaded headset and a quill-type stem with expander wedge or plug (photo 10-21). The larger clamp size also allows a larger stem shaft diameter to be used, since it does not have to meet a thin quill.

On the other hand, the bar height adjustment is much easier to vary with a threaded headset and quill stem. Varying the height of a threadless headset stem requires moving spacers around and readjusting the headset each time (covered in Chapter 11, of *Zinn and the Art of Mountain Bike Maintenance*). Adjustment range is also sharply limited.

I recommend getting a strong, stiff stem from a manufacturer with a good reputation. The last thing you want to break on a bike is your stem! Choose one with the length and angle that work for you. Appendix A deals with sizing yourself on the bike and can come in handy when choosing stems.

A front-opening stem (photo 10-22) is nice for someone who travels with their bike a lot. Instead of throwing off your headset adjustment by removing the stem to fit the bike in a box or bag, you can pull the bar off. Reassembling the bike takes far less time.

A partial stem upgrade consists of replacing the stem bolts with titanium ones. For most threadless headset stems, for about 20 bucks you can get a three- or four-bolt kit to replace the steel handlebar- and steerer-clamp bolts.

10.3 HANDLEBARS

The handlebar is your first route of control of the bike. It had better be intact and at a comfortable reach for you to accomplish this task well.

10.3A Handlebar Choice

There are so many types of bars on the market, that your choice may not be easy. You may be looking for a super-light one, but do not risk your neck unnecessarily on one not in wide use.

Generally, better bars will be lighter and, sometimes, stiffer. Your choices, besides brand, include materials, bend, and length (photo 10-23). Riser bars often have clamp-on stiffener options, too.

There are good bars made out of aluminum, steel, titanium, carbon, or a combination. On the other hand, there are lousy bars made out of any of these materials as well. Get one that you know other riders have used for a long time without breakage.

The bend is a matter of personal preference. If you can try various bars, or

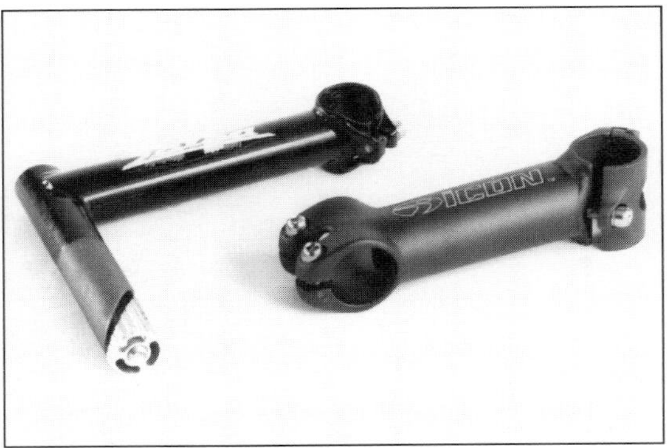

10-21
Quill-type stem with expander wedge (left) for threaded headset and clamp-on stem for threadless headset (right).

10-22
3T Forge Ahead stem with the front removed to show front-opening design.

other people's bikes with different bars, you can find the shape you like most. Generally, cross-country riders prefer single-bend bars, although the bend angle preference depends on the rider. Also, the way the bar ends are angled changes depending on bar bend. Some bars make the bar ends stick out at an odd and unusable angle.

Riders who concentrate on riding downhill or slalom and less on climbing will prefer a higher position with a double-bend bar.

On cross-country single-bend bars, there is very little choice of bar length. If you have wide shoulders, get the widest bar you can. If you need more width, use a bar end that gets you a little more lateral room by being mounted outboard of the clamp or by having a very narrow clamp. Also, double-bend

STEERING DAMPERS

The handlebars can be yanked back and forth from the rider's hands when bouncing down a rough descent at speed. A steering damper can slow the twisting of the wheel by bumps. Like a damper in a fork or a screen door, it stiffens up against fast movement. The principle is usually that of forcing a piston with a hole in it through some oil. The bigger the hole, the faster it can be moved, and vice versa. Slow movements of the handlebars are resisted very little by the damper.

Some dampers are cylindrical units that fit over the top of the headset (10-24), some fit down inside the top of the steering tube, and some are linear, screen-door-type shocks that attach to the down tube and one side of the fork crown.

GRIP INSTALLATION TIP

from Steve Driscoll, ATI's Gripologist

During the 1997 season, the hot thing among team mechanics was to use "Spray 99," 3M's super-strength spray adhesive. The grips slide on nicely and stay in place, once the glue sets up. WD-40 used to be the magical stuff in BMX. It lubricates the grip for sliding it on easily, and it bonds well after evaporating.

Now, however, our new secret formula for 1998 is to use the new Shimano citrus degreaser. It eats into the grip and bonds it really well to the bar. It evaporates very quickly. The problem with the 3M adhesive spray is that it is very messy. Your fingers and everything you touch sticks to it. WD-40 doesn't bond as well, and it evaporates more slowly than the Shimano degreaser.

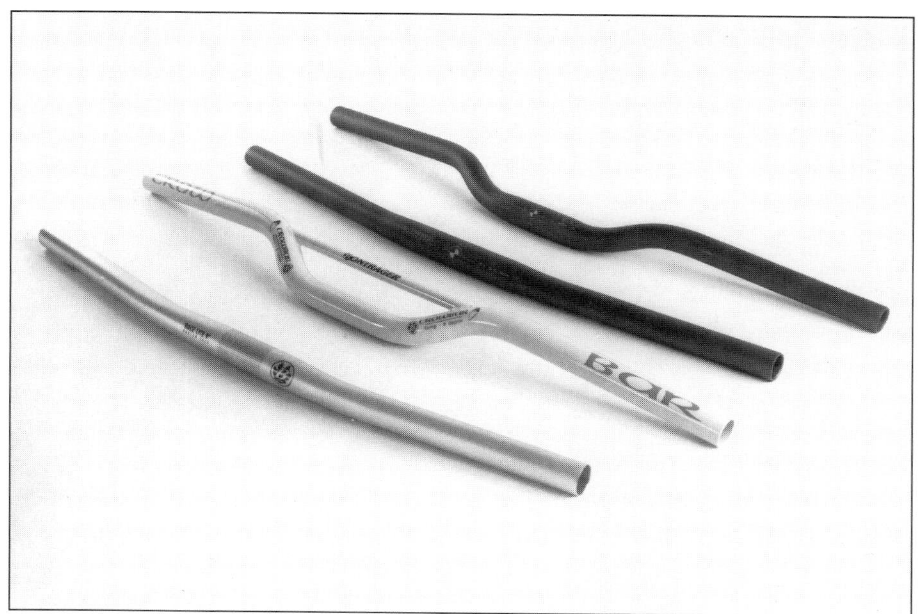

10-23
Bar choices include materials, bend, length, stiffener options.

10-24
Dampenator hydraulic steering damper. This one fits over the headset and does not work with triple-clamp forks.

bars are often longer than single-bend bars. A lower stem and one of these bars may get you where you want to be. Be aware that some double-bend bars might have too little straight section to accommodate all of the grips, shifters, brake levers, and bar ends you may want to fit.

Conversely, a smaller person may wish to cut the bars down. Make sure you cut the same amount off either end!

10.3B Grips

Since you grab the bars via the grips, you should not take grip choice or mounting lightly. The shape and thickness will affect your comfort and control. The grip length will depend on your hand size and whether you are using twist shifters or shift levers. You do not want the grips to slip. Usually, installing them with rubbing alcohol, which lubricates and evaporates, will hold them in place well, but many World Cup team mechanics have their own secret methods (see sidebar on page 117). Downhillers often use twisted wire to hold their grips in place.

10.4 BAR ENDS

Bar ends are not a must, but many riders prefer them. Bar ends offer some alternative hand positions and upper-body extensions, which can decrease fatigue on a long ride. When climbing in or out of the saddle, bar ends can provide a more effective handle to pull on. At high speeds on pavement, you can achieve a lower, more aerodynamic position on long bar ends.

10.4A Clamping Bar Ends to Handlebars

Care must be taken when clamping bar ends to some lightweight handlebars. Some thin bars come with cylindrical aluminum inserts to slide into the ends to support the bar under the bar-end clamp. Use them if they come with your bar. I have seen bars snap off right at the bar end.

Some carbon-fiber and thermoplastic bars will not accept bar ends or will only accept certain ones. Check with the manufacturer before putting bar ends on a composite bar.

With any lightweight bar, and especially with a composite bar, be sure that the bar end's clamp compresses the bar uniformly. It should work like a stem's handlebar clamp or a seat binder and pull uniformly around the circumference. If it does not, it will mash and ovalize the bar, weakening it dramatically. With a composite bar, if you hear a cracking noise as you tighten the bolt, stop!

10.4B Bar-End Shape

Choose a bar-end shape that suits you best.

If you will be using Shimano Rapid-fire Remote shifters, you will need a full-length bar end that curves inward, is round in cross-section, and has the standard diameter of 7/8 inch (22.2 mm).

If you want to keep weight down and just want something to pull up on during a climb, then short, straight super-light bar ends will be fine.

If you want more positions to get comfortable on, or if you want to pull with greater reach, get full-length bar ends with room to grab inboard of the bend.

If you will not be using remote shifters, you can choose the cross-sectional shape that best fits your hand. Some bar ends have very nice ovalized cross-sections or pistol-grip finger grooves.

11

SUSPENSION FORKS

Peace, Sancho.
Thou seest
my suspension.
—Miguel De
Cervantes, *Don
Quixote,* 1615

As you may have guessed, this chapter is primarily about front suspension. A thorough treatment of rigid forks already exists in Chapter 13 of *Zinn and the Art of Mountain Bike Maintenance.*

This chapter elaborates on the function, diagnosis, maintenance, and fine-tuning of telescoping suspension forks (photo 11-1). There is also a section on retrofitting a suspension fork to your bike. In the back of the chapter is a fork adjustment/troubleshooting guide.

Before you set to work evaluating and making adjustments, make sure that the fork has at least an hour of riding on it. If it is well used, make sure it is in good working condition. You will find out how to evaluate a fork's need for service in section 11.1 below and how to get it in good working condition in section 11.2.

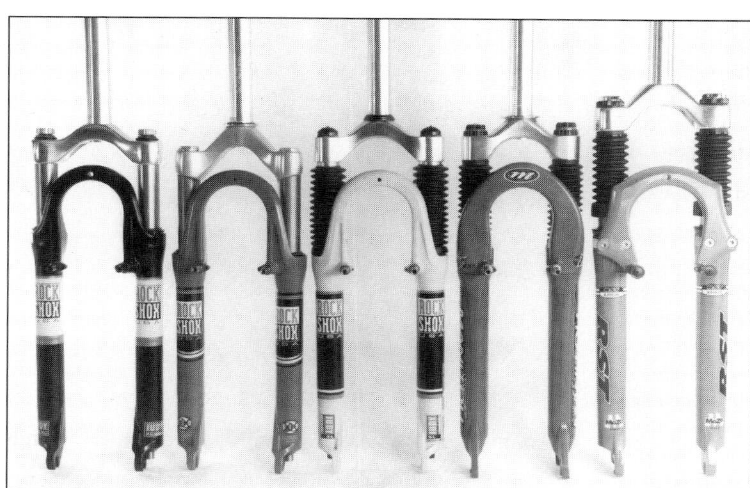

11-1
Telescoping cross-country suspension forks. From left: Rock Shox Judy XC (with disc brake mounts), Rock Shox SID, Rock Shox Judy SL with Total Air cartridges, Manitou SX-Ti, and RST Mozo Pro.

11.1 EVALUATING A FORK'S WORKING CONDITION

Don't get lured into thinking your fork is working fine, especially if it has been awhile since it was serviced. It is amazing how you can think your fork is working great until you take it apart and grease it. It usually works so much better afterwards that it feels like a different fork! You never noticed the degradation in performance, because it was so gradual.

Mileage on the fork since the last service is not as important as how many stream crossings or how much dust you rode through. You might figure your fork is getting beat when there is a lot of mud around the tire and brakes, but riding in dry conditions can do it as well. Moab dust can kill a fork's operation in a couple of days and ruin the sliders and bushings not long thereafter if you do not clean and lube it as soon as it gets dry.

Newer forks require less maintenance than models of a few years ago. Improved seals keep dirt out better, better bushings maintain the fork alignment longer, and damping cartridges can take more heat and slamming about before blowing out. Older fork models used to quickly get bad "notching." Fork boots, which were rare not so many years ago, are stock items on almost all forks now. (Incidentally, you should *always keep fork boots on* your fork's inner legs unless you have a mechanic that tears your fork down after every ride, or at least every race. Even if you have a Rock Shox SID (photo 11-1, second from left) which came without boots, adding the extra weight of boots protects your investment and increases the amount of time you can spend riding rather than working on your fork.)

A fork needing service will take more force to get it moving initially, and it will not return quickly, smoothly, or completely. You may notice while riding that the fork just seems slow. It will feel like the compression and rebound damping are turned up high. It moves slowly because it is gummed up!

FORK EVALUATION TIP

from Doug Bradbury, Inventor of the Manitou Suspension Fork and Tomac Bike Designer

You can tell if your fork has become notchy while the bike is standing still. Stand next to the bike, pull the front brake and push down on the bars lightly. Gradually increase the pressure; don't just push it hard! Notice how much pressure it takes before the fork finally moves. If the fork does not compress as you push harder and harder, and then it finally goes down chunk, chunk, chunk like a set of stairs, you've got a dry fork. That is notching.

If you cannot find any notching, and the fork begins sliding in smoothly under a relatively gentle push, then you've got a pretty clean fork.

11.2 SERVICING A DRY FORK

To get a dry, notchy fork moving properly again, you need to have clean, well-lubricated inner legs, bushings, and dust wipers.

This section applies to Rock Shox Judy and SID, all Manitou forks since 1995 (except Spyder), and RST Mozo Pro forks. Of the many other forks on the market, some come apart similarly, and some do not. I cannot include all of them, so I included those that are similar and most common on high end bikes (and hence most likely to see hard use and need overhaul). Consult your owners manual for different forks.

You need not remove the fork from the bike; just disconnect the front brake cable and remove the front wheel.

1. Unscrew the compression bolts on the bottoms of the fork legs until there are only a few threads still engaged (photo 11-15). If the bolts are not backing out, you are turning the dampers and the shafts along with them, and you may need to tighten the spring preload adjuster on top of the crown (photo 11-16) all of the way down (or put some more air in a SID).

A 5-mm Allen wrench is required to turn the compression bolts on a pre-1997 Rock Shox Judy. Both bolts on 1997–98 Judys and SIDs take an 8-mm hex key; you have to yank the aluminum adjuster knob out of the left one to get at it (this is easier said than done—use a pair of pliers padded with a rag).

On a Manitou Mach 5, Pro, FX, SX, or X-Vert, the right bolt takes a 4-mm hex key, and the large aluminum bolt on the left leg requires an 8-mm hex key. That 8-mm hex opening is concealed beneath the plastic damper-adjustment knob, which must be pulled out by hand to get at the bolt; it should come out easily.

Note **There is no consistency of wrench size for the compression bolt on various forks; it varies from 4- to 8-mm hex-key size and beyond depending on brand and model (photo 11-2).**

Note There is no need to remove the fork brace; if you do remove it, be very careful not to overtighten the brace bolt or the brake post, since it is pretty easy to strip the threads in the aluminum or magnesium outer legs. Do use Loctite on the threads. Current Rock Shox and Manitou forks have integral fork braces that cannot be removed.

Both bolts are 4 mm on an RST Mozo.

The bolts on a Total Air aftermarket cartridge are 5 mm.

WARNING: Do not unscrew the 5-mm bolt in the center of Manitou's 8-mm aluminum bolt. This is the damping adjuster, and if you unscrew it beyond its gentle stop, you will break it. This will create an oil spill and a bill for a new damping unit.

2. Before unscrewing the bolts completely (while they are still threaded in a few turns), tap the bolts with a mallet (photo 11-3) until the inner legs are free from the lower bushings. Remove the bolts. Pull the entire assembly that includes both lower legs and the fork brace off the inner legs (photos 11-4 and 11-5). Watch out; some forks have an oil bath that pours out when you remove the bolts. Oil from a blown cartridge may also pour out.

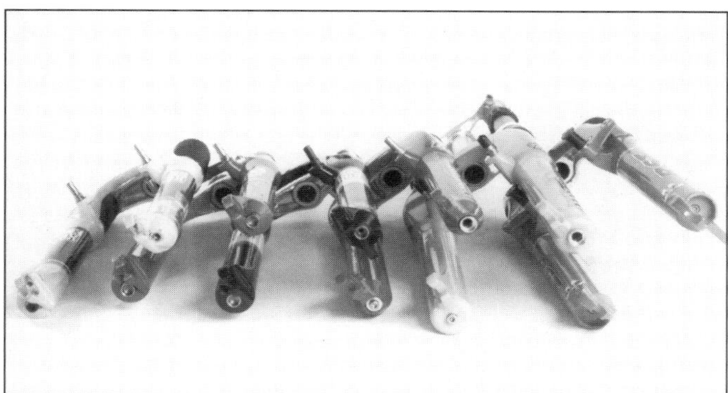

11-2
Different forks have different-sized compression bolts on the bottom of the fork legs.

11-3
Tapping the loosened bottom compression bolts with a mallet to free the inner legs from the lower bushings.

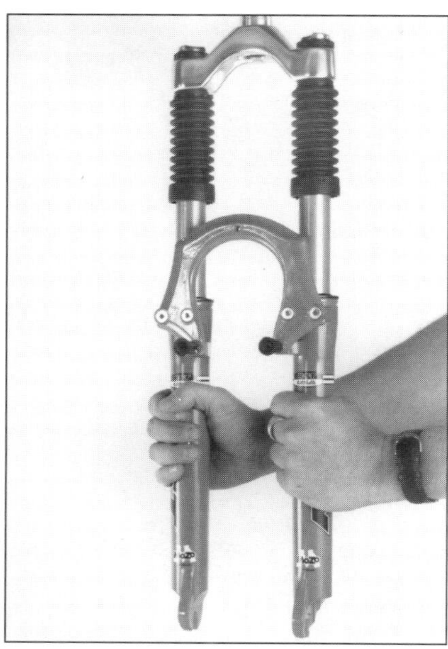

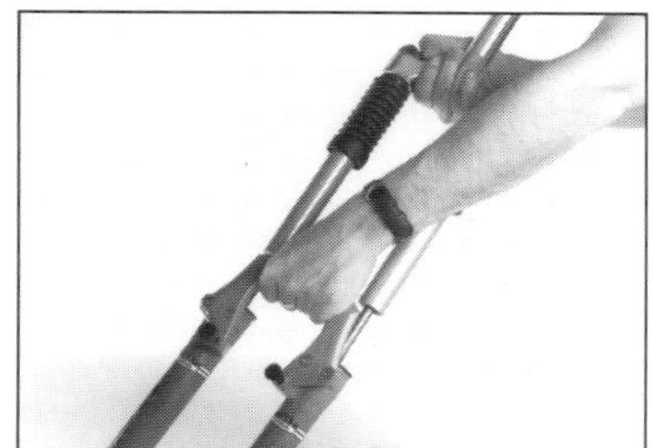

11-4 and 11-5
Pulling RST Mozo Pro lower legs and fork brace off the inner legs.

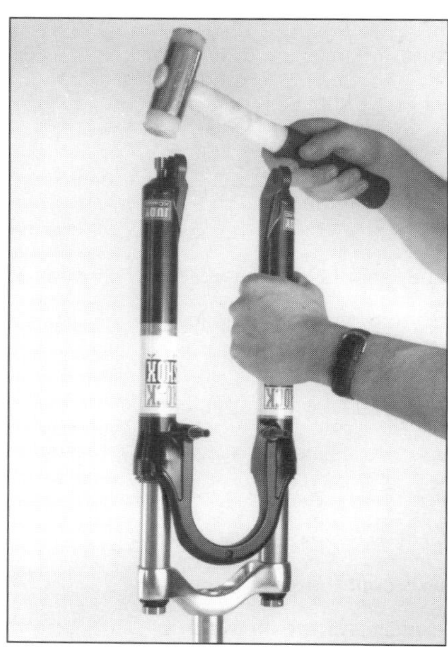

Note **On the EFC, Mach 5, and later Manitou models, there is an orange elastomer around the damper shaft that extends from the right inner leg (photo 11-7). It is a good idea to clean and grease it, but, if you remove it, be ready to catch the steel ball that will fall out. This is the "detent" ball for the damper that makes the clicks in the damper adjustment.**

3. With a clean, lint-free rag, clean the inner legs (photo 11-6).

Inspect the damper shaft for surface abrasion damage and bending. Check for oil leaking around the shaft seal. On forks with a separate damping cartridge, like Rock Shox, you can remove the circlip at the bottom of the inner leg (photo 11-8) and pull the cartridge out for inspection (photo 11-9). Cartridges in older Rock Shox forks were in the left leg; now they are in the right leg due to the extra stress of a disc brake attached to the left leg. Use a piece of PVC tube to knock the cartridge (or neutral shaft) out. Make sure you replace the circlip sharp edge down. A chopped-off old cartridge body works great for seating the circlip again.

Do not push the damper shaft up and down. It is meant to be supported in the fork to move up and down in perfect alignment. All it takes is a little side load on the shaft by pushing on it when it is not supported in this way and you have a mess. If you're unlucky, oil will squirt out around the seal because you pushed the shaft to the side at the seal and opened a gap there.

4. Clean the wiper seals and bushings inside the outer legs. There are two bushings in each outer leg: one at the top and one more way down at the bottom. You need to reach the bottom one with the rag wrapped around a long rod (photo 11-10).

5. Apply a thin layer of *non-lithium* grease (better yet, use a specialty suspension lube like Judy Butter or Englund Slick Honey) to the bushings and wipers in the outer legs. To grease the lower bushings, use a long rod (make sure it is clean), slather grease on the end of it, and reach down to the lower bushings with it. Fill the space between the top bushing and the dust wiper with grease (photo 11-11). *Do not* grease the spacer separating the upper and lower bushings. It will put pressure on the inner leg and bind the spacer.

6. Grease the inner legs (photo 11-12). Make sure that you grease anywhere that there is contact between parts. (Grease the springs well, too, so they do not drag inside the inner legs.)

7. Slide the outer legs gently over the inner legs (photo 11-13). Take care not to damage the upper dust wipers or the lower bushings. Push the outer legs on completely. It may help if you spread the outer tube and fork brace assembly slightly while you rock it side to side to engage the bushings on the inner legs.

8. Put a medium-strength Loctite on the shaft bolts (anti-seize on titanium ones). Put them back in the bottom of the outer legs, engaging the threads in the damper and neutral shaft. Push the inner legs in further, if the bolt threads do not engage.

HOT TIP: To keep the fork lubricated better, make an oil bath in your fork. Squirt a little light oil (15-weight) or ATF (10 cc) in through the bolt holes before replacing the bolts (photo 11-14). It keeps lubricant splashing around inside as you ride.

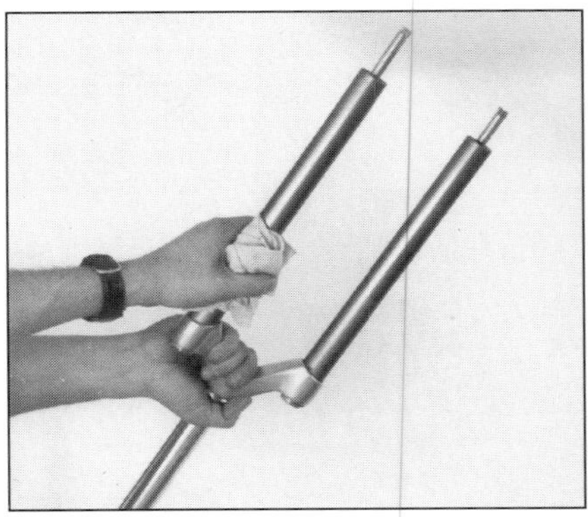

11-6
Wiping the inner legs with a clean, lint-free rag.

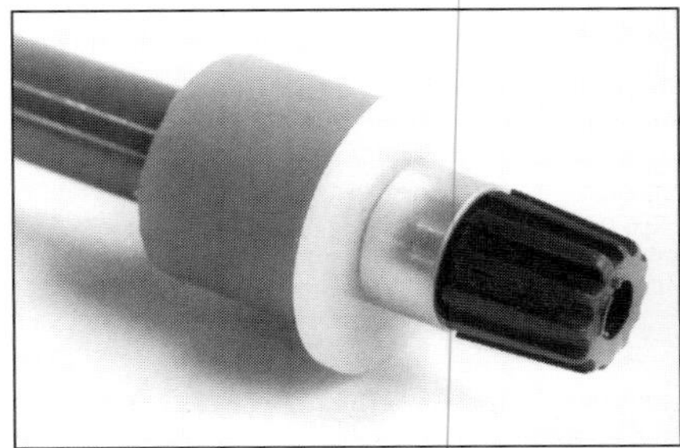

11-7
The elastomer around the damper shaft extending from the left inner leg of a Manitou fork. The elastomer is both a bottom-out bumper and a spring for the detent ball it conceals under it, which provides the click stops in the damping adjustment.

11-8
Removing the circlip at the bottom of Rock Shox Judy inner leg.

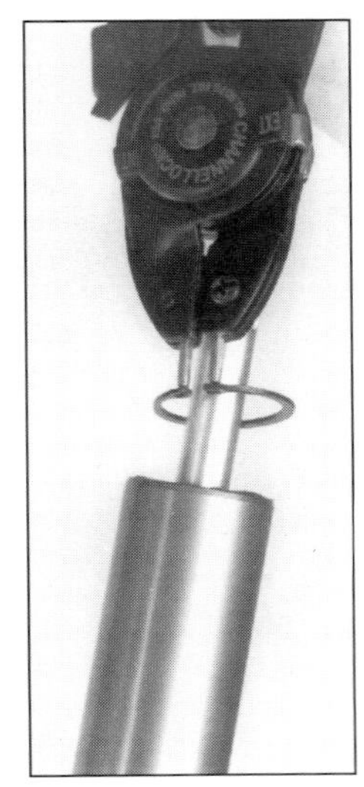

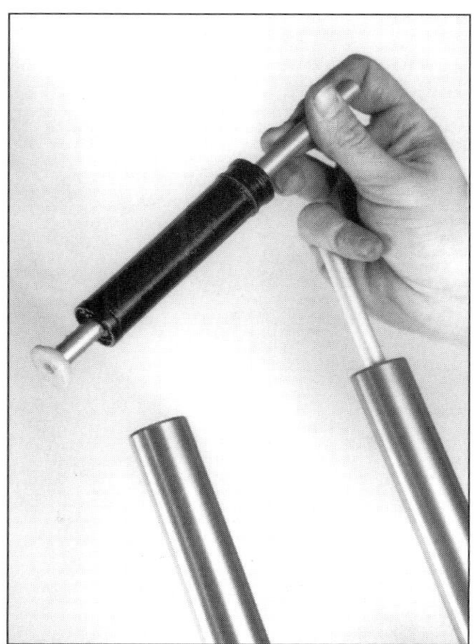

11-9
Inspecting a Rock Shox Judy cartridge for oil leakage.

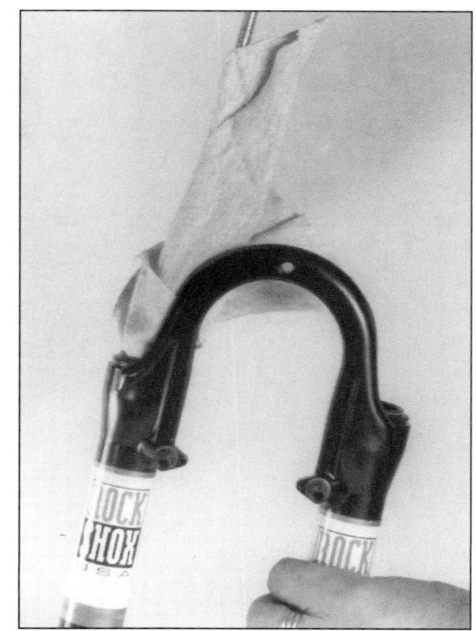

11-10
Cleaning the lower bushing in a Judy with a rag wrapped around a long rod.

11-11
Greasing a Judy top bushing and dust wiper and the space between them.

11-12
Greasing the inner legs.

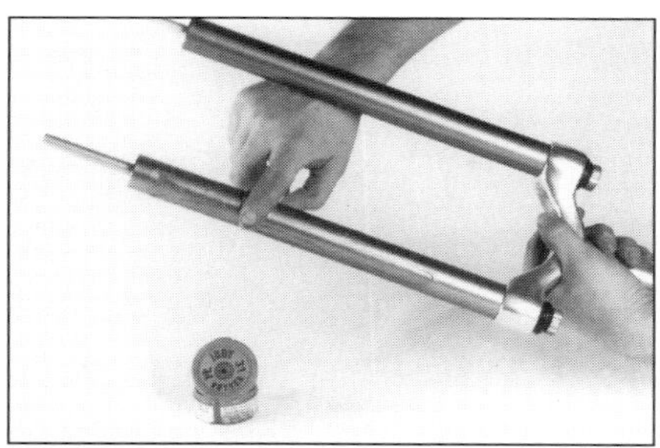

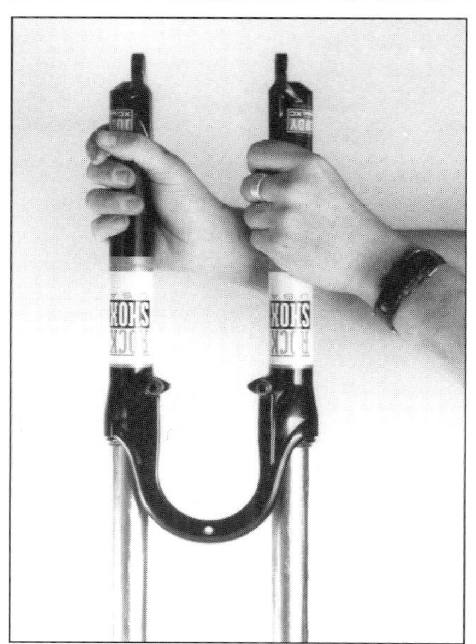

11-13
Left: Sliding the outer legs gently over the inner legs, rocking and spreading the outer legs as needed.

11-14
Right: Making an oil bath. Squirt 10 cc or so of automatic transmission fluid in through the bottom bolt holes to keep the fork lubed better.

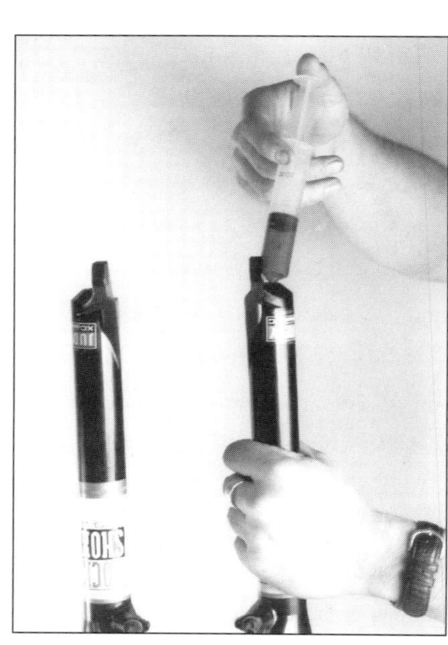

An oil bath eliminates the need for greasing the lower bushing. Judy and SID forks for 1998 come stock with 10 cc of oil sloshing in there. Do not put in more than 10 cc; if you put in too much oil, you can hydrolock your fork and thus limit its travel. Also, *never, never, never* put an oil bath in a pre-1998 Rock Shox Indy. There is no key way to let oil out of the compression bolt hole; the oil compressed by the tightening of the bolt will blow out the fork leg casting!

9. Tighten the bolts down with a torque wrench (photo 11-15). Rock Shox recommends 60 inch-pounds of torque; Manitou recommends 110–130 inch-pounds. Do not exceed 50 inch-pounds for a SID to avoid expanding the thin aluminum damper and neutral leg shafts. Getting RST bolts tight may require removing the spring stack and holding the top of the compression bolt with an 8-mm hex key.

Note: this entire process is unnecessary with 1999 Manitou SX forks, which have a grease fitting on each leg. All you do to lube the fork is pump the special Manitou grease into the grease parts with a thin-tipped bicycle grease gun.

11.3 SPRING PRELOAD

The spring preload is the amount that the spring is compressed when at rest. It determines the magnitude of the initial force that must be overcome before the fork compresses at all.

Most high-end coil/elastomer-sprung forks have a preload adjuster knob on the top of the fork crown. Tightening the knob compresses the spring (photo 11-16). Preload does not affect the "spring rate" of a coil spring, due to a coil's rate being linear; preload *does* affect the spring rate of an elastomer or air spring, however, due to their rates being progressive (see section 11.4 below).

High preload damages a spring, particularly an elastomer, by giving it a permanent "set." The spring is always being compressed, even when you are not riding! Get the spring right with minimal preload (see General Recommendations, section 11.7).

Tightening the top cap into the fork crown (with the preload adjuster fully unscrewed) should not preload the spring. If you have to push down on the cap to engage the threads, cut some length off the elastomer (cut straight!) so that the top cap contacts the top of the spring 1–3 mm before it is tight. If you have preloaded the spring with the top cap, the spring rate may be too high with the preload backed off, yet too soft with the next softer spring.

11.4 SPRINGS

The spring is what holds you up (i.e., *suspends* you). It is intended to isolate the rider and bicycle from impact forces. Without frictional losses, the spring will return the energy by springing back just as forcefully as it was compressed. The spring, at least in a high-end fork with a damper, is *not* intended to dissipate the energy of the impact (i.e., to control the speed of the compression or the rebound); that is the job of damping.

The spring medium in a fork can be a steel or titanium coil, a synthetic elastic polymer (elastomer), or compressed air. Springs are adjustable in most forks, either by replacing the coil or elastomer or by varying air pressure. If you have any question about how to change the spring, consult section 13-12 or 13-16 in Chapter 13 of *Zinn and the Art of Mountain Bike Maintenance*, Second Edition.

"Spring rate" is measured in units of force and determines the stiffness of a spring; it is the amount of force required to compress a spring a unit distance. In the English system, spring rate is measured in pounds of force required to compress a spring 1 inch. Springs, be they elastomers or coils, often are color-coded for spring rate. A coil's spring rate is dependent on the stiffness of the metal, the wire diameter, the number of coils, and the diameter of the coils. An MCU (Micro Cellular Urethane) elastomer's spring rate is dependent on its durometer rating (i.e., hardness) and the amount of air trapped in the mixture.

You can measure spring rate yourself. If you stand a 70-pound spring up on a scale, it should compress 1 inch when you push on it with a force registering 70 pounds on the scale (photo 11-17). You should be aware that springs can vary greatly from their rating. Two 70-pound springs might actually register 68 and 75.

A coil spring has a "linear" spring rate. A constant increase in force on a coil spring results in a constant increase in deflection until it reaches the end of its travel. Compressed air or an MCU has a "progressive" spring rate. A constant increase in force on an MCU results in an ever-smaller increase in deflection. In other words, a 50-pound coil spring requires 50 pounds of force to move it the first inch, 100 pounds to move it the second inch, etc., while a 50-pound MCU requires 50 pounds of force to compress it the first inch, but it may take 150 pounds to move it the second inch.

Many newer forks use springs that are a combination of a coil and an MCU

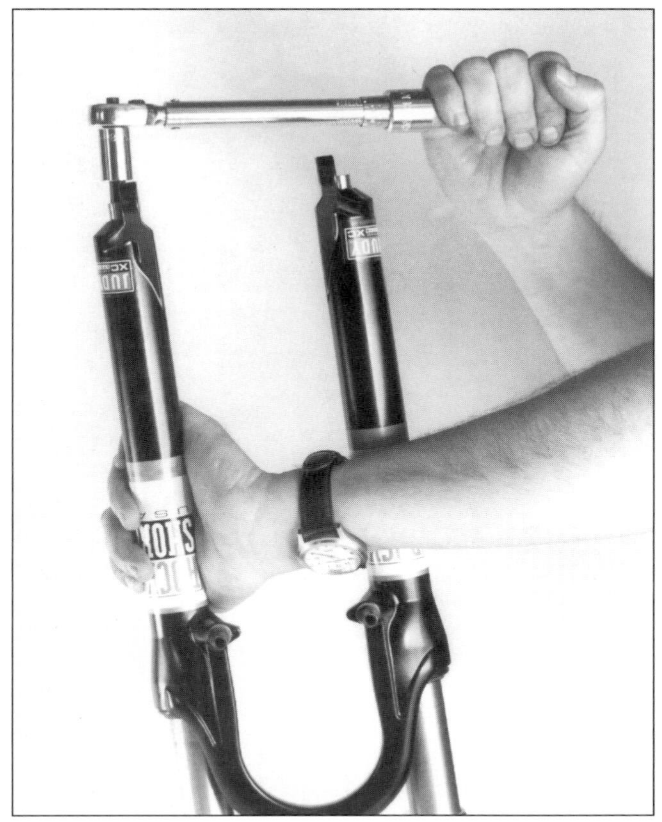

11-15
Turning Rock Shox Judy compression bolt with a torque wrench.

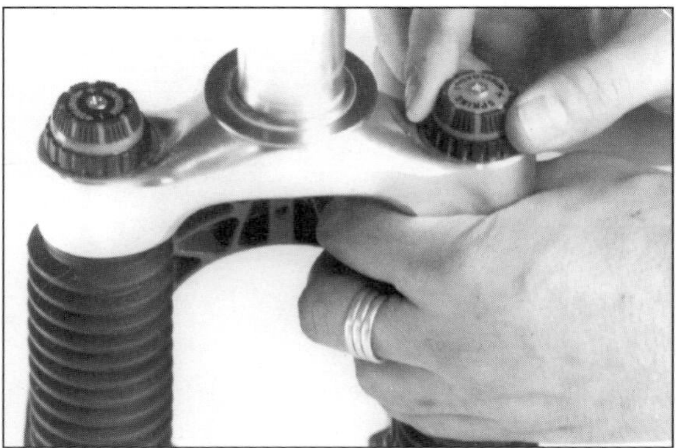

11-16
Adjusting spring preload on a Manitou SX-Ti fork.

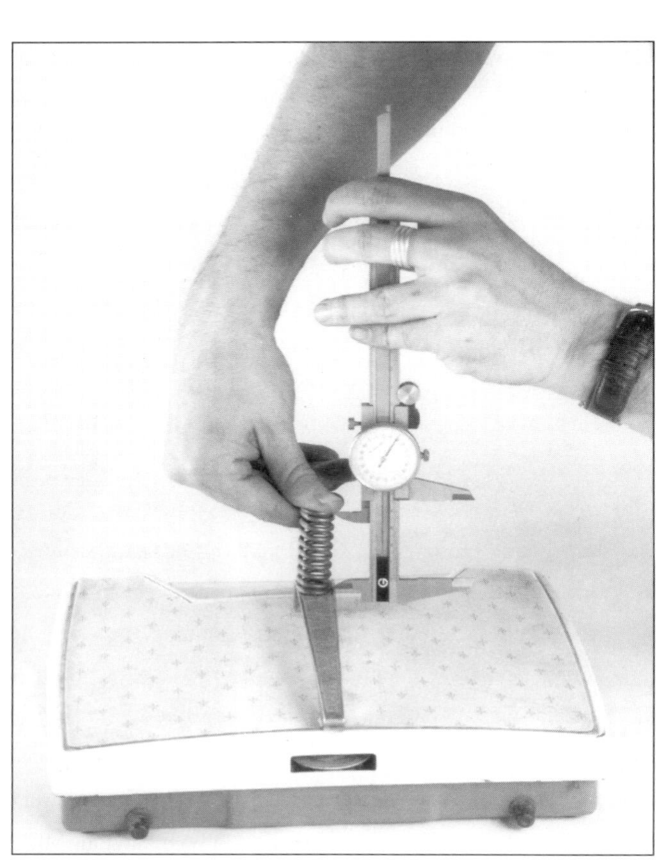

11-17
Measuring spring rate, which is the force registered in pounds to compress a spring 1 inch. Putting the scale and the spring in a large vise is a more accurate way to measure spring rate.

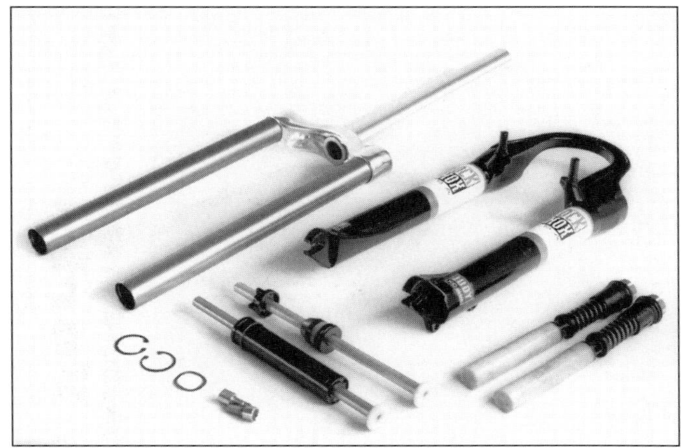

11-18
An exploded Rock Shox Judy with Type II (coil/MCU) springs.

11-19
Open the top of the air chamber on a Rock Shox SID with an adjustable wrench.

11-20
Adjusting air volume in a SID by turning the piston at bottom of chamber with an 8-mm hex key.

(photo 11-18). The idea is that you can benefit from the best characteristics of each. The MCU can react quickly to small impacts due to its light spring rate, while it takes a higher activation energy to get a coil moving. On repeated medium impacts, the coil gives a lively feel. A coil's linear spring rate keeps it responding the same way to force increases no matter how much travel has been used up, and it rebounds with all of the energy it absorbs. On big hits, the progressive spring rate of the MCU is beneficial by stiffening up when the fork approaches full travel, protecting the rider from bottoming out harshly.

Grease the inside of the inner legs before putting coil or elastomer springs inside. Grease the top cap threads as well.

Without a fork, I recommend setting your spring rate as soft as you can get away with. If you need a spring in between one that you find too stiff and one that is too soft, throw one of each in (i.e., the stiffer spring in one leg and the softer spring in the other). In more recent forks, the rigidity of the larger legs and crown braces makes it possible to run mismatched springs in the two sides.

See more on spring choice and how it interacts with damping in General Recommendations, section 11.7.

When you pull out springs, inspect them for deformation or cracking; replace damaged ones. Slather every spring with Judy Butter or Slick Honey before installing it.

Newer air-sprung forks have "negative" coil springs that are always working against the air spring, trying to compress the fork. The Rock Shox SID (photo 11-1, second from left), and the Englund Total Air cartridge (photo 11-31) have this feature. The intent is to make the air spring's progressive spring rate more linear and to react faster to small bumps.

Reducing the air chamber volume on an air-sprung fork makes the spring rate ramp up more rapidly, while increasing the air chamber volume gives you a softer spring at the end of the stroke. On older air-sprung forks (e.g., Rock Shox Mag 20, 21, and others), you reduce the volume of the air chamber by pouring some oil into it, and you increase the volume by pouring some oil out. On a Rock Shox SID, you reduce the air volume by moving the piston up, and increase it by moving the piston down. Open the top of the air chamber with a 22-mm wrench (photo 11-19). Unscrew the piston at the bottom of the chamber with an 8-mm hex key to reduce the chamber air volume (photo 11-20) and vice versa. You can also pour oil into a SID to reduce air volume, if you wish. You want to have at least 5 ccs of oil in there to lube the glide rings.

To get more compliance on small bumps with your SID, you can move the circlip for the negative spring down to a lower groove in the cartridge shaft (there are seven grooves to choose from). Move the circlip up for the opposite effect. Bigger riders use a higher groove, smaller riders use a lower one. The negative spring compresses the fork and gets the air spring moving sooner.

11.5 DAMPING

Damping controls the speed of movement of the spring in a suspension system by dissipating kinetic energy as heat. The spring and the damping work together to isolate the rider from impacts and control the speed of compression and rebound. A rubber super-ball dropped on the ground illustrates undamped energy return. The ball has little internal damping, so it takes awhile to stop bouncing. Damping would reduce the height of each bounce and stop it faster. When you have a spring-loaded screen door that slams shut, you know what a difference damping makes when you install a damper to slow the door's return.

Spring return on most high-end forks, as on most screen doors, is controlled by a cylindrical hydraulic damper filled with oil. A shaft with a piston on it moves through the oil. Holes (orifices) in the piston and/or shaft allow oil to move past the piston. Some systems, like the Englund Total Air cartridge, use compressed air moving through the orifices instead of oil, but the principle is the same.

When the piston moves slowly, the oil can move through the holes quickly enough to create little resistance to movement. When the piston tries to move quickly, however, the oil cannot move as quickly through the holes, and the resistance to movement of the piston goes up rapidly with increasing piston speeds. The size and number of these orifices can be varied to adjust the amount of resistance to piston movement. Some forks have an adjuster screw on the damper. Depending on which way you turn it, it closes down or opens up orifices.

You can think of a damper by sticking your hand out the window of a moving car. Your hand represents the piston, and the moving air represents the oil. With your hand flat against the wind and your fingers together, it takes a lot of force to keep your hand from being blown backward. If you spread your fingers, representing opening damper orifices, your hand moves through the air more easily.

Thin, ring-shaped shims on either side of the piston can separate compression and rebound damping. A shim may be held fixed against the piston by a circlip so it can flex away from the piston, or it may be held against the piston by a spring so that it can slide away from the piston against the spring. The shim slides or flexes away from the piston when oil flows out of a hole in the piston underneath the shim, and it stays against the piston when oil tries to flow the other direction. For example, a shim on top of the piston stays flat against the piston and blocks oil moving into the orifice as the piston moves up through the oil on compression. When the piston moves back down, the shim flexes or slides away from the piston and allows oil to flow up out of the orifice. This would make the fork slow to move on compression and quick on rebound.

Shim stacks can be changed to affect damping action. The variables in shims are: 1) outer diameter (the inner diameter of all of the shims should be the same to fit the piston shaft), 2) thickness, and 3) position in the stack. A shim of larger outer diameter resists oil flow more than a smaller one. A thicker shim will not flex as much as a thinner one and will resist oil flow and slow the fork action more. A shim closer to the piston will oppose oil flow more than one farther away.

Since a spring, especially a coil spring, is elastic and returns most of the energy it absorbs, it does not heat up much. A damper, however, prevents the spring from absorbing all of the energy and from returning all that it does absorb. The damping oil dissipates the energy by heating up. The hydraulic oil will break down over time from getting so hot and need to be changed. An oil change in a 1996-1997 Manitou cartridge is demonstrated in photos 11-21 to 11-27. Follow the procedure in the captions.

As I mentioned in Chapter 8 with regard to hydraulic brakes, oil can expand in volume when it gets hot. In a damper, this can result in lockup of the system, just as in brakes. There are different means of dealing with this problem. One easily conceptualized version is the "open oil bath" inside a Marzocchi Bomber fork. The outer leg is full of oil, a far greater volume than in the damping cylinder alone. Oil is free to move between the open damping cylinder and the area around it. The larger oil volume stays cooler, resulting in less fluid expansion and contraction. The free damping oil lubricates the fork as well. A Bomber still requires frequent oil changes because the oil gets contaminated by powdered aluminum in the open leg created by the fork's movement. Fortunately changing oil in a Bomber is easy.

Manitou also uses higher oil volume to dissipate heat in its TPC system. The twin-piston damper (no spring) in the left leg has about three times the volume of

11-21 to 11-27

Changing oil in Manitou single-piston damper (a clear display model is shown for clarity):

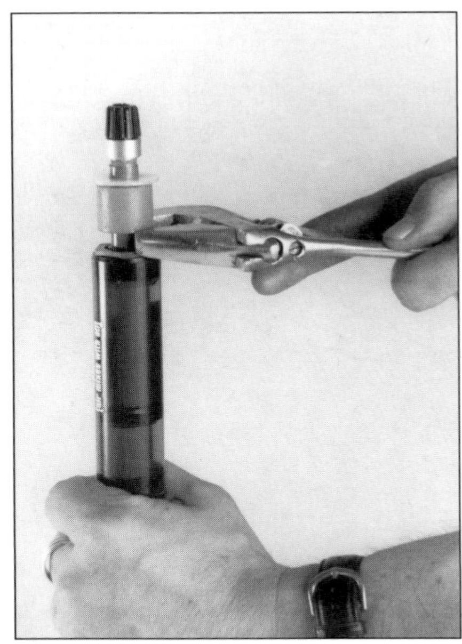

11-21

Unscrew the end nut on the Manitou damper.

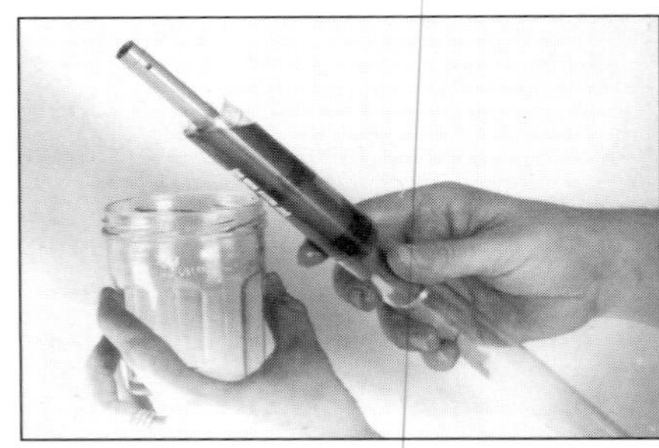

11-22

Pour out the old oil.

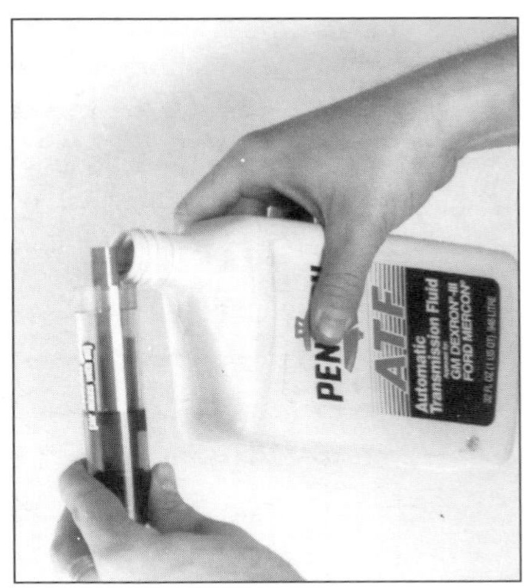

11-23

Pour in ATF or fork hydraulic fluid to top.

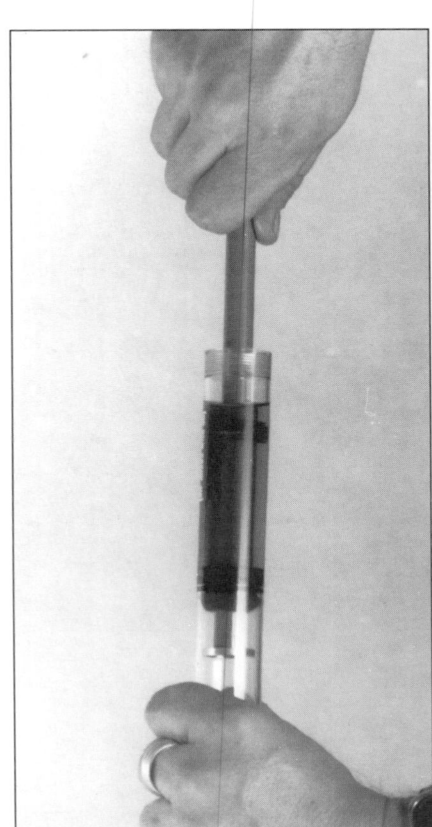

11-24

Stroke the shaft a few times to get any air bubbles out. Top off with ATF again.

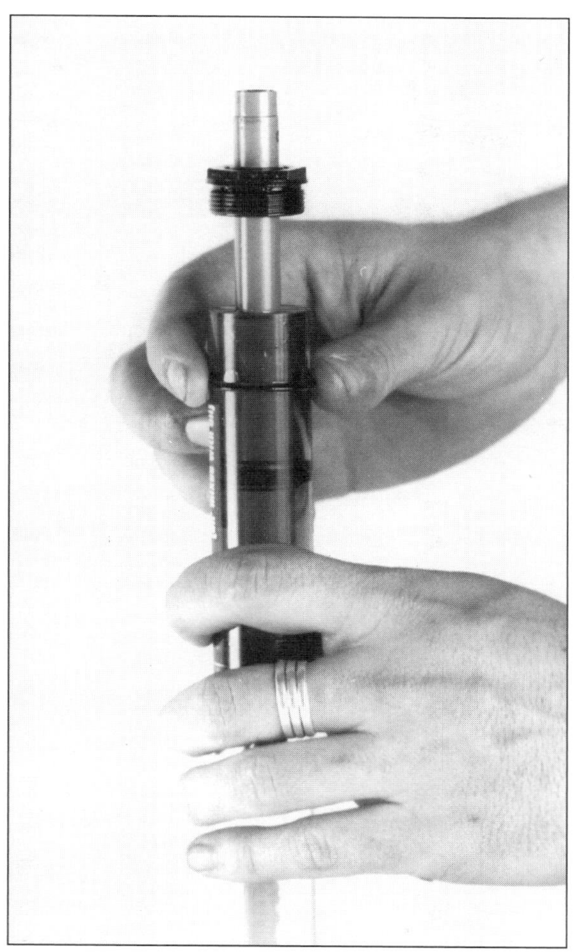

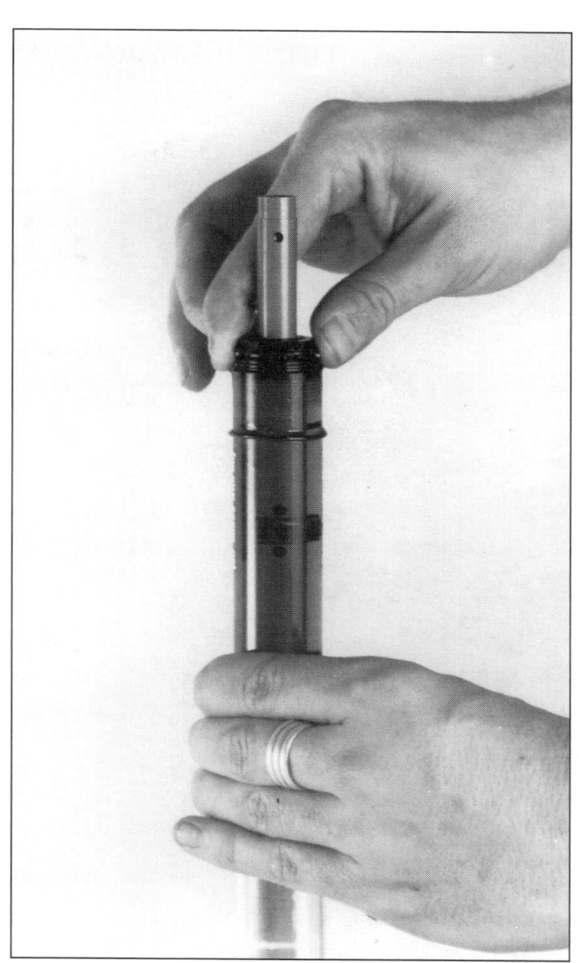

11-25
Remove the O-ring from below the lip of the end nut and slide it down onto the leg.

11-26
Upper right: Tighten the end nut down by hand. With the O-ring removed from the nut, air and excess oil are vented out through a small hole beneath the lip of the nut. (*Note:* A Manitou damper is not actually a "cartridge," since it is not a separate, complete unit. To prevent air from infiltrating a Rock Shox cartridge [photo 11-9] as you close it back up, you can submerge it in hydraulic oil as you reassemble it.)

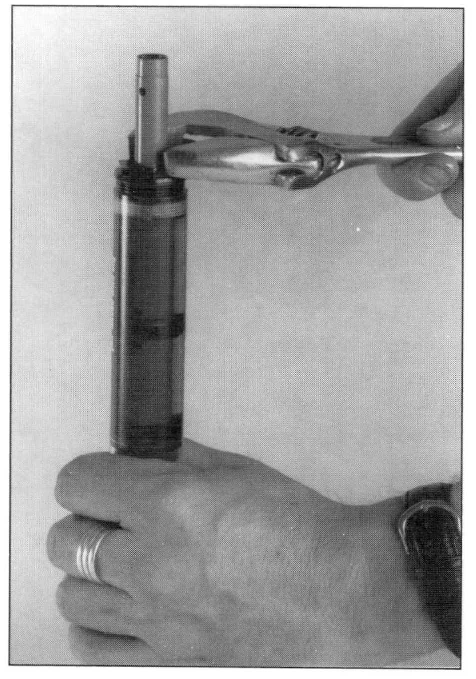

11-27
Replace the O-ring and tighten the end nut with a wrench. Replace the detent ball and bottom-out bumper on the damper shaft (bumper is shown in photos 11-7 and 11-21).

just about any cartridge or Manitou's old damper (photo 11-28). It can go a long time between oil changes (a couple seasons for most riders). Another cool feature of the twin-piston design is that you no longer have to worry about allowing air to get into the damper; any extra air simply rises to the top of the chamber. Changing oil in a TPC fork is a snap. You just pull out the top piston (carefully work it past the threads), pour out the old oil, and pour in new oil. Don't worry about air bubbles, and just set the oil height (using a ruler or a dipstick) to the level below the top stated in the manual for the particular fork model.

Air in closed dampers is a bummer, because it is compressible, whereas the oil is not. The damper thus does not perform as it should.

Dampers must deal with the compression stroke and the rebound stroke. It makes sense to make these two damping functions separately adjustable, because you do not necessarily want the fork to respond with the same speed to impact as to rebound. The next two sections deal with these adjustments.

As with setting your spring rate, I recommend setting your damping as light as you can get away with. See more on this in General Recommendations, section 11.7.

11.5A Compression Damping

Compression damping controls the speed of compression of the fork on impact. A fork with compression damping can have a lighter spring than one without it, since the damper shares the load with the spring more and more as the speed increases. This allows for a wider range of performance. The softer spring will be more supple over small, low-speed hits, and the compression damping will resist bottoming the spring on hard, high-speed hits.

While changing compression damping in most dampers also affects rebound damping, a fork with a single damper usually has an adjustment for one or the other. For instance, Rock Shox Judy cross-country forks generally have an adjustment in the bottom of the damping cartridge for compression damping and not for rebound. Judy downhill forks have a second cartridge in the opposite leg with adjustable rebound damping.

Some downhill forks have dual-stage compression damping. That way, compression damping can be set light for smoothness over fast stutter bumps, while the second stage can be set stiffer so that the fork will not dive when braking.

11.5B Rebound Damping

Rebound damping controls the speed of the fork's return to full extension. Rebound damping is particularly important with coil springs, since these springs have almost no frictional energy loss; they store and then return upon rebound almost all of the energy they absorb. MCUs (elastomers with trapped air inside them) will not return with as much energy, since they absorb some energy internally.

Rebound damping settings are dictated by trail conditions. If the ground is wet and soft, you do not need a quick springback, since the ground is already forgiving. A slow return might give you better traction on a slippery surface.

While changing the rebound damping adjustment also can affect compression damping, a fork with a single damper usually has an adjustment for one or the other. For example, pre-1998 Manitou Mach 5 and SX cross-country forks generally have an adjustment in the bottom of the damping cylinder for rebound damping and not for compression.

Current Manitou forks have a "TPC" Twin Piston Chamber in the left leg that has two separate pistons on separate shafts (photo 11-28). (There are no springs in the left leg; all of the springs are in the right side and are twice as stiff as the springs in one side of a 1997 Manitou single-piston fork set up the same.) The rebound damping adjuster knob on the bottom of the leg controls the size of the orifices in the piston on the end of the lower shaft. The compression damping adjuster knob on the top of the fork crown, or an internal seat screw controls the size of the orifices in the piston on the end of the upper shaft.

11.6 SAG

Sag, or ride height, is the amount the fork compresses when you just sit on the bike when it is not moving. Obviously, sag is not dependent on damping because there is no movement involved. Sag is only dependent on spring stiffness. (Well, if your fork is really dirty, sag is also dependent on the amount of friction preventing the fork from moving.)

Sag is affected by changing your springs and/or your spring preload adjustment. A good rule of thumb is to set your springs so that sag uses up one-quarter of the fork's travel. Measuring travel and sag is explained thoroughly in

Chapter 13, section 13-10 of *Zinn and the Art of Mountain Bike Maintenance*, Second Edition.

11.7 GENERAL SUSPENSION TUNING RECOMMENDATIONS

These recommendations are intended to enable you to get the most out of your suspension, and following them will maximize your comfort and control on any course. Efficiency and control on downhill sections will be maximized, and efficiency and speed will generally be maximized throughout rough cross-country courses as well.

These recommendations apply to both downhill and cross-country bikes and anything in between. With full-suspension bikes, follow the same recommendations for the rear end, so that the front and rear are balanced. More on rear suspension in Chapter 13.

Riding plush suspension is at odds with the prevailing mindset bike riders had when suspension first hit the market. Everyone was afraid of soaking up pedaling forces in the suspension, and they set their forks up to be firm and counteract that. Many World Cup cross-country racers today use high tire pressures and stiff suspension out of similar concerns. You may want to consider *not* following their lead, since their needs are different from those of most riders. World Cup cross-country courses are usually relatively smooth, riders are light, and they are very concerned about avoiding pinch flats and going uphill fast on fine roads. You will be much happier and not so beat up when you get off the bike if you set everything softer and lighter.

11-28
Clear display models of Manitou TPC twin-piston damper (right) and Manitou's old single-piston damper (left). The TPC fills the entire left leg, and doubly stiff springs are used in the right leg. The cartridge has separate adjustments for compression and rebound damping. The old system had springs in both legs and the short damper under the left-leg springs.

11-29
Older Rock Shox Judy elastomer stack (left) and newer Type II coil/MCU spring (right).

On a rough course, efficiency is higher with plush suspension. When a big bump slams the tire up and back, much less energy and speed are lost if all that moves up and back is the wheel, rather than you and the bike.

Make setting changes in small increments. It is easy to overadjust. It takes a leap of faith, I know, to believe that twisting a little knob a half-turn is going to make any difference when you are flying down a rocky descent.

Make only one adjustment at a time.

Suspension tuning is affected by: 1) rider weight, 2) rider ability, 3) riding speeds, 4) course conditions, 5) rider style, and 6) position on the bike. If any or all of these things change, so should the tuning adjustments.

SOFTEN UP: Use the softest springs you can with little or no preload. You want to bottom out occasionally, but not frequently. If you are bottoming out too much, how do you know whether to change your compression damping or your spring rate? To separate the two, notice the speed of the fork's compression. If the compression is slow, yet you are still bottoming out, your spring is too soft. You would be getting beaten up on the intermediate hits, or, when bottoming out on a big hit, it would be harsh through the entire stroke. Consequently, you want to stiffen the spring rate and lighten the compression damping. The ride height (again, use up 25 percent of stroke when you sit on the bike) dictates some of your spring rate.

Preload makes the spring rate ramp up faster, not to mention wearing it out faster. If you can use a stiffer spring and back off on preload, you will be a lot happier for it.

LIGHTEN UP: Set the *compression damping* to blow off quickly. Your plush spring won't bottom out harshly anyway! The compression damping should be set low enough that on big hits you use up all of your travel, but high enough that the bars are not smacking you in the hands when you hit bottom.

Tighten up the *compression damping* if you are blowing through the stroke and getting smacked in the hands too hard.

If you have no damping adjuster, you can play with oil viscosity. (See photos 11-21 to 11-27 for oil-change procedure.) You can change the oil in your damper and go up 2.5 points in oil weight if the fork is moving too fast. Conversely, you can lighten the damping up with lighter oil, especially in winter. There is less adjustment range when lightening up the oil, since dampers already come with light (five-weight or so) oil.

Lighten up the *rebound damping* to return as quickly as possible without "pogo-ing." Some forks adjust rebound damping at the bottom, some at the top, and some you have to take apart and change the shim stacks or the oil viscosity; read your manual.

You want a lively rebound, since a sluggish return will allow the fork to pack up (e.g., as you go over stutter bumps, water bars, or closely spaced rocks, the fork will get shorter and shorter).

Tighten up the *rebound damping* if the fork springs back too fast. The rebound should not be so light that you are getting bounced. On soft ground, increase rebound damping for better traction.

SPEED UP: Rebound and compression damping should be speed-sensitive in a good fork. Don't worry about settings that feel good at low speeds being too light for high speeds; the fork will get stiffer as you hit things faster. At all speeds, you want the fork to pop back as quickly as possible without kicking back.

HEAT UP: Damping is temperature sensitive. Oil is thick and sluggish in the cold, but when it gets hot, your fork gets really lively. You will need to adjust accordingly in summer, with stiffer springs and firmer damping adjustments.

COOL OFF: You can lighten up your springs and damping adjustments even more in the cold of winter. Your overall speeds are slower, the grease and oil in the fork are thicker, and the elastomers and coil springs are stiffer. Lighter oil in the damper will help.

If you have a full-suspension bike, you will want to have the front and rear suspension balanced. Flip to Chapter 13 to see about that.

The high-tech way suspension settings are adjusted for well-sponsored downhillers is by wiring the bike and fork with displacement-measuring rods, accelorometers, speedometers on both wheels, gyroscopes, timers, and strain gauges connected to a portable computer. Computer down-loading of suspension performance allows damping and spring rate to be precisely tuned for specific courses.

11.8 TESTING YOUR FORK

To set your fork up well, you need to evaluate its performance objectively. Consistency is key. You must be able to separate out factors like course selection, speed,

FORK SETUP TIPS

from Doug Bradbury

A good rule of thumb comes from the old moto-cross school: You want to bottom out a couple of times (front and rear) on a course. If the suspension is never bottoming out, the spring is too stiff or the compression damping is too high. Your body is taking too much impact.

Err on the side of having too light springs and damping. Use the softest springs you can with little or no preload, and set your compression and rebound damping as light as you can. (At 180 pounds, Bradbury rides on Manitou's softest blue elastomers and goes very fast down hills.)

Light *rebound damping* allows your tire to get back on the ground as fast as possible, such as after you go over a bump. If the tire takes its sweet time to get back on the ground, you have already hit something else! If you feel like you're returning from a bungee jump, tighten up the rebound setting.

Adjust *compression damping* so that it absorbs quickly through the system and lets the spring work. You may have the perfect spring for your weight, but if your damping is set too high, you can't get the piston through the oil. It is moving so slowly that you are already past the obstacle before the fork has moved! You also don't want it to move through so quickly that it smacks in and bottoms out harshly. When you are at the highest point of the rock you just hit, you want your fork travel used up.

Avoid using the *preload* adjuster as much as you can. You may think you can get where you want by cranking up your preload. You'll say, "My preload's up about four turns, and, O.K., I'm bottoming out once just fine. Boy, on the big hits, I can take it; I've really got my compression damping and rebound damping right, everything's feeling good." Problem is, the initial little stutter bumps are driving you crazy, and the fork feels really stiff over them because the spring stiffens up too fast. Instead of increasing preload, use a stiffer spring and as little preload as possible—just enough to snug up your spring.

position, riding style, fatigue, and so on to really be able to tell the difference between one suspension setup and another.

Pick out a section of rough trail at least 100 meters long with a climb on it and a sharp turn. Go back and forth climbing and descending to see how each change you make affects performance. Be consistent with your riding style. This allows you to see what each adjustment really does.

A short trail test section is a benefit, so you can remember everything that happened. Short sections encourage frequent retesting, which is always useful. Ideally, a test course will not be longer than 20 minutes and will be similar to and as rough as the most demanding courses you ride or race on.

Get familiar with what your suspension adjustments do. Ride the course with rebound damping backed all of the way out. Then ride it with rebound damping tightened down to its maximum setting. Do the same with preload, spring rate, and, if your fork allows, compression damping.

Just make one change at a time, so you can isolate what each change does. Record everything you do in writing.

Keep a notebook by where you store the bike. Write your observations down right after the ride while it is fresh in your mind. If you wait until you have time to work on your bike, you will forget what was bugging you about it and what you wanted to work on.

11.9 TEARING A FORK APART

First off, make sure you have a service manual for your fork. The owners manuals that come with Marzocchi and older Manitou forks are quite thorough and useful. Even the little manual for an RST has an exploded diagram. This is not the case with Rock Shox and recent Manitous, however. The owners manual only explains the simplest adjustments and has no disassembly instructions or exploded diagrams. Rock Shox and Manitou service manuals *do* exist, however. Make sure you get one.

Be patient when taking the fork apart, and build up your confidence and comfort level. Don't take it completely apart the first time. The first time, just switch springs. The next time, take it down a step further. Spring changes and simple disassembly procedures are explained in Chapter 13 of *Zinn and the Art of Mountain Bike Maintenance*, Second Edition.

A good bike shop can be a great resource for learning how to tear apart forks. Hang out in the shop and watch them work on forks, or watch mechanics in the technical support vehicles of fork companies at major races. Technical support personnel are often willing to answer questions, when they are not under the gun just before a race start. Some shops offer clinics on fork maintenance and tuning.

Tear apart as many forks as you can; it's really a kick and can build confidence (and sometimes drive you crazy). You can always call your fork manufacturer's tech support line if you get stuck with your fork halfway put back together. Suspension will become much less intimidating. Once your fork is no longer a black box to you, you will tend to service it more often, adjust it better, and keep its performance higher.

Remember that most designers of high-end forks intended that disassembly be simple.

11-10 INCREASE OR DECREASE TRAVEL

By getting a damping cartridge and neutral leg different in length from what is currently in the fork, you can change the travel of most forks. Consult your fork service manual for parts needed and procedures.

Be aware that the bushing placement on some early-model Judy XCs makes it a poor idea to increase travel. A small percentage of these will disengage from the stanchions.

11-11 UPGRADING INTERNAL FORK PARTS

You can get more performance out of a stock fork in many cases by replacing the springs and/or dampers with aftermarket ones. This is especially true with midrange forks that have no damping cartridge; you can replace the MCU or MCU/coil spring with a coil- or air-spring/damper combination and get more boing with less pogo.

11-11A Coil Springs

Coil springs lend more liveliness to old elastomer forks but require more damping to control the quicker absorption and more powerful return of a coil. Simply replacing the MCU stack with coil springs in older Judys or Manitou EFCs or Mach 5s can put too much strain on the damping cartridge and require a change in shim stack or a new cartridge.

FORK TEAR-DOWN TIPS

from Doug Bradbury

You can take apart a Manitou and some of the other fork brands down to the last nut. You can get to the point where you are changing the shim stacks on the damper pistons. They are not as complex as you think, but there are lots of small parts to keep track of. Good service manuals and patience are a must to do it properly. Use your manual! Use your manual! Use your manual! And cleanliness is next to godliness.

When you make fork adjustments, only make one change at a time! You may think you know exactly what it needs and that you can get it just right by changing a few things at once. Don't do it. When you go out and ride, you will have no concept of what is going on.

Change your spring. Once you get the spring correct, come back and change rebound damping. Once you get that correct, then change compression damping.

Write down every adjustment setting and how it worked while riding! When you change things, you can get lost very quickly without good records. In the middle of the night when you are remembering a ride and trying to figure out what to change, if you look at some old numbers, you may suddenly get it.

Manufacturers continually improve upon their forks year after year, often by adopting some ideas from aftermarket parts made for their own forks. For instance, older Judy internals leave something to be desired by today's standards. The old cartridge is made of plastic and tends to heat up and blow. The elastomer stack (photo 11-29) has little Judy Jax plastic spacers between them that allow the elastomers to snake around inside the fork and get mashed asymmetrically. The fork legs and crown are nice and stiff, though. Aftermarket coil springs and aluminum damping cartridge can turn an old Judy into a hot fork. Rock Shox followed the lead of companies making such aftermarket Judy upgrades by coming up with the Type II coil/MCU spring (photo 11-29) and new dual coils. Many fork manufacturers sell new spring and cartridge kits to upgrade their own old models to current internals. For instance, you can replace the MCU stack in a Judy with a Type II MCU/coil one, or you can slap the MCU/coil stack from a Manitou SX or SX-Ti into a Mach 5 or EFC. A cheap, under $10 upgrade is to replace one elastomer in a Mach 5 with a coil spring.

A fork like a Rock Shox Indy that has no damping cartridge gets much better with the addition of one. One such option is Risse's hydraulic damper and coil spring set (photo 11-30) to replace the stock MCU/coil spring.

11-11B Air Springs

The Englund Total Air (photo 11-31) can lighten up a Judy (or Indy or Manitou) while making it more adjustable. Air pressure is easy to adjust, and the Total Air uses compressed air as both the spring medium *and* the damping medium. The Total Air has both a rotating damping adjuster as well as adjuster shafts that can be interchanged for faster or slower action. Total Air comes stock in some 1998 White Bros. forks.

11-11C Upgrading for Small Riders

A rider under 100 pounds (even one under 120 pounds) is going to have a hard

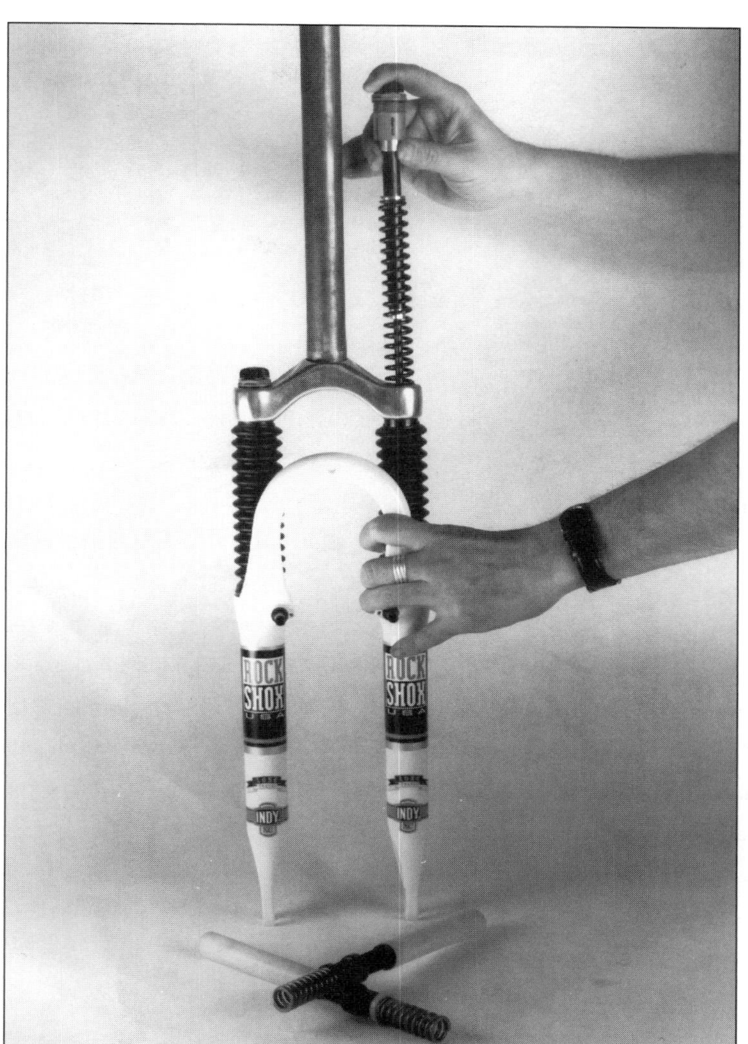

11-30
Risse hydraulic damper and coil spring set being inserted into a Rock Shox Indy.

11-31
Englund Total Air system for a Judy.

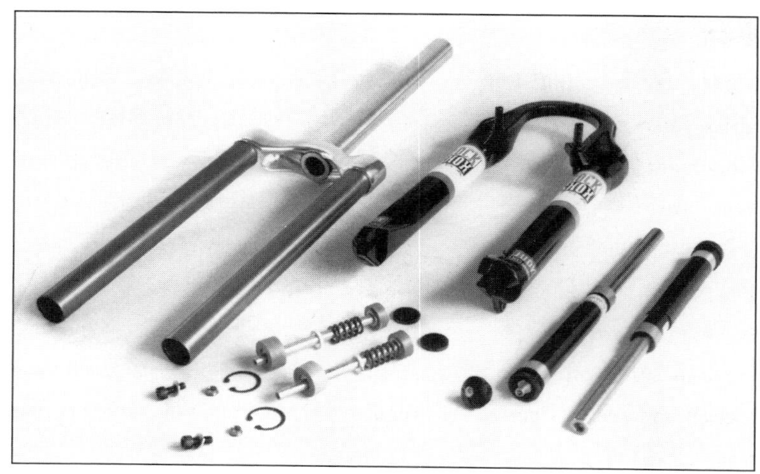

time getting an elastomer or coil spring fork to move. The initial amount of force to get the fork moving will simply be too high. If you are setting up bikes for adolescents, for example, they would be better off with a lightweight rigid fork than they would having to lug around a suspension fork that will not compress under them.

Trying to make an MCU plush enough for a small person is tough. I tried to make a Rock Shox Quadra work for my daughter when she was nine. I got the softest elastomer available and then turned down the diameter in the center section in steps, like a turned candlestick holder. That still was not enough. She simply could not overcome the spring and the internal friction of the fork.

A good solution with a small rider is to put a soft spring in one leg and no spring in the other. If you have a TPC fork that already only has springs in one leg, replace the spring with a soft spring from a pre-1998 dual-spring Manitou.

I have also had great success with small riders using air springs coupled with negative springs. The beauty of an air spring is that it can be set very low; you can pump an air fork up to one psi if you want! Problem is, without a negative spring, the initial stiction of the fork is still a problem. If you set the air pressure low enough that they can get the fork to move, it will be too soft once it is moving.

A negative spring is designed to eliminate this problem. It pulls down on the fork all of the time. So, for instance, if there is no air pressure in the fork, it compresses itself. Three options for an air fork with a negative spring are to retrofit Englund Total Air cartridges into an existing MCU or MCU/coil spring fork or to buy a Rock Shox SID fork or a White Bros. fork that has the Total Air built in.

11-11D Disc Brake Mounts

If you want to avoid buying an entire new fork to accommodate your bitchin' new disc brake, you can get new outer legs with disc brake tabs (photo 11-32) for your old fork.

11-12 HOW OFTEN SHOULD YOU MAINTAIN YOUR FORK?

As with knowing when to oil a chain, you will soon learn just how often to maintain your fork once you get into the habit of maintaining it. When you get into the fork and find lots of gum and dirt, then you know you waited too long. There are many variables determining when to work on a fork, and it depends on where and how much you ride.

Trying other forks will help you recognize the condition of yours. A new fork feels great because you have been riding your old fork at well below its best performance. A better fork that is clean will feel way better!

If you disassemble, clean, and grease the inner legs and bushings frequently, you will less frequently face costly repairs, such as replacing bushings and damping cartridges. Perform maintenance more often than you think it's needed.

As an example of service periods, see the table from Manitou's *Suspension Tuning for Performance Manual* on page 137 (these time intervals assume the rider has fork boots installed):

Fork Maintenance Tips from Arlo Englund, Inventor of Total Air Front and Rear Shocks

Any person tuning a fork should seriously consider maintenance to ensure that there is no unnecessary friction. Stiction is the worst enemy of mountain bike suspension.

When lubing a fork (e.g., the seals, wipers, and bushings), using just any off-the-shelf grease is less than desirable. Experiment with different brands of specially formulated suspension lubricants to find one that will provide you with the smoothest action.

11-13 BUSHINGS

Bushings are the wide cylindrical rings in the top and bottom of each lower leg on which the upper leg slides. The bushings must be quite slick and fit tightly (but not *too* tightly) to keep the fork legs moving smoothly and in line with each other. They can be made out of any slick material; nylon or oil-impregnated steel are common choices.

Most people neglect fork bushings as a maintenance item, and it is a bad idea to do so. If the bushings are worn, the cartridge will get wrecked quickly, since the cartridge shaft will not be moving straight up and down. The side load on the shaft will allow oil to come around the seals. You will know it, because oil will drip out of the bottom of your fork leg, and your damping will feel very light or nonexistent.

Check if your bushings are worn by grabbing the front brake and pushing the bike back and forth and feel for play. Be

SUSPENSION TUNING

Severe Conditions (mud, rain, snow)		
Riding Frequency/Duration:	*Frequent/Long*	*Sporadic/Short*
Clean and grease inner legs and bushings every:	1–2 weeks	3–4 weeks
Grease spring stack:	as needed	as needed
Change oil in cartridge as needed or every:	2–3 months	as needed

Normal Conditions		
Riding Frequency/Duration:	*Frequent/Long*	*Sporadic/Short*
Clean and grease inner legs and bushings every:	6–8 weeks	3–4 months
Grease spring stack:	as needed	as needed
Change oil in cartridge as needed or every:	2–3 months	as needed

aware that most bushings are originally set up a little loosely so that they will move freely and account for manufacturing tolerances.

Bushings can be easier to interchange than you may think. For example, you can make a bushing puller for a Manitou by gluing a long 5-mm hex key into a neutral leg, with which you can hook the lower bushings and drag it out. The same tool can be used to tap in the new bushing. Every fork manufacturer has special bushing puller and installation tools for its forks. Bushing change may realistically be a job for a shop, if you do not want to buy or make the tools. Changing bushings is worth it, though, since you can wreck your inner legs and damping cartridge if you ride with worn-out bushings.

11.14 FORK FLEX

Flex in a suspension fork can allow your front wheel to go places other than where you had planned. It also can result in the brakes banging the rim. Newer forks have more rigid lower leg/fork brace assemblies to combat this. Triple-clamp forks (photo 11-33) and stronger frames designed for them increase rider control by eliminating flex, as do stiffer

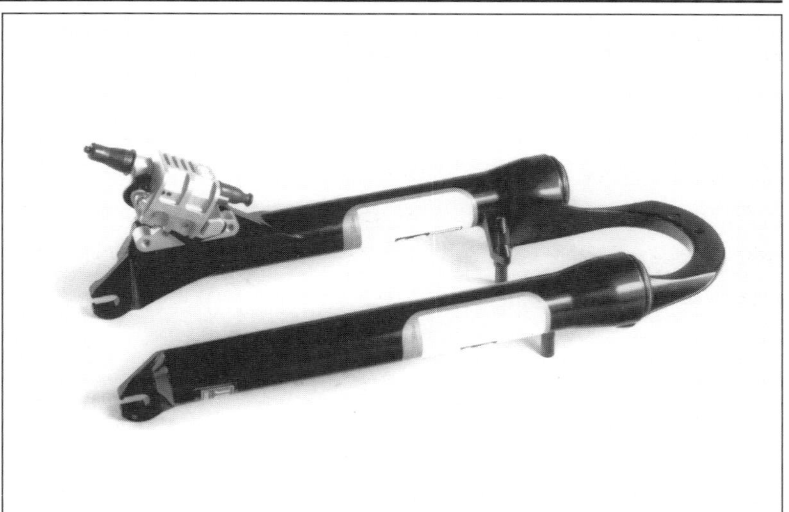

11-32
Disc brake mount option on a pair of Judy lower legs.

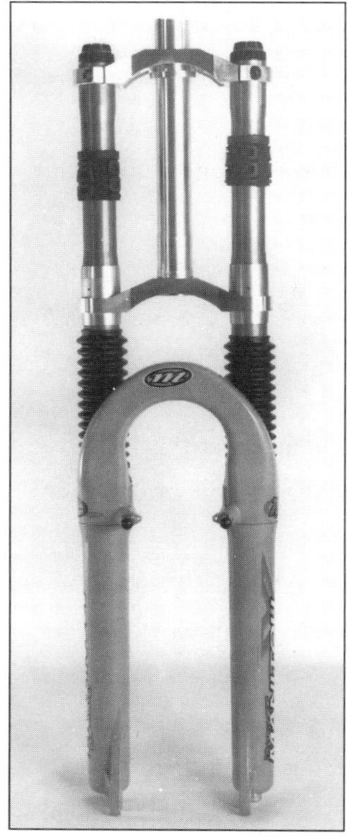

11-33
Triple-clamp Manitou X-Vert fork.

hubs (photo 5-22). Bolt-on hubs with giant axles are a huge improvement in rigidity and control for downhillers.

11.15 RETROFITTING A SUSPENSION FORK TO YOUR BIKE

You can slap any fork with a long enough steerer of the right diameter on any frame. It may not always be a great idea, though. Here are some considerations to keep in mind when doing it.

11.15A Effects to Consider

STEERER DIAMETER: You will want to make sure that the fork has the same steering tube diameter as the one the frame was built for. For most current mountain bikes, that will be 1 1/8 inches.

STEERER LENGTH: The steering tube needs to be long enough to fit the headset parts on, and in the case of a threadless steerer, the stem as well. A threadless steerer needs to be around 10 cm longer than your head tube, while a threaded steerer needs to be about 4 cm longer than the head tube. The steerer will need to be cut to length. More on this in Chapter 11 of *Zinn and the Art of Mountain Bike Maintenance.*

A triple-clamp fork needs to have both the steerer and the stanchion tubes long enough for your frame.

FORK LENGTH: You should know that a longer fork will *increase your bottom bracket height, decrease your head angle,* and *raise your handlebars.* These things will have the effect of slowing down your steering by increasing your fork trail (the distance from the tire's ground contact point to the intersection point of the steering axis and the ground), and transferring more of your weight from the bars to the saddle.

Note A fully compressed fork will tend to oversteer, because the fork trail is small, and a fully extended fork will tend to understeer, because the fork trail is large. (The fork trail changes because the head angle changes with compression and extension; the fork rake—the forward offset of the front hub ahead of the steering axis—does not change.)

Your center of gravity will also get higher with a longer fork. Obviously, in the fork's fully compressed state, these heights and angles will be about the same as with a rigid fork.

11.15B Triple-Clamp Forks

You do not want to slap a triple-clamp fork (photo 11-33) on just any bike. You need to have exceptionally strong head-tube joints on the frame to handle the extra stress the fork will apply. The super-stiff fork can act like a bottle opener and pry the head tube right off a frame that is not sufficiently reinforced in that area.

11.16 SUSPENSION FORK ADJUSTMENT/TROUBLESHOOTING GUIDE

This section was stolen from Manitou's *Suspension Tuning for Performance Manual* (with permission, or course).

Two important things to keep in mind:

1. A bottoming sensation (even if the fork is not bottoming) may actually be caused by the inability of the bike and rider to overcome an overly stiff spring or excessive damping.
2. A harsh sensation (even if the bike has soft springs) may actually be caused by a spring rate too soft for the bike and rider, causing the suspension to ride with much of the travel compressed (i.e., packed up).

Spring Rate

TOO SOFT: Bottoming of fork, high preload needed, front end too low on downhills.

TOO HARD: Fork rarely or never bottoms (e.g., fork does not use full travel).

Spring Preload

TOO LITTLE: Excessive static sag, front end too low entering turns, oversteering.

TOO MUCH: Not enough static sag, fork feels stiff/harsh, understeering, poor low-speed tight-turning ability.

Rebound Damping

TOO LITTLE: Fork extends too quickly and wheel springs up from ground after landing from jump, difficulty in maintaining a straight path though rocks, front end attempts to climb the berm/groove while cornering, high ride height, understeering.

TOO MUCH: Harsh feeling, especially through successive rapid hits, bottoming after several successive large hits, failure to rebound after landing from jump, low ride height, oversteering, bottoming occurs even though compression damping and spring rate are correct.

Compression Damping

TOO LITTLE: Bottoming, fork dives while braking, oversteering, fork is unstable.

TOO MUCH: Harsh feeling, fork rarely or never bottoms, high ride height despite soft spring and/or little preload, understeering.

Common Front Suspension Symptoms and Some Fixes

Fork too hard
1. Decrease rebound damping
2. Decrease spring rate
3. Decrease oil viscosity
4. Increase spring rate**

Fork too soft
1. Increase spring rate
2. Increase oil viscosity
3. Replace worn out oil
4. Put oil in (empty) cartridge

**If you are running a spring rate that is too soft for your weight and ability, you can be misled into thinking that the spring rate is too stiff. This is because you are using up the fork travel before you begin to ride. Furthermore, the fork is working in a stiffer spring-rate range on smaller hits, giving the impression of the fork being harsh and stiff. This is where the ride-height (sag) adjustment is important.

Front end searching/nervous descending:
1. Increase rebound damping
2. Increase spring preload
3. Increase spring rate

Front end "knifes"/oversteers:
1. Decrease rebound damping
2. Increase spring preload
3. Increase spring rate

Front end pushes or washes out in turns:
1. Increase rebound damping
2. Decrease spring preload
3. Decrease spring rate

No response to small bumps:
1. Decrease rebound damping
2. Decrease spring preload
3. Decrease spring rate

12

SADDLES AND SEATPOSTS

His saddle forced him to fly.
—Edmund Spenser, *The Faerie Queene*

This chapter is primarily devoted to comfort (and, of course, performance, which is improved when you are comfortable).

12.1 Saddles

There are a number of reasons to upgrade a saddle. Light weight is certainly one of them, but the primary reason is comfort. By comfort I do not always mean the comfort of your butt, either; I am also talking about efficiency. Biomechanical efficiency is dependent on your muscles and skeleton being in a comfortable position.

If a saddle's rails have a longer straight section, it will allow you a greater range of fore and aft adjustment. If you are at the limit of the adjustment of your saddle in one direction or the other, you would benefit from a

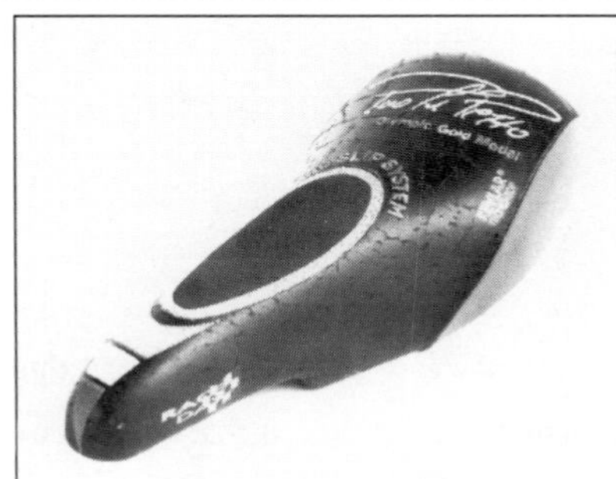

12-1
Selle San Marco Paola Pezzo Race Day saddle with chopped ears and soft Lycra perineal-protecting spot.

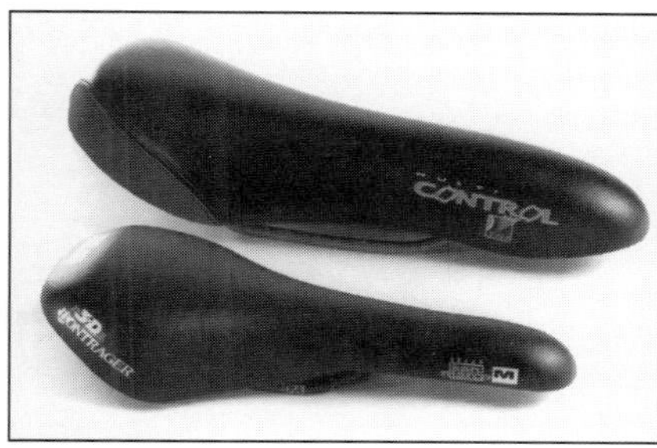

12-2
Oversized Tioga DH Control saddle (top). Standard-sized Selle San Marco Bontrager 3-D saddle with chopped ears and tail (bottom).

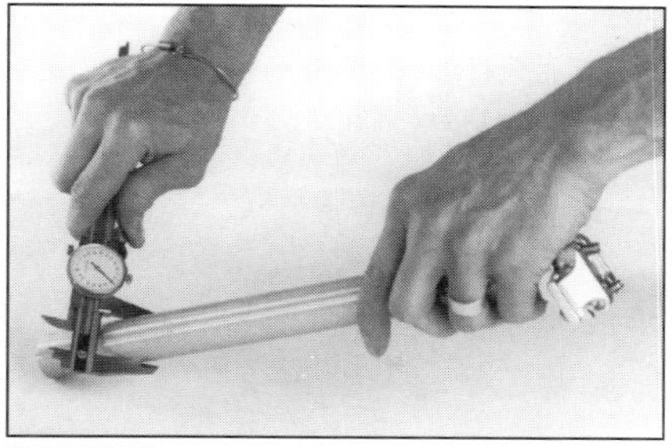

12-3
Measuring seatpost diameter with caliper.

saddle with more adjustability (or a seatpost that has more offset in whichever direction you need). Saddles do vary widely in the length of the straight section of their rails; compare some!

A saddle with chopped-off ears at the back (photo 12-1) will make it easier for you to slide on and off the back end of the saddle. Chopping the rear top edge down at an angle also can aid with sliding off and back on quickly (photo 12-2, bottom). These features allow you to descend faster with more comfort when going over steep drops. You can get your weight back over the rear tire quickly when you need it, and get back on easily to resume pedaling.

For a bigger rider, a stronger saddle (try one with steel rails and a tough base) will not break and land you on the rotating rear tire.

Some people prefer stiffer saddles, others prefer softer. The same goes for narrow vs. wide at the nose. Experiment to find what you like.

Perineal protection is useful to protect tender body parts against the bouncing of mountain bike riding. For men, reducing prostate damage and damage to blood vessels associated with erectile activity is a good idea. Women also seem to be much happier when their soft tissues are not getting bashed against a hard surface. One example of perineal protection is the saddle in photo 12-1. It has a very soft spot under the black Lycra oval. The shell is concave beneath it, and the Lycra gives way there.

Saddles with suspended rails also can afford extra comfort. A saddle that is connected to the rails through some sort of elastic media can take the edge off hard jolts.

Some downhillers sometimes prefer a huge, long, soft saddle (photo 12-2, top). The saddle allows all sorts of positioning options, being so long. Its narrow shape does not restrict pedaling. The soft padding can be nice when hitting big rocks at over 50 mph.

12.2 Seatposts

Remember always to grease the post before insertion. Grease it annually, so it does not get stuck. If it does, there is a section on freeing a seized seatpost in Chapter 10 of *Zinn and the Art of Mountain Bike Maintenance.*

12.2A Considerations for All Seatposts

The first thing you want to make sure is that the seatpost is the right diameter for

12-4
American Classic seatpost with butted walls.

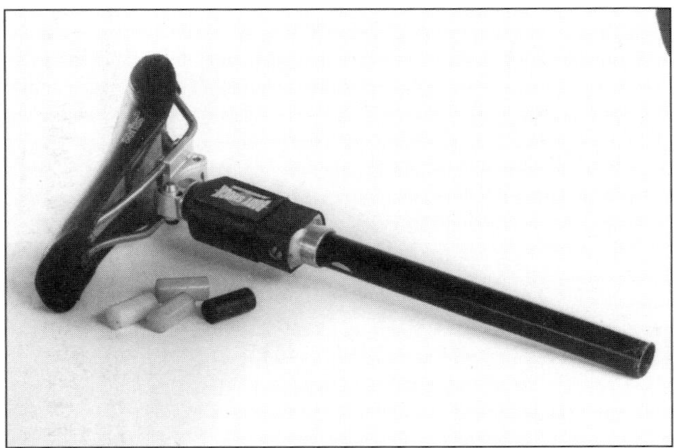

12-5
Answer Body Shock seatpost with elastomers pulled out.

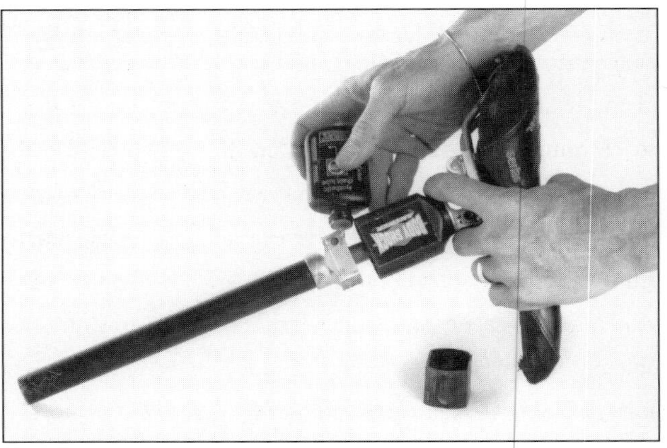

12-6
Lubing Body Shock bearings with lower dust cover pulled off.

your bike. You can measure it with a caliper (photo 12-3). To determine if it will fit your frame, you can measure the inside of your frame's seat tube with a caliper. Be aware that the seat tube clamp area can be ovalized and give you an odd reading. Go by the frame manufacturer's seatpost size recommendation, and try posts of that size first. You may find yourself going up or down a size to get it right.

If your seatpost slips, cut a shim for it. If an in-between post size would be ideal, this may be your best option. If, for example, you have a 27.0-mm post that slips, yet a 27.2 mm would be too big, cut a section out of an aluminum can to slip in between the seat tube and the post. Curve the edges to avoid tearing your flesh. Start with a big piece, and keep cutting it down until you get one that just fits in with the post.

The post should be long enough to be inserted beyond the limit line when you have it set to the height you want. You may need to shop around if you are a long-legged person riding on a small frame.

To get the correct fore-aft position of your saddle, look for a post with the proper setback for you. Some posts have the clamp centered over the post shaft, which works for riders who like a forward position. Most posts have some offset of the clamp behind the shaft, which riders who like to power the pedals from farther back will prefer.

A seatpost should have a strong shaft. A weak post can bend or break, especially with the length of exposed post above the seat tube that most sloping-top-tube mountain bikes require. Strength and stiffness can be achieved by making the shaft walls thicker, by using a stronger material for the post, or by butting the shaft. In the case of a seatpost, butting usually refers to making the post thicker along the front and back of the shaft than on the sides (photo 12-4). This keeps weight down while increasing strength.

You also want a seatpost with a strong clamp. Some cheaper posts just cannot take the beating a strong mountain bike rider will give it. Ideally, the clamp will have a flat surface on the bottom half to support each rail over the full length of the clamp. Clamps that only touch each rail at two points (e.g., where the clamp is simply a bisected cylinder only clamping the rail at each outer edge of the cylinder) can concentrate more stress on sections of a lightweight saddle rail, resulting in breakage.

12.2B Suspension Seatposts

There are two basic types of suspension seatposts: telescoping (photo 12-5) and parallelogram pivot (photo 12-7) versions. Softride beam suspension had a brief period of popularity but seems to have almost disappeared from the market.

A common feature of most suspension seatposts is one-size-fits-all sizing. A diameter around 1 inch (25.4 mm) seems to be common—a size that very few, if any, mountain bike frames accept. This means, of course, that the post requires a shim to fit your frame. Suspension post manufacturers usually stock cylindrical shims of various sizes to fit common frames. There is at least one manufacturer (USE) that offers a complete line of shim sizes for every frame (USE shims can be used with some other brands of suspension posts as well).

Another feature of a suspension post is that you cannot measure your seat height without sitting on the bike. Seat height is dependent on the sag of the post when you get on it. Your seat height adjustment will have to change as you change springs or preload.

While you ride, your seat height and reach to the stem and bars change. With a telescoping post, seat height changes a lot and handlebar reach changes very little; with a pivoting seatpost, the opposite is true. Either way, by giving you the continuous feedback of your leg or arm reach changing, a suspension post encourages you to smooth out your pedaling style. You do not want to be causing it to bob up and down (or back and forth) from pedaling alone.

12.2C Tuning a Suspension Seatpost to Your Riding Style

Tuning a seatpost is much like tuning a fork, except you usually do not have a separate damper to adjust. A suspension post typically counts on the internal damping of elastomers (and your legs) to control its speed of movement.

You can raise the force required to start the spring moving by increasing the preload, which affects ride height, too. With an elastomer spring, this also increases the spring rate, due to the progressive nature of elastomers. It also shortens the life of the elastomers by deforming them, giving them a permanent set more quickly.

Telescoping Posts

With a telescoping suspension post (photo 12-5), the most common spring is a stack of elastomers. There are less common or discontinued telescoping posts with other spring types, like air or coils.

On an elastomer-sprung telescoping post, change the springs by unscrewing the cap inside the bottom end of the post (photo 12-5). The elastomers are color-coded, as in an elastomer fork. Put in the combination of elastomers that gives you the spring rate you like best. Make sure you grease the elastomers with a good fork grease.

If you want a plush ride, set your spring rate so that you use up 25 percent of the travel in sag (ride height) when you sit on it. If you pedal smoothly, it will not bob much on a smooth surface, but it will be quite active riding over bumps. If you prefer less variation in seat height while pedaling and want the equivalent of a rigid post except when you slam into something hard, use stiffer springs.

Tighten the bottom cap in so it just contacts the elastomers and pushes on them slightly. Ride it like that (preferably on the test course you selected for fork tuning (see Chapter 11, section 11-8), switching springs around until you find a combination that feels the best to you. If you want small adjustments, increase the preload (by tightening the bottom cap).

Keep your post moving freely by frequently cleaning and lubricating the shaft and the bushings or bearings it moves on (photo 12-6). Keep the dust boot on when riding to keep the mechanism clean.

Parallelogram Pivot Posts

With a parallelogram pivot suspension post, the saddle travels in an arc about the lower pivot point, rather than along the line of the seatpost shaft. The idea is that hitting a bump throws you back, and a pivoting seatpost allows your body to move back and down. A compressing telescoping post moves you down and slightly forward, since the seat tube is angled forward.

High-end pivoting posts have a parallelogram mechanism (photo 12-7) with a pivot at each of the four corners, like a rear derailleur. This keeps the saddle level throughout the movement. Rudimentary pivoting posts have a single pivot, which causes the saddle to tip back as the post pivots back.

Some pivoting posts use an elastomer spring, others a coil. The spring as well as the preload on the spring can be changed. On the Moxey post pictured in photo 12-7, the spring is a parallelogram-shaped block of elastomer with a hole in it. A pivot pin can be removed (once the preload screw is backed off completely!) in order to open the parallelogram and interchange springs.

On impact, the Moxey elastomer parallelogram block deforms, ovalizing the round hole in its center. When the impact is large enough to close the hole, the spring rate ramps up steeply and prevents harsh bottoming. The elastomer is much stiffer once the hole is closed; its freedom of movement is greatly reduced.

The Moxey preload adjuster is a bolt on the back of the post behind the seat clamp. Tightening the preload screw pulls the parallelogram back and deforms the elastomer. The preload is set on near maximum in photo 12-7. As you can see, increasing the preload on this type of post reduces the total travel.

With a parallelogram post, every time you hit a bump, the saddle swings back, and the reach to the bars increases. This can be disconcerting. I find that I like to run a Moxey post with a lot of preload, notwithstanding all that I have said about minimizing preload on forks and rear shocks. This keeps the saddle in a smaller fore-aft range, never ending up very far forward. It helps avoid getting pitched forward when dropping over something steep. High preload and a stiff elastomer also minimizes bobbing during pedaling. Bobbing is more prevalent with a parallelogram post than with a telescoping post due to reduced internal friction. On a telescoping post your weight is binding the shaft against the bearing surface at the back of the post.

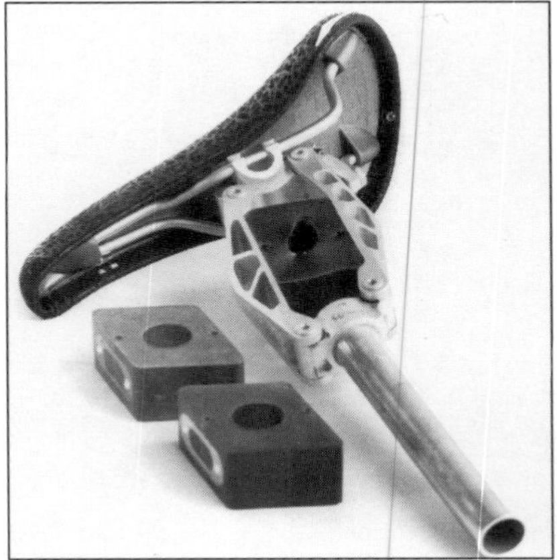

12-7
Moxey pivoting post with various elastomers. The preload screw is at the top rear of the parallelogram.

A Power Post Mount parallelogram post minimizes bobbing and reach variation with a hydraulic damping cartridge inside the shaft. It has cylindrical elastomers inside the shaft that can be changed or preloaded like those in a telescoping post.

Remember to frequently clean and lubricate the pivots on the post.

13

FRAMES

To endure torments of heat and cold extreme, like frames that virtue hath disposed . . .
—Alighieri Dante, *The Divine Comedy: Purgatory*

This chapter is devoted to two things: prepping any frame for assembly of components, and tuning rear suspension.

Chapter 14 of *Zinn and the Art of Mountain Bike Maintenance* has sections on checking frame alignment, aligning dropouts, repairing threads and bent frame fittings, repairing dents and paint chips, and inspecting a frame for crash damage, cracks, and tube rippling. I will not duplicate those efforts here.

13.1 Prepping a New Frame for Assembly

Before putting parts on a new frame, you want to be sure that they are going to work properly once installed. This includes making sure that all of the bearing surfaces are parallel so that the bearings turn smoothly, making sure the wheels will line up with each other, and making sure that the rear derailleur will be in alignment.

13.1A Reaming and Facing Head Tube

The head tube must be properly sized internally so that the headset cups can be press-fitted into the head tube. The internal bore of the ends of the head tube must be aligned (co-linear) so that those pressed-in cups line up with each other. The head tube end faces must be cut so that they are parallel. This will ensure that the headset bearings are parallel and will thus turn without binding.

All these things are not necessarily guaranteed on a new frame off the shelf. Manufacturing techniques vary, but most frames are not reamed and faced after completion, although many retail bike shops perform these steps on all frames sold.

Even if a head tube looks reamed on the inside and faced on the ends, these steps may have been performed on the head tube when it was simply a tube, before it got attached to the other frame tubes. Obviously, it is quicker and simpler to turn a tube on a lathe than it is to jig up an entire frame for machining. Problem is, welding the head tube causes nonuniform heat expansion and contraction, since the top and down tubes are welded only to one side. This tends to bow the tube toward the welds, meaning that even nicely machined end faces and internal bores will no longer be parallel.

You can ream and face the head tube with a hand-operated reaming and facing tool (photo 13-1). A long center shaft running through a centering collar keeps the cutters lined up with the opposite end of the head tube. A disc-shaped facing cutter with teeth on its bottom side is paired with a separate cylindrical reamer with teeth on its outer diameter.

Make sure the teeth are clean, free of metal chips, and wet with cutting oil before starting. Assemble the tool according to its directions; there are slight differences in all tools, and it never hurts to read before you cut. You run the risk of making a blunder on your expensive frame.

Keep turning the tool, in a forward direction *only*, until the reamer has gone all of the way in and the facer has cut a new surface all of the way around the end face of the tube. Increase spring tension at the bottom end as needed by tightening the threaded nut. Remove the tool by pulling it straight up and out. *Do not* turn the handles in the reverse direction, as you will dull the tool. Cutters can be sharpened by a machinist specializing in tool sharpening, but it is expensive, and it can only be done so many times, especially on the reamer. Sharpening a reamer slightly reduces its diameter, and hence its usefulness, each time. It is best to avoid dulling the tools as much as possible. This is done by keeping them cool and well lubricated with cutting fluid, turning them only in the forward direction, and putting high pressure on the facing cutter when you start so that it takes a deep cut, rather than sliding on the surface before biting in.

13.1B Tapping Bottom Bracket Shell

Tapping (cutting threads with threading taps) a bottom bracket shell ensures that the bottom bracket cups will thread in smoothly. The threads in either end of the shell not only need to be cut to the specified diameter, depth, and thread pitch to fit the cups, but they also need to be lined up with each other to ensure that the cups share the same centerline and hence maintain parallel bearings.

Bottom bracket tap sets have a left-hand-threaded tap for the drive side, and a right-hand-threaded tap for the left side of the shell. For mountain bikes, the tap size is 1.37 inches x 24 threads per inch. The handles have a pilot shaft to keep the two taps lined up with each other. Both taps are started simultaneously from either side to line up each other (photo 13-2). Make sure you use cutting oil on the taps, and, *above all*, make sure you put the left-hand-thread tap into the drive side of the shell! Clean any grit or chips out of the shell before inserting the taps.

Correct tapping method for any threads is to turn the tap forward and back, rather than just driving the tap forward, which can destroy the threads you are making by dragging a huge metal burr over them. It can also result in getting the tap stuck. Turn the tap in the cutting direction about 1/8 turn, then back about half that much to break off the chip, forward 1/8, back 1/16, and so forth. Make sure you supply enough coolant (cutting fluid) and go slowly enough that the taps do not get hot. This is particularly important in a titanium frame, whose shell can stretch around the taps and bind them.

13.1C Facing Bottom Bracket Shell

Most drive-side bottom bracket cups have a flange that tightens flat against the shell face, and some left-side cups have a lock ring that also goes up against the shell face. Cutting the faces of the shell so that they are parallel ensures that the cup orientation will not be thrown off when the lock ring or flange is tightened against the face.

A Park facing cutter is held by the same tap handles. It requires that the taps be fully inserted as guides for the pilot shaft (photo 13-3). The cutter pressure is supplied by your pushing inward on the handle. A Campagnolo facing cutter has its own handle with a fatter pilot shaft that slides inside separate thread guides that are tightened in against each other from either side after the taps are removed. Cutting pressure is supplied by a spring tightened with a nut against the opposite end of the shell.

Proceed by a similar process as facing the head tube, turning the cutter clockwise only, and supplying enough pressure to take a deep cut, rather than having the cutter skate across the surface. Keep cutting until you have created a new surface all the way around.

13.1D Tapping Other Frame Threads

If the bottle boss bolts do not go in easily, tap the water-bottle bosses (photo 13-4). If the brake bolts do not easily thread all the way in, tap the cantilever

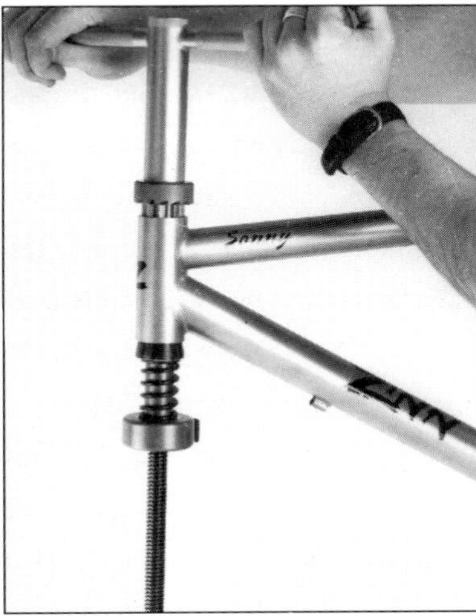

13-1
Reaming and facing head tube.

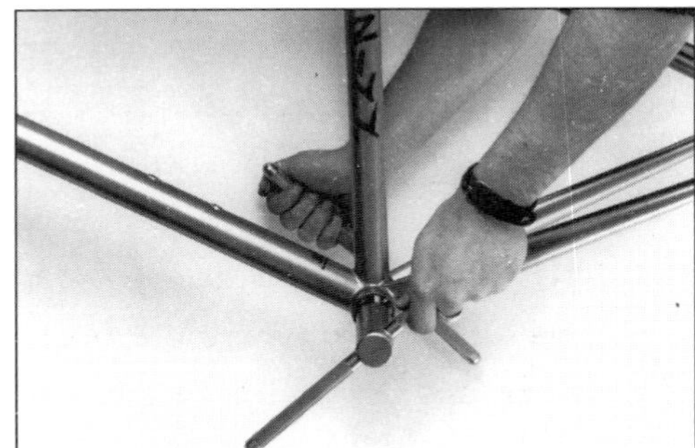

13-2
Tapping bottom bracket threads.

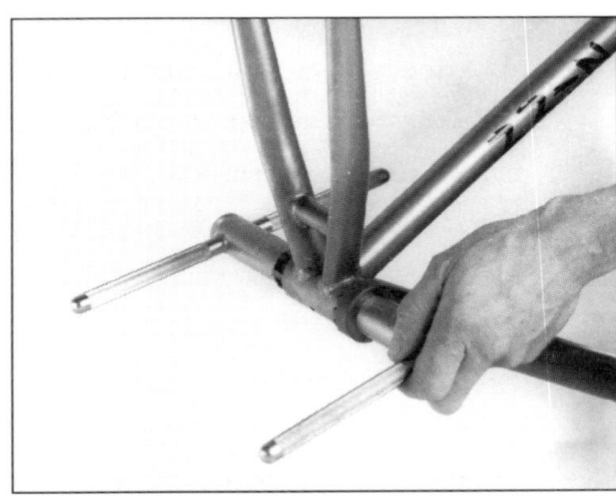

13-3
Facing bottom bracket shell.

posts (photo 13-5). Frames that have a welded-on seat binder sometimes require tapping to clear out paint and burrs from the seat-tube slotting process. If the derailleur does not thread into the dropout derailleur hanger, tap that, too.

As I mentioned with regard to tapping a bottom bracket shell, use cutting oil and turn the tap forward a bit, back a bit, forward a bit, and so on, to avoid getting it jammed. If you get a small tap like this jammed, you can easily break it off in the frame. Taps are brittle; be careful with them! If you *do* get one jammed, take it to an expert for extraction, preferably before you break it off.

13.1E Checking and Adjusting Derailleur Hanger Alignment

The derailleur hanger should be parallel to the plane of the frame and wheels in

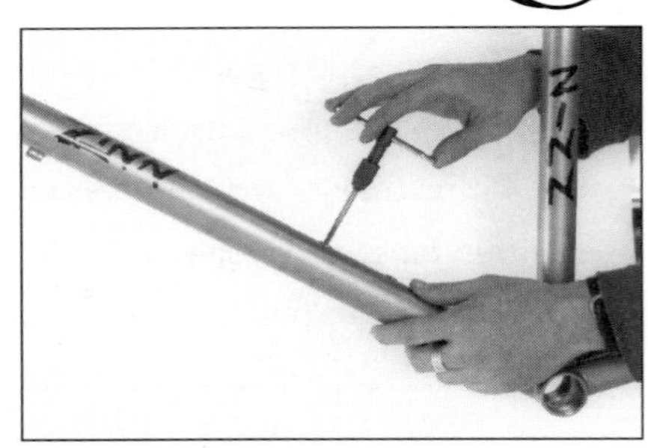

13-4
Tapping water-bottle bosses.

Tap sizes:

Bottom bracket shell:	1.37 inches x 24 T.P.I.
Bottle boss and rack boss:	5 mm x 0.8
Cable guide mounting hole under bottom bracket shell:	5 mm x 0.8
Some fender mount and reflector/cable clamp holes:	5 mm x 0.8
Cantilever boss and seat binder:	6 mm x 1
Rear derailleur hanger:	10 mm x 1

13-5
Tapping cantilever post.

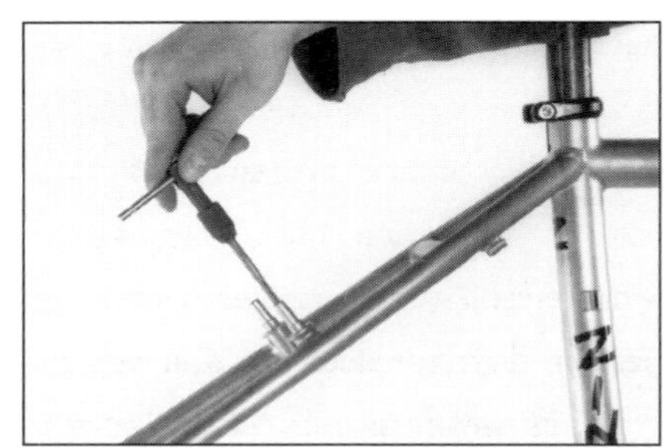

order to make the rear derailleur work properly. You can check its alignment and correct the alignment with a tool like Park's hanger alignment gauge (photo 1-14).

Put a true wheel in the frame. Thread the alignment tool into the derailleur hanger. With Park's tool, slide the gauge out on the square tube to the rim. Slide the rod inward until it touches the rim (photo 13-6). Swing the tool around its full arc (it will be stopped by the seatstay and chainstay or swingarm; you cannot check in the part of the arc the chain occupies), sliding the gauge to keep the rod against the rim.

If the distance between the tool arm and the rim varies as it arcs around, then the derailleur hanger is bent. If it is, find the place where the tool arm is closest to the rim, and set the gauge rod against the rim there. Pull outward on the tool a bit (photo 13-7) until there is a small amount of space between the gauge rod and the rim when you stop pulling. Reset the gauge rod against the rim and go around the arc again, checking the gauge spacing from the rim. If the distance from the rim to the gauge rod still varies, find the closest point again, bend outward on the tool there, and recheck around the rim again. Continue until it is as good as you can get it, accounting for the fact that there is some play in the tool and the wheel. You cannot get the accuracy down to the thousandths, or even hundredths of an inch; that kind of accuracy is unnecessary for a derailleur, anyway.

13.1F Checking a Frame after a Crash

If your frame has sustained damage in a crash, you do not want to ride it again, at least until you have assessed the damage and, if required, fixed it.

You should clean up the frame and then look for ripples, crimps, dents, stretched paint, and cracks, especially at the joints. You should also check the frame's alignment. Chapter 14 of *Zinn and the Art of Mountain Bike Maintenance* has detailed sections on frame inspection and checking alignment.

13.2 Tuning Rear Suspension

Everything I have said about front suspension applies equally to rear suspension. Please review Chapter 11 for an explanation of suspension spring rates, preload, compression damping, rebound damping, and so on. Many of the same recommendations for setting up forks apply to rear suspension as well.

These general recommendations apply to cross-country full-suspension bikes (photo 13-8) as well as to downhill versions (photo 13-9).

13.2A Evaluating a Swingarm's Working Condition

You can tell if your suspension needs some lubrication while the bike is standing still. Stand next to the bike, pull the rear brake and push down lightly on the saddle. *Gradually* increase the pressure; don't just push it hard! Notice how much pressure it takes before the bike finally compresses. If the swingarm does not compress as you push harder and harder, and then it finally goes down chunk, chunk, chunk, like a set of stairs, you've got a dry system. You need to clean and lubricate the pivots and the shock. There is no point to tuning the suspension until you have it moving smoothly.

If the swingarm begins compressing smoothly under a relatively gentle push, then you have a pretty clean, well-lubricated system.

13.2B Pivot Maintenance

Figure on cleaning and greasing pivot bushings after at least every 40 hours of riding. Inspect them for wear frequently. Check for wear by feeling for lateral play and binding with the shock deflated or disconnected. Check the bushings for scoring and ovalization, and lubricate any squeaky ones. Replace any worn bushings. All of this applies to pivot bearings as well, although they should wear longer than bushings as long as they are kept greased.

13.2C Testing Rear Suspension

Just as with your fork, you need to evaluate rear suspension performance objectively. Consistency is the key to separating out factors like course selection, speed, position, riding style, fatigue, and so on, to really be able to tell the difference between one suspension setup and another. Use the same test course you set up in Chapter 11, section 11.8 to evaluate your rear suspension. Ride the course with damping adjustments set on either extreme to see what they do.

As with a fork, make only one adjustment at a time.

13.2D Shock Types

Standard shock types are: *coil-over,* in which a coil spring surrounds a hydraulic damper/compressed air chamber; *elastomer-over,* which is the same thing with elastomer doughnuts surrounding it instead of a coil; *air-oil,* in which compressed air is the spring coupled to an oil damper; *air-air,* in which compressed air does the suspending as well as the damping; and *undamped* elastomers or coils.

13.2E Shock Maintenance

Keep the shock shaft, shaft seals, and bottom-out bumper clean. Clean them after every ride, but *do not* use high-pressure water on them.

Keep the bushings in the "eyes" (mounting holes on either end of the shock) clean and greased. Grease the bushings once a month and/or every 40 hours of riding.

Do a shock oil change at least once a year. The oil inside degrades over time, and damping is reduced. If you notice a damping loss, you need an oil change.

13.2F Sag

Sag, or ride height, is the amount the bike compresses when you just sit on it. Ride height is not dependent on damping because there is no movement involved; it is only dependent on spring rate and preload.

Sag is affected by changing your springs and/or your spring preload adjustment. A good rule of thumb is to set your springs so that sag uses up one-quarter of the bike's travel.

On a coil-over shock, measure the shock shaft when you are off the bike. Have someone else measure it again when you are sitting on it. If less than 75 percent of the shaft length is still showing, increase spring rate or preload. If more than 75 percent of the shaft length is showing, decrease spring rate or preload. You can also measure the travel and sag either with a zip tie around the shock body of air shocks or, with any shock, you can measure the height of the saddle above the ground at unloaded height, ride height, and full compression.

If you have used more than six preload turns of the spring collar to reach 25 percent travel usage in ride height, you need a stiffer spring.

Warning: Excessive preload on a soft spring can cause the spring to fail.

If preload is zero and you get 25 percent sag, you're there!

On steep downhill courses, more of your weight will be shifted to the front of the bike, so more sag in the rear is a good idea.

13.2G Front and Rear Compatibility (i.e., Balance)

If you have a full-suspension bike, you will want to have the front and rear suspension balanced so that everything is working together. Use the following procedure (stolen from Manitou's *Suspension Tuning for Performance Manual*) to determine whether or not the suspension is balanced reasonably well.

Hold the bike upright on level ground. While standing next to the bike, lightly pull on the front brake, place one foot on the pedal closest to you while the crank arm is at bottom dead center, and push down on the pedal with your foot. If the bike maintains a level attitude as the suspension is compressed, the spring rates are well balanced. Next, sit on the bike and take a riding posture. If one end drops noticeably more than the other, the front and rear are not compatible, and you need to readjust the spring preload and/or spring rate to achieve a better balance.

13.2H General Suspension Tuning Recommendations

These recommendations will look famil-

13-6
Checking derailleur hanger alignment with a Park alignment gauge. Swing the arm around, keeping the gauge rod lined up with the rim, and see if the spacing between the end of the gauge rod and the rim changes.

13-7
Aligning a bent derailleur hanger with a Park alignment gauge. Pull outward on the tool arm at the point where the gauge rod is closest to the rim.

13-9
Four-bar suspension system on a downhill bike.

iar if you read the front suspension chapter. They are also based on the rule of thumb that comes from the old moto-cross school: You want to bottom out a couple of times on the front and rear on a course. If the suspension is never bottoming out, the spring is too stiff or the compression damping is too high.

Make setting changes in small increments. It is easy to overadjust.

Make only one adjustment at a time.

Once you have balanced your front and rear end, any adjustment you make to the front you should also make to the rear, and vice versa.

Read your manual for your frame as well as for your shock adjustment methods and recommendations.

Suspension tuning is affected by: 1) rider weight, 2) rider ability, 3) riding speeds, 4) course conditions, 5) rider style, and 6) rider's position on the bike. If any or all of these things change, so should the tuning adjustments.

Soften up: Use the softest springs you can with little preload. You want to bottom out occasionally, but not frequently. If you are bottoming out too much, you need to change your compression damping or your spring rate. If the compression is slow, yet you are still bottoming out, your spring is too soft. You will feel beaten up on the intermediate hits, or, when bottoming out on a big hit, it will be harsh through the entire stroke. Stiffen the spring rate and lighten the compression damping. The ride height (again, you use up 25 percent of stroke when you sit on the bike) dictates some of your spring rate.

Preload makes the spring rate ramp up faster. If you can use a stiffer spring and back off on preload, you are a lot happier for it, and your spring life will be longer.

Lighten up: Set the *compression damping* to blow off quickly. Your plush spring won't bottom out harshly, anyway! The light compression damping should be set high enough that on big hits you use up all of your travel, but the bars are not smacking you in the hands when you hit bottom.

Tighten up the *compression damping* if you are blowing through the stroke and getting smacked in the hands too hard.

If you have no damping adjuster, you can play with oil viscosity. Find out what oil weight you have from your manual, the shock manufacturer, or a shop. Rely on manufacturer recommendations to help you decide on your new oil weight. Heavier oil slows the shock; lighter oil speeds it up. Changing the oil in your shock is a good idea, even if you like its performance. Replacing the oil is necessary periodically, since it breaks down with use, and there are little worn bits of your shock floating in it, sometimes even on a new shock. Using lighter oil in winter and heavier in summer is also a good policy.

Lighten up the *rebound damping* to return as quickly as possible without pogoing.

You want a lively rebound, since a sluggish return will allow the suspension to pack up (as you go over stutter bumps, water bars, or closely spaced rocks, the bike will ride lower and lower). On soft ground, more rebound damping may make for better traction.

Again, if you have no damping adjuster, change your oil viscosity. Change the oil in your shock to a heavier weight to slow it down. Conversely, lighten the damping up with lighter oil, especially in winter.

Tighten up the *rebound damping* if the bike springs back too fast. The rebound should not be so light that you are getting bounced. Tighten it up for climbs, if you have a quick adjuster.

Speed up: Rebound and compression damping are speed-sensitive in a good shock. Don't worry about settings that feel good at low speeds being too light for high speeds; the shock will get stiffer as you hit things faster. At all speeds, you want the shock to pop back as quickly as possible without kicking back.

Heat up: Damping is temperature sensitive. Oil is thick and sluggish in the cold, but when it gets hot, your shock gets really lively. You will need to adjust accordingly in summer, with stiffer springs and firmer damping adjustments.

Cool off: You can lighten up your springs and damping adjustments even more in the cold of winter. Your overall speeds are slower, the grease and oil in the shock are thicker, and elastomer-over and coil-over springs will be stiffer. Lighter oil in the shock will help.

13.21 On-the-Fly Rebound Damping Adjustment

If you can adjust your rear suspension rebound on the fly, turn it up when you climb. It does not need to throw you up as much when you hit things, as you are going much slower, anyway. You will climb much faster this way. Some shocks have a shifter-operated damping lockout that is really key for this purpose.

Reduce the rebound damping when you head back down.

13.2J Downhill Adjustment Recommendations

Again, you are looking for a setup in which your front and rear shocks bottom out on the biggest bump on the course *at race speed.*

On *rougher courses,* increasing spring rate (or preload) will keep you from bottoming out so much. Compensate for small bumps by reducing rebound damping to keep the shock from packing in on successive hits. If the bike is bucking, increase damping a bit.

On *smoother courses,* try decreasing spring rate (or preload) and increasing damping. Negotiating turns will usually be the major challenge, and the lower ride height (sag) provided by the softer springs will keep you closer to the ground. The greater sag will also increase the amount of negative fork travel (the amount the wheel can go *down*) available, which will help maintain tire traction in turns and when braking. Higher compression damping, while making the shock absorption slower, will still be fast enough to deal with isolated bumps, and it will eliminate harshest bottoming out. Higher rebound damping will reduce the bouncing of the bike after the isolated bumps.

Where there is no general rough or smooth characterization of the course, set up your suspension to perform best on the sections in which you have the most trouble for the most elapsed time. In other words, don't set it up ideally for a tricky section you get through in a couple seconds; set it up for a challenging section on which you will spend half a minute.

13.2K Tearing Apart a Shock

Many mechanics who are great at mechanical systems are leery of hydraulic items like shocks. Hydraulic systems are often a simpler means of accomplishing the same thing that would require a zillion different parts from a mechanical system. Once people get inside a rear shock, they are often amazed at how few parts there are. Just make sure you use your manual and keep track of all of those parts!

As with fork dampers, shim stacks on shock pistons can be changed to alter damping.

Replacement oil and springs can be obtained at many bike shops. So can knowledgeable shock service.

Special tools are recommended for many shock services, such as replacing air valves, glide rings, shaft bushings, shaft seals, and pivot eye bushings. It may not make sense for you to own these tools, in which case a good relationship with a shock-literate shop is in order.

13.2L Changing Suspension Travel

Many full-suspension frames allow for adjustment of the travel without switching to a different shock by attaching the shock in a different spot. Some bikes have oval shock mounts with an offset hole. Reversing the holes changes the travel.

Similarly, bottom bracket height and head angle can be changed by varying the shock mount as well.

Note **Sometimes bucking can be caused by too much damping, not just by too little. Heavily damped shocks will respond so slowly that they will pack in over repeated bumps, giving you a rigid bike and low ride height.**

13-8
Unified rear triangle full-suspension design for cross-country.

14

SCHOOLS OF BICYCLE MECHANICS, FRAME BUILDING, AND RIDING AND RACING SKILLS

To further hone your wrenchin'—and ridin'—skills, you may want to consider one of the following mechanical courses or an off-road riding school. Food and lodging are included with longer courses at most schools.

14.1 PROFESSIONAL BIKE MECHANICS AND FRAME BUILDING SCHOOLS

Barnett's Bicycle Institute

Classes range from one-day frame preparation and machining courses and two-day wheel-building classes up to 23-day intensive classes. Students can take sets of classes depending on interests.

Mechanical certification available.

Proprietor: John Barnett

Prices: Range from $120 for one-day classes to $1,550 for 23-day courses, plus price of Barnett's manual textbook ($150)

Contact: B.B.I., 2755 Ore Mill Dr., #14, Colorado Springs, CO 80904-3162, 719/632-5173, fax 719/632-4607; e-mail: bbinstitute@juno.com; website: www.bbinstitute.com

CABDA Service School

CABDA stands for Chicago Area Bicycle Dealer's Association.

Complete mechanical class is five days long. All other classes are two-day weekend courses.

No certification courses, but students do get a pass/fail certificate.

Instructor: Vance Blume

Prices: $195 for weekend courses; $495 for five-day courses.

Contact: CABDA, 18440 Governor's Hwy, Homewood, IL 60430; 708/798-2004, fax 708/798-2208; website: www.cabda.com

United Bicycle Institute

Mechanics classes, certification classes, and frame building classes.

Most classes last two weeks, but are offered back to back so students can take classes for one month.

DT wheel-building certification course.

Students are tested to receive certifications.

Two steel frame-building classes and a titanium frame-building class. All frame-building classes are two weeks long, and students complete a frame during the course.

Proprietor: Ron Sutphin

Prices: Ten different classes ranging from $375 for three-day bicycle assembly class to $2,500 for titanium frame-building class.

Contact: U.B.I., 423 Williamson Way, P.O. Box 128, Ashland, OR 97520; 541/488-1121, fax 541/488-3485; website: www.bikeschool.com

14.2 RIDING TECHNIQUE SCHOOLS AND COURSES

Bicycling in Balance

Full mountain bike skills instruction including innovative balance-enhancing techniques that quickly and dramatically increase confidence, skill, and safety whether racing or riding off-road. All skill levels welcome.

Blair Lombardi is unique in offering classes that teach a rider of any skill level to use and understand their body's inherent balance mechanisms for mountain bike riding. Novice riders leave with professional cornering and descending skills after three private lessons.

Private and group classes, two-day clinics in Marin County and ongoing group classes at Marin Recreation Center are offered.

Students receive pocket lesson books.

Proprietor: Blair Lombardi

Prices: Private lessons: $200 for three two-hour classes. Groups of over three: $160/person for four-to-six two-hour classes.

Contact: Bicycling in Balance, 169 Los Angeles Blvd., San Anselmo, CA 94960; 415/456-4251; e-mail: inbalance@earthlink.net; website: http://home.earthlink.net/~inbalance/

Dirt Camp

Courses ranging from one-hour lessons to half-day clinics to week-long camps.

Junior development camps and racing camps are offered.

Certification courses offered in conjunction with IMBA to train and certify mountain bike instructors and guides.

Proprietor: Dan Pullman

Prices: Ranging from a $25 group rate for a one-hour class up to $1,350 for a week-long camp.

Contact: Dirt Camp, 120 Old Ridgefield Rd., Wilton, CT 06897; 800/711-3478 (800/711-DIRT), or 203/762-9199; fax 203/762-5421; website: www.dirt-camp.com/mtb

John Howard School of Champions

Two-day courses to five-day camps with John Howard, a many-time national and world champion in road, mountain bike, and triathlon.

Proprietor: John Howard

Prices: $125–$895

Contact: J.H.S.O.C., 1705 Old Mill Rd., Encinitas, CA 92024; phone/fax 760/944-3787; e-mail: jhschool@aol.com

West Coast School of Mountain Biking

Day camps and clinics, and three- and four-day camps, including women's camps and youth camps.

Proprietor: Joan Jones

Prices: Day clinics: up to $120; camps: $350–$465

Contact: W.C.S.M.B., P.O. Box 64160, Kluge Rd., Coquitlam, B.C. Canada V3J7V6; 604/931-6066, FAX 604/931-7433; e-mail: wcsmb@rogers.wave.ca; website: home.bc.rogers.wave.ca/wcsmb

W.O.M.B. (Women On Mountain Bikes)

One and two-day clinics for women (and men) on riding skills, basic mechanics, safety, and fitness.

Proprietor: Andrea Tollefsrud

Prices: $25–$40

Contact: W.O.M.B., P.O. Box 4148, Boulder, CO 80306; 303/494-7062; e-mail: atmtnbike@aol.com

W.O.M.B.A.T.S. Camp

Beginning in 1984, the first mountain bike camps were camps for women founded by former national and world mountain bike champion Jacquie Phelan who founded W.O.M.B.A.T.S. (Women's Mountain Bike and Tea Society) in 1986. W.O.M.B.A.T.S. is intended to increase the enjoyment of mountain biking for women. Courses are available in many parts of the U.S. and Canada for four to five days.

Prices: Starting at $600.

Contact: W.O.M.B.A.T.S., P.O. Box 757, Dept. C, Fairfax, CA 94978; 415/459-0980, fax 415/459-0832; e-mail: jacquie@batnet.com; website: www.wombats.org

Note: Some ski resorts also offer mountain biking skills courses during the summer.

APPENDICES

Appendix A: Troubleshooting

This index is intended to assist you in finding and fixing problems. If you already know wherein the problem lies, consult the Contents for the chapter covering that part of the bike. If you are not sure which part of the bike is affected, this index can be of assistance. It is organized alphabetically, but, since people's descriptions of the same problem vary, you may need to look through the entire list to find your symptom.

This index can assist you with a diagnosis and can recommend a course of action.

SYMPTOM	LIKELY CAUSES	ACTION
bent wheel	1. misadjusted spokes 2. broken spoke 3. bent rim	true wheel replace spoke replace rim
bike pulls to one side	1. wheels not true 2. tight headset 3. pitted headset 4. bent frame 5. bent fork 6. loose hub bearings 7. tire pressure really low	true wheels adjust headset replace headset replace or straighten frame replace or straighten fork adjust hubs inflate tires
bike shimmies at high speed	1. frame cracked 2. frame bent 3. wheels way out of true 4. loose hub bearings 5. headset too loose 6. flexible frame/heavy rider	replace frame replace or straighten frame true wheels adjust hubs tighten headset replace frame
bike vibrates when braking	see chattering and vibration when braking under "strange noises" below	
brake doesn't stop bike	1. misadjusted brake 2. worn brake pads 3. greasy rims 4. sticky brake cable 5. steel rims in wet weather 6. brake damaged 7. sticky or bent brake lever 8. air in hydraulic brake lines 9. disc brake pads worn through	adjust brake replace pads clean rims lube or replace cable use aluminum rims replace brake lube or replace lever bleed brake lines replace disc brake pads
chain falls off in front	1. misadjusted front derailleur 2. chain line off 3. chainring bent or loose	adjust front derailleur adjust chain line replace or tighten
chain jams in front between chainring and chain stay —called *chain suck*	1. dirty chain 2. bent chainring teeth 3. chain too narrow 4. chain line off 5. stiff links in chain	clean chain replace chainring replace chain adjust chain line free links, lube chain
chain jams in rear	1. misadjusted rear derailleur 2. chain too wide 3. small cog not on spline 4. poor frame clearance	adjust derailleur replace chain re-seat cogs return to dealer
chain skips	1. worn chain 2. misadjusted derailleur 3. worn rear cogs 4. dirty or rusted chain 5. tight chain link 6. bent rear derailleur 7. bent derailleur hanger 8. loose derailleur jockey wheels 9. bent chain link 10. sticky rear shift cable	replace chain adjust derailleur replace cogs and chain clean or replace chain loosen tight link replace derailleur straighten hanger tighten jockey wheels replace chain replace shift cable
chain slaps chainstay	1. chain too long 2. weak rear derailleur spring 3. terrain very bumpy	shorten chain replace spring or derailleur ignore noise
derailleur hits spokes	1. misadjusted rear derailleur 2. broken spoke 3. bent rear derailleur 4. bent derailleur hanger	adjust derailleur replace spoke replace derailleur straighten or replace
knee pain	1. poor shoe cleat position 2. saddle too low or high 3. foot rolled in or out	reposition cleat adjust saddle replace shoes or get orthotics
pain or fatigue when riding, particularly in the back, neck, and arms	1. incorrect seat position 2. too much riding 3. incorrect stem length or angle 4. poor frame fit 5. incorrect stem height	adjust seat position build up miles gradually replace stem replace frame adjust stem height
pedal(s) move laterally, clunk or twist while pedaling	1. loose crank arm 2. pedal loose in crank arm 3. bent pedal axle 4. loose bottom bracket 5. bent bottom-bracket axle or axle 6. bent crank arm 7. loose pedal bearings	tighten crank bolt tighten pedal to crank replace pedal or axle adjust bottom bracket replace bottom bracket replace crank arm adjust pedal bearings
pedal entry difficult (clip-in pedals)	1. mud-clogged cleat 2. release tension set high 3. shoe sole knobs too tall 4. cleat guide on pedal loose or gone 5. cleat loose	clean cleat reduce release tension trim knobs tighten or replace tighten cleat bolts
pedal release difficult (clip-in pedals)	1. release tension set high 2. loose cleat on shoe 3. dry pedal spring pivots 4. dirty pedals 5. bent pedal clips 6. dirty cleats 7. cleat worn	reduce release tension tighten cleat oil spring pivots clean and lube pedals replace pedals or clips clean, lube cleats replace cleat
pedal release too easy (clip-in pedals)	1. release tension set too low 2. cleats worn out 3. pedal worn out or broken	increase release tension replace cleats replace pedal
rear shifting working poorly	1. misadjusted derailleur 2. sticky or damaged cable 3. loose rear cogs 4. worn rear cogs 5. stretched/damaged chain 6. see also *chain jams in rear* and *chain skips* above	adjust derailleur replace cable seat and tighten cogs replace cogs replace chain
resistance (while coasting or pedaling)	1. tire rubs frame or fork or true wheel 2. brake drags on rim	make axle adjustments adjust brake

	3. tire pressure really low	inflate tire
	4. hub bearings too tight	adjust hubs
	5. hub bearings dirty/worn	overhaul hubs
	6. mud packed around tires	clean bike
resistance (while pedaling only)	1. bottom bracket too tight	adjust bottom bracket
	2. bottom bracket dirty/worn	overhaul bottom bracket
	3. chain dry/dirty/rusted	clean/lube or replace
	4. pedal bearings too tight	adjust pedal bearings
	5. pedal bearings dirty/worn	overhaul pedals
	6. bent chainring rubs frame	straighten or replace
	7. chainring rubs frame	adjust chain line

STRANGE NOISES

Weird noises can be hard to locate; use this to assist in locating them.

SYMPTOM	LIKELY CAUSES	ACTION
chattering and vibration when braking	1. bent or dented rim	replace rim
	2. loose headset	adjust headset
	3. brake pads toed out	adjust brake pads
	4. wheel way out of round	true wheel
	5. greasy sections of rim	clean rim
	6. loose brake pivot bolts	tighten brake bolts
	7. flexible seat stays	use brake booster plate
clicking noise	1. cracked shoe cleats	replace cleats
	2. cracked shoe sole	replace shoes
	3. loose bottom bracket	tighten bottom bracket
	4. loose crank arm	tighten crank arm
	5. loose pedal	tighten pedal
creaking noise	1. dry handlebar/stem joint	put grease inside stem clamp
	2. loose seatpost	tighten seatpost
	3. loose shoe cleats	tighten cleats
	4. loose crank arm	tighten crank arm bolt
	5. cracked frame	replace frame
	6. dry, rusty seatpost	grease seatpost
	7. cartridge BB moving inside threaded cup	smear grease inside cup
	8. see *squeaking noise* below	see *squeaking noise* below
rubbing or scraping noise when pedaling	1. crossed chain	avoid extreme gears
	2. front derailleur rubbing	adjust front derailleur
	3. chainring rubs frame	longer bottom bracket *or,* move bottom bracket over
rubbing or scraping noise (when coasting)	1. tire dragging on frame	straighten wheel
	2. tire dragging on fork	straighten wheel
	3. mud packed around tires	clean bike
	4. brake dragging on rim	adjust rim
	5. dry hub dust covers	clean and lube
squeaking noise	1. dry hub or BB bearings	overhaul hubs or BB
	2. dry pedal bushings	overhaul pedals
	3. squeaky saddle	replace saddle
	4. dry suspension pivots	overhaul suspension
	5. rusted or dry chain	lube or replace chain
	6. dry suspension fork	overhaul fork
	7. dry suspension seatpost	overhaul seatpost
squealing noise when braking	1. brake pads toed out	adjust brake pads
	2. greasy rims	clean rims and pads
	3. loose brake arms	tighten brake arms
	4. flexible seat stays	use brake booster plate

Appendix B: Gear Development

The gear table on the following page is based on a 26-inch (66-cm) tire diameter. Your gear development numbers may be slightly different if the diameter of your rear tire, at inflation, with your weight on it, is not 26 inches. Unless your bike has 24-inch wheels or some other nonstandard size, these numbers will be very close.

If you want to have totally accurate gear development numbers for the tire you happen to have on at the time, at a certain inflation pressure, then you can measure the tire diameter very precisely using the procedure below. You can come up with your own gear chart by plugging your tire diameter into the following gear development formula, or by multiplying each number in this chart by the ratio of your tire diameter divided by 26 inches (the tire diameter we used).

CHAINRING TEETH

COG TEETH	20	22	24	26	28	30	32	34	36	38	39	40	41	42	43	44	45	46	47	48	49	50	51	52	53	COG TEETH
11	47	52	57	61	66	71	76	80	85	90	92	95	97	99	102	104	106	109	111	113	116	118	121	123	125	**11**
12	43	48	52	56	61	65	69	74	78	82	84	87	89	91	93	95	97	100	102	104	106	108	111	113	115	**12**
13	40	44	48	52	56	60	64	68	72	76	78	80	82	84	86	88	90	92	94	96	98	100	102	104	106	**13**
14	37	41	45	48	52	56	60	63	67	70	72	74	76	78	80	82	84	85	87	89	91	93	95	97	98	**14**
15	35	38	42	45	49	52	55	59	62	66	68	69	71	73	75	76	78	80	81	83	85	87	88	90	92	**15**
16	33	36	39	42	45	49	52	55	58	61	63	65	67	68	70	72	73	75	76	78	80	81	83	85	86	**16**
17	31	34	37	40	43	46	49	52	55	58	60	61	63	64	66	67	69	70	72	73	75	76	78	80	81	**17**
18	29	32	35	38	40	43	46	49	52	55	56	58	59	61	62	64	65	66	68	69	71	72	74	75	77	**18**
19	27	30	33	36	38	41	44	47	49	52	53	55	56	57	59	60	62	63	64	66	67	68	70	71	73	**19**
20	26	29	31	34	36	39	42	44	47	49	51	52	53	55	56	57	59	60	61	62	64	65	66	68	69	**20**
21	25	27	30	32	35	37	40	42	45	47	48	50	51	52	53	54	56	57	58	59	61	62	63	64	66	**21**
22	24	26	28	31	33	35	38	40	43	45	46	47	48	50	51	52	53	54	56	57	58	59	60	61	63	**22**
23	23	25	27	29	32	34	36	38	41	43	44	45	46	47	49	50	51	52	53	54	55	57	58	59	60	**23**
24	22	24	26	28	30	32	35	37	39	41	42	43	44	45	47	48	49	50	51	52	53	54	55	56	57	**24**
25	21	23	25	27	29	31	33	35	37	39	41	42	43	44	45	46	47	48	49	50	51	52	53	54	55	**25**
26	20	22	24	26	28	30	32	34	36	38	39	40	41	42	43	44	45	46	47	48	49	50	51	52	53	**26**
27	19	21	23	25	27	29	31	33	35	37	38	39	39	40	41	42	43	44	45	46	47	48	49	50	51	**27**
28	18	20	22	24	26	28	30	32	33	35	36	37	38	39	40	41	42	43	44	45	46	46	47	48	49	**28**
30	17	19	21	23	24	26	28	29	31	33	34	35	36	36	37	38	39	40	41	42	42	43	44	45	46	**30**
32	16	18	20	21	23	24	26	28	29	31	32	33	33	34	35	35	37	37	38	39	40	41	41	42	43	**32**
34	15	17	18	20	21	23	24	26	28	29	30	31	31	32	33	33	34	35	36	37	37	38	39	40	41	**34**
38	14	16	16	18	19	21	22	23	25	26	27	27	28	29	29	30	31	31	32	32	33	34	35	36	36	**38**
	20	**22**	**24**	**26**	**28**	**30**	**32**	**34**	**36**	**38**	**39**	**40**	**41**	**42**	**43**	**44**	**45**	**46**	**47**	**48**	**49**	**50**	**51**	**52**	**53**	

CHAINRING TEETH

Measure Diameter of Your Tire

1. Sit on the bike with your tire pumped to your desired pressure.
2. Mark the spot on the rear rim that is at the bottom, and mark the floor adjacent to that spot.
3. Roll forward one wheel revolution, and mark the floor again where the mark on the rim is again at the bottom.
4. Measure the distance between the marks on the floor; this is the tire circumference at pressure with your weight on it.
5. Divide this number by π (3.14159) to get the weighted wheel diameter.

Note: *This roll-out procedure is also the method to measure the wheel size with which to calibrate your bike computer, except you do it on the front wheel with most computers.*

The formula is:

Gear development = (number of teeth on chainring) x (wheel diameter) ÷ (number of teeth on rear cog)

To find out how far you get with each pedal stroke in a given gear, multiply the gear development by 3.14159265 (π).

Appendix C: Bike Fit

Mountain Bike Fitting

If you are getting a new bike, you might as well get one that fits you properly. The simple need to protect your more sensitive parts should keep you away from a bike without sufficient stand-over clearance, but there are a lot of other factors to consider as well. You need to make certain that your bike has enough reach to ensure that you don't bang your knees on the handlebar; you also need to check that your weight is properly distributed over the wheels so that you don't end up going over the handlebars on downhills or unweighting the front end on steep climbs. An improperly sized bike will cause you to ride with less efficiency and more discomfort. So take some time and find out how you can pick the properly sized bike.

I've outlined two methods for finding your frame size. The first is a simple method of checking your fit to fully assembled bikes at your local bike shop. The second is a bit more elaborate, since it involves taking body measurements. This more detailed approach will allow you to calculate the proper frame dimensions whether the bike is assembled or not.

Selecting the Size of a Built-Up Bike

Stand-over Height

Stand over the bike's top tube and lift the bike straight up until the top tube hits your crotch. The wheels should be at least 2 inches off the ground to ensure that you can jump off the bike safely without hitting your crotch. There is no maximum dimension here. If you have 5 inches of stand-over height or more, that is fine, as long as the top tube is long enough for you and the handlebar height can be set properly for you.

Note: If you have 2 inches of stand-over clearance over one bike, do not assume that another bike with the same listed frame size will also offer you the same stand-over clearance.

Manufacturers measure frame size using a variety of methods. They also slope their top tubes differently, and use different bottom bracket heights, all of which affect the final stand-over height.

All manufacturers measure the frame size up the seat tube from the center of the bottom bracket, but the top of the measurement varies. Some manufacturers measure to the center of the top tube ("center-to-center" measurement), some measure to the top of the top tube ("center-to-top"), and others measure to the top of the seat tube (also called "center-to-top"), even though there is wide variation in the length of the seatpost collar above the top tube. Obviously, each of these methods will give you a different "frame size" for the same frame.

No matter how the frame size is measured, the stand-over height of a bike depends on the slope of the top tube. Top tubes that slant up to the front are common, so stand-over clearance is obviously a function of where you are standing. With an up-angled top tube, stand over it a few inches forward of the nose of the saddle, and then lift the bike up into your crotch to measure stand-over clearance.

A bike with a suspension fork will have a higher front end than a bike with a rigid fork would, since the suspension fork has to allow for travel. This makes it difficult even to compare listed frame sizes from the same manufacturer to determine stand-over height.

Stand-over height is also a function of bottom bracket height above the ground. There is substantial variation here, especially with bikes with rear suspension whose bottom brackets are often very high so that ground clearance is still sufficient when the suspension is fully compressed.

Unless the manufacturer lists the stand-over height in its brochure and you know your inseam length, you need to actually stand over the bike.

Another note: If you are short and cannot find a frame size small enough for you to get at least 2 inches of stand-over clearance, consider a bike with 24-inch wheels instead of 26-inch.

Knee-to-Handlebar Clearance

With one foot on the ground and one foot on the pedal, make sure your knee cannot hit the handlebar. Do this standing out of the saddle as well as seated and with the front wheel turned slightly, to make sure that the knee will not hit when you are in the most awkward pedaling position you might use.

Handlebar Reach and Drop

Ride the bike. See if the reach feels comfortable to you when grabbing the bars or the bar ends. Make sure it is easy to grab the brake levers. Ensure that your knees do not hit your elbows as you pedal. And be sure that the stem can be raised or lowered enough to achieve a comfortable handlebar height for you.

Note: Check that your toe does not hit the front tire.

Choosing a Frame Size Based on Your Body Measurements

You will need a second person to assist you.

By taking three easy measurements, most people can get a very good frame fit. When designing a custom frame, I go through a more complex procedure than this, involving more measurements. For picking an off-the-shelf bike, this method works well.

Measure Your Inseam

Spread your stocking feet about 2 inches apart, and measure up from the floor to a broomstick held level and lifted firmly up into your crotch. You can also use a large book and slide it up a wall to keep the top edge horizontal—as you pull it up as hard as you can—into your crotch. You can mark the top of the book on the wall and measure up from the floor to the mark.

Measure Your Inseam Plus Torso Length

Hold a pencil horizontally in your sternal notch, the U-shaped bone depression just below your Adam's Apple. Standing up straight in front of a wall, mark the wall with the horizontal pencil. Measure up from the floor to the mark.

Measure Your Arm Length

Hold your arm out from your side at a 45-degree angle with your elbow straight. Measure from the sharp bone point directly behind your shoulder joint to the wrist bone on your little finger side.

Find Your Frame Seat Tube Length

Subtract 34 cm to 42 cm (13.5 inches to 16.5 inches) from your inseam length. This length is your frame size measured from the center of the bottom bracket to the top of a horizontal top tube. If the frame you are interested in has a sloping top tube, you need a bike with an even shorter seat-tube length. With a sloping-top-tube bike, project a horizontal line back to the seat tube (or seatpost) from the top of the top tube at the center of its length. Mark the seat tube or seatpost at this line. Measure from the center of the bottom bracket to this mark; this length should be 34 cm to 42 cm less than your inseam measurement.

Also, if the bike has a bottom bracket higher than 29 cm (11 1/2 inches), subtract the additional bottom-bracket height over 29 cm from the seat-tube length as well.

Generally, smaller riders will want to subtract close to 34 cm from their inseam, while taller riders will subtract closer to 40 cm. There is considerable range here. The top-tube length is more important in a frame than any specific "frame size," and if you have a short torso and arms, you can use a small frame to get the right top-tube length as long as you can raise your bars as high as you need them.

You really want to make sure you have plenty of stand-over clearance, so do not subtract less than 34 cm from your inseam for your seat-tube length; this should ensure at least 2 inches (5 cm) of stand-over clearance. If you are short and cannot find a bike small enough for you to get at least 2 inches of stand-over clearance, consider one with 24-inch wheels instead of 26-inch ones.

Find Your Top-Tube Length

To find your torso length, subtract your inseam measurement from your inseam-plus-torso measurement. Add this torso length to your arm length measurement. To find the top-tube length, multiply this arm-plus-torso measurement by a factor in the range between 0.47 and 0.5. If you are a casual rider, use 0.47; if you are a very aggressive rider, use 0.5; and if you are in between, use a factor in between. This top-tube length is measured horizontally from the center of the seat tube to the center of the head tube. Obviously, the horizontal top-tube length is more than the length measured along the top tube on a sloping top-tube bike.

Find Your Stem Length

Multiply the arm-plus-torso length you found in step 5 by 0.10 up to 0.14 to find the stem length. Again, a casual rider will multiply by 0.10 or so, while an aggressive rider will multiply by closer to 0.14. This is a starting stem length. Make your final decision on the stem length once you are sitting on the bike and can see what feels best.

Positioning of Your Saddle and Handlebars

The frame fit is only part of the equation. Except for the stand-over clearance, a good frame fit is relatively meaningless if the seat setback, seat height, handlebar height, and handlebar reach are not set correctly for you.

Saddle Height

When your foot is at the bottom of the stroke, lock your knee without rocking your hips. Do this sitting on your bike on a trainer with someone else observing. Your foot should be level, or the heel should be slightly higher than the ball of the foot. Another way to determine seat height is to take your inseam measurement (found under "Choosing a Frame Size Based on Your Body Measurements," above) and multiply it by 1.09; this is the length from the center of the pedal spindle (when the pedal is down) to one of the points on the top of the saddle where your butt bones (ischial tuberosities) contact it. Adjust the seat height (Chapter 10) until you get it to the proper height.

Note: These two methods yield similar results, although the measurement-multiplying method is dependent on shoe sole and pedal thicknesses. Both methods yield a biomechanically efficient pedaling position, but if you do a lot of technical riding and descending, you may wish to have a lower saddle for better bike-handling control.

Saddle Setback

Sit on your bike on a stationary trainer with your cranks horizontal and your foot at the angle it is at that point when pedaling. Have a friend drop a plumb line from the front of your knee below your kneecap. You can use a heavy ring, washer, or some similar weight tied to a string for the plumb line. The plumb line should bisect the pedal axle or pass up to 2 cm behind it (you will need to lean the knee out to get the string to hang clear). A saddle centered in this manner encourages smooth pedaling at high rpms, while 2 cm behind the pedal spindle encourages powerful seated climbing.

You may want to move your saddle a bit forward of this if you have trouble keeping your front wheel down on steep climbs. Your upper body may relax more on steep climbs with this more forward position.

Slide the saddle back and forth on the seatpost until you achieve the desired fore-aft saddle position. Set the saddle level or very close to it. Recheck the seat height in Step 1 above, since fore-aft saddle movements affect seat-to-pedal distance as well.

Handlebar Height

Measure the handlebar height relative to the saddle height by measuring the vertical distance of the saddle and bar up from the floor. How much higher the saddle is than your bar (or vice versa) depends on your flexibility, riding style, overall size, and the type of riding you prefer.

Aggressive and tall cross-country riders will prefer to have their saddle 10 cm or more higher than the bars. Shorter riders will want proportionately less drop, as will less-aggressive riders. Riders doing lots of downhills will want their bars higher; downhill racers often have no drop from saddle to bar, and mountain bike slalom riders' bars are usually higher than their saddles. Generally, people beginning mountain-bike riding will like their bars high and can lower them as they become more comfortable with the bike, with going fast, and with riding more technical terrain.

If in doubt, start with 4 cm of drop and vary it from there. The higher the bar, the greater the tendency is for the front wheel to pull up off the ground when climbing, and the more wind resistance you can expect. Change the bar height by raising or lowering the stem or by switching stems and/or bars.

Setting Handlebar Reach

The reach from the saddle to the handlebar is also very dependent on personal preference. More-aggressive riders will want a more stretched-out position than will casual riders. This length is subjective, and I find that I need to look at the rider on the bike and get a feel for how he or she would be comfortable and efficient.

A useful starting place is to drop a plumb line from the back of your elbow with your arms bent in a comfortable riding position. This plane determined by your elbows and the plumb line should be 2 cm to 4 cm horizontally ahead of each knee at the point in the pedal stroke when the crank arm is horizontal-forward. The idea is to select a position you find comfortable and efficient; listen to what your body wants.

Vary the saddle-to-bar distance by changing stem length, not by changing the seat setback position, which is based on pedaling efficiency and not on reach.

Note: *There is no single formula for determining handlebar reach and height. I can tell you that using the method of placing your elbow against the saddle and seeing if your fingertips reach the handlebar is close to useless. Similarly, the oft-suggested method of seeing if the handlebar obscures your vision of the front hub is not worth the brief time it takes to look, being dependent on elbow bend and front-end geometry. Another method involving dropping a plumb bob from the rider's nose is dependent on the handlebar height and elbow bend and thus does not lend itself to a well-defined relationship for all riders.*

Bar-End Position

The bar ends should be set in a range between horizontal and pointing up 15 degrees. Find the position you find comfortable for pulling on when climbing standing or seated, and for when pedaling seated for long stretches on paved roads.

Note: Do not use the bar ends to raise your hand position by pointing them vertically up. If you want a higher hand position, get a taller or more up-angled stem, and/or a higher-rise handlebar. Bar ends are not meant to be stood straight up and held on to for cruising along sitting up high; that is the mountain bike equivalent of flipping a road drop bar upside down to lift the hands. As with the road bar equivalent, you cannot reach the brakes when you need them.

Appendix D: Glossary

adjustable cup: the non-drive-side cup in the bottom bracket. This cup is removed for maintenance of the bottom-bracket spindle and bearings, and it adjusts the bearings. Term sometimes applied to top headset cup as well.

AheadSet: a style of headset that allows the use of a fork with a threadless steering tube.

Allen key (Allen wrench, hex key): a hexagonal wrench that fits inside the head of the bolt.

anchor bolt ("cable anchor," "cable-fixing bolt"): a bolt securing a cable to a component.

axle: the shaft about which a part turns, usually on bearings or bushings.

axle overlock dimension: the length of a hub axle from dropout to dropout, referring to the distance from locknut face to locknut face.

b knuckle: the upper pivot on a rear derailleur containing the derailleur hanger bolt.

barrel adjuster: a threaded cable stop that allows for fine adjustment of cable tension. Barrel adjusters are commonly found on rear derailleurs, shifters, and brake levers.

BB: (see "bottom bracket").

bearing: a unit that by rolling reduces friction between two surfaces.

binder bolt: a bolt clamping a seatpost in a frame, a bar end to a handlebar, a handlebar inside a stem, or a threadless steering tube inside a stem clamp.

bottom bracket (BB): the assembly that allows the crank to rotate. Generally, the bottom bracket assembly includes bearings, an axle, a fixed cup, an adjustable cup, and a lock ring.

bottom-bracket shell: the cylindrical housing at the bottom of a bicycle frame through which the bottom-bracket axle passes.

bottom-out: the point at which a suspension fork or swingarm will not compress any further.

brake boss (brake post or pivot; cantilever boss, post, or pivot): a fork- or frame-mounted pivot for a brake arm.

brake caliper: the part of a brake that contains the brake pads and squeezes them against the braking surface.

brake modulation: the ability to easily alter the braking force during braking.

brake pad (brake block): a block of rubber or similar material used to slow the bike by creating friction on the rim or other braking surface.

brake post: (see "brake boss").

brake shoe: the metal pad holder that holds the brake pad to the brake arm.

braze-on: a generic term for most metal frame attachments, even those welded or glued on.

brazing: a method commonly used to construct steel bicycle frames. Brazing involves the use of brass or silver solder to connect frame tubes and attach various "braze-on" items including brake bosses, cable guides, and rack mounts to the frame.

bushing: a metal or plastic sleeve that acts as a simple bearing in pedals, suspension forks, suspension swing arms, and jockey wheels.

butted tubing: a common type of frame tubing with varying wall thicknesses. Butted tubing is designed to accommodate high stress points at the ends of the tube by being thicker there.

cable (inner wire): wound or braided wire strands used to operate brakes and derailleurs.

cable anchor: (see "anchor bolt").

cable end: a cap on the end of a cable to keep it from fraying.

cable-fixing bolt: (see "anchor bolt").

cable hanger: cable stop on a fork- or seat-stay arch used to stop the brake cable housing for a cantilever or U-brake.

cable housing: a metal-reinforced exterior sheath through which a cable passes.

cable housing stop: (see "cable stop").

cable stop: a fitting on the frame, fork, or stem at which a cable housing segment terminates.

cage: two guiding plates through which the chain travels. Both the front and rear derailleurs have cages. The cage on the rear also holds the jockey pulleys.

caliper: (see "brake caliper").

cantilever boss: (see "brake boss").

cantilever brake: a brake that relies on tension in a straddle cable to move two opposing arms, pivoting on frame- or fork-mounted posts, toward the braking surface of the rim.

cantilever pivot: (see "brake boss").

cantilever post: (see "brake boss").

cartridge bearing: ball bearings encased in a cartridge consisting of steel inner and outer rings, ball retainers, and sometimes bearing covers.

cartridge damper: a self-enclosed suspension damping unit that controls the spring movement.

cassette hub: a rear hub that has a built-in freewheel mechanism. Also called a "freehub."

chain: a series of metal links held together by pins and used to transmit energy from the crank to the rear wheel.

chain line: the imaginary line connecting the center of the middle chainring with the middle of the cogset. This line should in theory be straight and parallel with the vertical plane passing through the center of the bicycle. This is measured as the distance from the center of the seat tube to the center of the middle chainring (an easy way to measure this is to measure from the left side of the seat tube to the outside of the large chainring, measure the distance from the right side of the seat tube to the inside of the inner chainring, add these two measurements, and divide the sum by two).

chain link: a single unit of bicycle chain consisting of four plates with a roller on each end and one in the center.

chainring: a multiple tooth sprocket attached to the right crankarm.

chainring-nut spanner: a tool used to secure the chainring nuts while tightening the chainring bolts.

chainstays: the tubes leading from the bottom bracket shell to the rear hub axle.

chain suck: the dragging of the chain by the chainring past the release point at the bottom of the chainring. The chain can be dragged upward and until it is jammed between the chainring and the chainstay.

chain whip (chain wrench): a flat piece of steel, usually attached to two lengths of chain. This tool is used to remove the rear cogs on a freehub.

chase, wild goose: (see "goose").

circlip (snap ring, Jesus clip): a C-shaped snap ring that fits in a groove to hold parts together.

clip-in pedal (clipless pedal): a pedal that relies on spring-loaded clips to grip the rider's shoe, without the use of toe clips and straps.

clipless pedal: (see "clip-in pedal").

cog: the sprockets located on the drive side of the rear hub.

coil spring: a cylindrically wound piece of metal wire or rod.

compression damping: the deadening or diminishing of the speed of the compression of a spring on impact.

cone: a threaded conical nut that serves to hold a set of bearings in place and also provides a smooth surface upon which those bearings can roll.

crank arm: the lever attached at the bottom-bracket spindle used to transmit a rider's energy to the chain.

crank arm-fixing bolt: the bolt attaching the crank to the bottom-bracket spindle on a cotterless drivetrain.

crankset: the assembly that includes a bottom bracket, two crank arms, chainring set, and accompanying nuts and bolts.

cross four: a wheel-building pattern that calls for each spoke to cross over four other spokes on its path from the hub to the rim.

cross three: a wheel-building pattern that calls for each spoke to cross over three other spokes on its path from the hub to the rim.

cross two: a wheel-building pattern that calls for each spoke to cross over two other spokes on its path from the hub to the rim.

crown: in a fork, the cross piece connecting the steering tube to the fork legs.

cup: a cup-shaped bearing surface that surrounds the bearings in a bottom bracket, headset, or hub.

damper: unit that controls a spring's movement. (See also "cartridge damper.")

damping: the control of a spring's movement by dissipating its energy as heat.

derailleur: a gear-changing device that allows a rider to move the chain from one cog or chainring to another while the bicycle is in motion.

derailleur hanger: a metal extension of the right rear dropout through which the rear derailleur is mounted to the frame.

diamond frame: the traditional bicycle frame shape.

disc (also "rotor"): the circular metal braking surface attached to the hub against which a disc brake presses the brake pads to stop the bike.

disc brake: a brake that stops the bike by squeezing brake pads against a circular disc attached to the wheel.

dish: a difference in spoke tension on the two sides of the rear wheel so that the wheel is centered.

double: a two-chainring drivetrain setup (as opposed to a three-chainring, or "triple," one).

double-clamp: a suspension fork style common for cross-country use, referring to the fork crown and the fork brace forming two clamps holding the fork together.

down tube: the tube that connects the head tube and bottom-bracket shell together.

drivetrain: the crank arms, chainrings, bottom bracket, front derailleur, chain, rear derailleur, and freewheel (or cassette).

drop: the perpendicular distance between a horizontal line passing through the wheel hub centers and the center of the bottom bracket.

dropouts: the slots in the forks and rear triangle where the wheel axles attach.

dust cap: a protective cap keeping dirt away from a part.

elastomer: a urethane spring used in suspension forks and swing arms.

ferrule: a cap for the end of cable housing.

fixed cup: the nonadjustable cup of the bottom bracket located on the drive side of the bottom bracket.

flange: the largest diameter of the hub where the spoke heads are anchored.

fork: the part that attaches the front wheel to the frame.

fork crown: the cross piece connecting the fork legs to the steering tube.

fork ends: (see "dropouts").

fork rake (rake): the perpendicular offset distance of the front axle from an imaginary extension of the steering tube centerline (steering axis).

fork tips (fork ends): (see "dropouts").

four cross: (see "cross four").

frame: the central structure of a bicycle to which all of the parts are attached.

freehub: a freewheel that is integral with a rear hub. Also refers to the hub itself, including the built-in freewheeling mechanism. Cassette hub.

freewheel: a removable cluster of cogs attached to a mechanism that rotates forward and not back, allowing a rider to stop pedaling as the bicycle is moving forward. *Verb:* to coast without pedaling.

front triangle (main triangle): the head tube, top tube, down tube, and seat tube of a bike frame.

goose chase, wild: (see "wild").

grip: padded tube on a handlebar end for the rider to hold onto.

Grip Shift: a shifter that is integrated with the handlebar grip of a mountain bike. The rider shifts gears by twisting the grip (see also "twist shifter").

guide pulley: (see "jockey wheel").

headset: the cup, lock ring, and bearings that hold the fork to the frame and allow the fork to turn in the frame.

head tube: the front tube of the frame through which the steering tube of the fork passes. The head tube is attached to the top tube and down tube and locates the headset.

hex key: (see "Allen key").

hub: the central part of a wheel to which the spokes are anchored and through which the wheel axle passes.

hub brake: a disc, roller, drum, or coaster brake that stops the wheel with friction applied to a braking surface attached to the hub.

hydraulic brake: a type of brake that uses fluid pressure to move the brake pads against the braking surface.

hydraulic/cable-actuated disc brake: a hydraulic disc brake in which a standard brake lever and cable transmit the braking force from the hand to the hydraulic brake caliper.

index shifter: a shifter that clicks into fixed positions as it moves the derailleur from gear to gear.

inner leg: in a suspension fork, one of the two tubes clamped into the fork crown on which the moving outer legs slide. Also called a stanchion or stanchion tube.

inner wire: (see "cable").

Jesus clip: (see "circlip").

jockey wheel or jockey pulley: a circular cog-shaped pulley attached to the rear derailleur used to guide, apply tension to, and laterally move the chain from rear cog to rear cog. Also called a guide pulley.

knob: a raised traction bump on a mountain bike tire.

linear spring rate: a characteristic of some springs in which the spring rate is a constant (i.e., the spring's stiffness is the same) as the spring is compressed until it bottoms out. Steel and titanium coil springs have relatively linear spring rates.

link: 1) a pivoting steel hook on a V-brake arm that the cable-guide "noodle" hooks into. 2) (see "chain link").

locknut: a nut that serves to hold the bearing adjustment in a headset, hub, or pedal.

lock ring: the outer ring that tightens the adjustable cup of a bottom bracket against the face of the bottom-bracket shell.

lock washer: a notched or toothed washer that serves to hold surrounding nuts and washers in position.

lower legs: (see "outer legs").

master link: a detachable link that holds the chain together. The master link can be opened by hand without a chain tool.

MCU: for "micro-cellular unit," a urethane elastomer with trapped air in the mixture used as a spring medium in some front- and rear-end suspension systems.

mounting bolt: a bolt that mounts a part to a frame, fork, or component. (see also "pivot bolt.")

needle bearing: 1) rod-shaped roller in a bearing. 2) a set of needle bearings arranged coaxially into a cylinder. 3) a set of needle bearings arranged radially in a disc shape.

nipple: a small threaded nut specially designed to receive the end of a spoke and fit the holes of a rim.

noodle: curved cable-guide pipe on a V-brake arm that stops the cable housing and directs the cable to the cable anchor bolt on the opposite arm.

outer legs: in a suspension fork, the outer tubes that slide on the inner legs, or stanchion tubes. Also called "sliders" or "lower legs." The front hub, fork brace, and brake are usually attached to the outer legs.

outer wire: (see "cable housing").

outer wire stop: (see "cable stop").

p knuckle: the lower pivot on a rear derailleur containing the jockey wheel cage pivot spring assembly.

p spring: the pivot spring inside the p knuckle.

pin spanner: a V-shaped wrench with two tip-end pins that is used for tightening the adjustable cup of the bottom bracket.

pivot bolt: a fixing bolt that fastens the brake arm to the frame or fork.

preload: (see "spring preload").

Presta valve: thin, metal tire valve that uses a locking nut to stop air flow from the tire.

progressive spring rate: a characteristic of some springs in which the spring rate increases (i.e., the spring gets stiffer) as the spring is compressed. Compressed air and elastomer springs have progressive spring rates.

quick release: 1) the tightening lever and shaft used to attach a wheel to the fork or rear dropouts without using axle nuts. 2) a quick-opening lever and shaft pinching the seatpost inside the seat tube, in lieu of a wrench-operated bolt. 3) a quick cable release on a brake. 4) a fixing mechanism that can be quickly opened and closed, as on a brake cable or wheel axle. 5) a fixing bolt that can be quickly opened and closed by a lever.

quill: the vertical tube of a stem that inserts into the fork steering tube. It has an expander wedge and bolt inside to secure the stem to the steering tube.

race: a ring-shaped surface on which the bearings roll freely.

radial: directed straight outward from the center. In wheel building, a pattern in which each spoke takes the shortest distance to the rim, contacting the rim (or, more accurately, its chord at that point) at a right angle.

Rapidfire shifter: an indexing shifter manufactured by Shimano for use on mountain bikes with two separate levers operating each shift cable.

rear triangle: the rear portion of the bicycle frame, including the seatstays, the chainstays, and the seat tube.

rebound damping: the diminishing of the speed of return of a spring on rebound (after compression).

rim: the outer hoop of a wheel to which the tire is attached.

roller-cam brakes: a brake system using pulleys and a cam to force the brake pads against the rim surface.

rotor: (see "disc").

saddle (seat): a platform made of leather and/or plastic upon which the rider sits.

Schrader valve: a high-pressure air valve with a spring-loaded air-release pin inside. Schrader valves are found on some bicycle tubes and air-sprung suspension forks as well as on adjustable rear shocks and automobile tires and tubes.

seal: a part designed to prevent elements like dirt, oil, grease, water, or air from passing from one side of a mechanical system to the other.

sealed bearing: a bearing enclosed in an attempt to keep contaminants out. (See also "cartridge bearing.")

seat: (see "saddle").

seat cluster: the intersection of the seat tube, top tube, and seat stays.

seatpost: the cylindrical part that connects the saddle to the bicycle frame.

sidepull cantilever brake: (see "V-brake").

skewer: a hub quick release or a shaft passing through a stack of elastomer bumpers in a suspension fork.

sliders: (see "outer legs").

snap ring: (see "circlip").

spider: a star-shaped piece of metal that connects the right crank arm to the chainrings.

spoke: metal rod that connects the hub to the rim of a wheel.

spoke nipple: (see "nipple").

spring: an elastic contrivance, which, when compression force is removed, returns to its original shape by virtue of its elasticity. The spring gives the "boing" to a suspension system; it holds the rider and bike up (i.e., it "suspends" the rider and bike). A suspension spring can be a metal coil, an elastic polymer, or compressed air.

spring preload: the initial loading of a spring so part of its compression range is taken up prior to impact. Preloading stiffens the spring.

spring rate: the amount of force it takes to compress a spring a unit distance.

sprocket: a circular, multiple-toothed piece of metal that engages a chain. (See also: "cog" and "chainring.")

stanchion (or stanchion tube): (see "inner leg").

stand-over clearance ("stand-over height"): the distance between the top tube of the bike and the rider's crotch when standing over the bicycle.

star nut ("Star-fangled nut"): a tanged nut that is forced down into the steering tube and anchors the stem bolt of a threadless headset.

steering axis: the imaginary line about which the fork rotates.

steering tube: the vertical tube on a fork that is attached to the fork crown and fits inside the head tube.

straddle cable: short segment of cable connecting two brake arms together.

straddle-cable holder: (see "yoke").

swingarm: the movable rear end of a rear-suspension frame.

threadless headset: (see "AheadSet").

three cross: (see "cross three.").

thumb shifter: a thumb-operated shift lever attached on top of the handlebars.

top tube: the tube that connects the seat tube to the head tube.

triple: a term used to describe the three-chainring combination attached to the right crank arm.

triple-clamp: a suspension fork style with extra-long inner legs common for downhill use, referring to a brace above the headset, the fork crown, and the fork brace forming three clamps holding the fork together.

twist shifter: a cable-pulling derailleur control handle surrounding the handlebar adjacent to the hand grip; it is twisted forward or back to cause the derailleur to shift (see also "Grip Shift").

two cross: (see "cross two").

U-brake: (Shimano trademark) a mountain bike brake consisting of two crossing arms each shaped like an inverted L affixed to posts on the frame or fork and actuated by pulling up on a straddle cable connecting the two arms.

upside-down fork: suspension fork on which the slider tubes attached to the hub are the inner legs and the stanchion tubes attached to the crown are the outer legs. The outer stanchions are open at the bottom to accept the sliders. An upside-down fork cannot be used with a rim brake.

V-brake: (Shimano trademark) a cable-operated sidepull cantilever rim brake consisting of two vertical brake arms with a cable stop on one arm and a cable anchor on the opposite arm.

wheelbase: the horizontal distance between the two wheel axles.

wild goose chase: (see "chase").

women's frame: (see "step-through frame").

yoke: the part attaching the brake cable to the straddle cable on a cantilever or U-brake.

Appendix E: Torque Table

If you have a torque wrench, these are the standard tightnesses recommended by Shimano, SRAM/Grip Shift, Rock Shox, Answer/Manitou, Marzocchi, RST, 3TTT, Avid, Formula, Hayes, and Magura for their products.

Unit conversion: Divide these numbers by 12 to convert them to foot-pounds (ft-lb). Multiply these numbers by 0.115 to convert to Newton-meters (N-m).

Brake Assemblies	
brake lever clamp bolt	50–70 inch-pounds
brake lever clamp-slotted screw	22–26 inch-pounds
brake mounting bolt	40–60 inch-pounds
brake cable fixing bolt	50–70 inch-pounds
V-brake pad fixing nut	50–70 inch-pounds
cantilever brake pad fixing bolt	70–78 inch-pounds
straddle cable yoke fixing nut	35–43 inch-pounds
Shimano V-brake leverage adjuster bolt	9–13 inch-pounds
Avid Arch Supreme arch-mounting bolt	35–40 inch-pounds
Hayes disc brake:	
rotor mounting bolts	45–55 inch-pounds
handlebar master cylinder clamp	15–20 inch-pounds
hose nut	40 inch-pounds plus 1 rotation
caliper bleeder	2 inch-pounds to seal
caliper bridge bolts	100–120 inch-pounds
banjo bolt	50–60 inch-pounds
caliper mount bolts	100–120 inch-pounds
Formula disc brake:	
rotor mounting bolts	42–47 inch-pounds
caliper mounting bolts	76–84 inch-pounds
valve couplers	101–111 inch-pounds
Magura rim brake:	
5-mm center bolt	52 inch-pounds
4-mm housing clamp bolt	35 inch-pounds
bleed screws	35 inch-pounds
brake line sleeve nuts	35 inch-pounds
Magura Gustav M disc brake:	
rotor mounting bolts	35 inch-pounds
master cylinder line fitting	35 inch-pounds
caliper mounting bolts	52 inch-pounds
Rock Shox disc brake:	
rotor mounting bolts	50 inch-pounds
caliper mounting bolts	50 inch-pounds
cable guide hardware	50 inch-pounds
Derailleur and Shifter Assemblies	
front derailleur cable-fixing bolt	44–60 inch-pounds
front derailleur clamp bolt	44–60 inch-pounds
rear derailleur cable-fixing bolt	44–60 inch-pounds
rear derailleur mounting bolt	70–86 inch-pounds
rear derailleur pulley center bolts	27–34 inch-pounds
Rapidfire SL shifter clamp bolt	44 inch-pounds
shifter clamp bolt-hex key	53–69 inch-pounds
shifter clamp bolt-slotted screw	22–26 inch-pounds
shift lever parts fixing screw	22–24 inch-pounds
Gripshift lever mounting screw	17 inch-pounds
Hubs, Cassettes, Quick Releases	
hub quick-release lever closing	79–104 inch-pounds
bolt-on steel skewer	65 inch-pounds
bolt-on titanium skewer	85 inch-pounds
quick-release axle locknut	87–217 inch-pounds
freehub cassette body-fixing bolt	305–434 inch-pounds
cassette cog lock ring	260–434 inch-pounds
Crank, Bottom Bracket Assemblies	
crank arm fixing bolt	357–435 inch-pounds
chainring fixing bolt	70–100 inch-pounds
cartridge bottom bracket cups	435–608 inch-pounds
standard bottom bracket fixed cup	609–695 inch-pounds
standard bottom bracket lock ring	609–695 inch-pounds
pedal axle to crank arm	307 inch-pounds or more
Seats, Stems	
seatpost clamp bolt	174–347 inch-pounds
seat tube clamp binder bolt	140 inch-pounds
stem handlebar clamping bolt	160–260 inch-pounds
stem expander bolt	174–260 inch-pounds
AheadSet stem clamp bolts	130 inch-pounds
Aheadset bearing preload	22 inch-pounds
3T Forge Ahead wedge bolt	MAX 177 inch-pounds
3T Forge Ahead handlebar clamp bolt	159–177 inch-pounds
Suspension Forks	
Rock Shox fork crown clamp bolt	60 inch-pounds
Rock Shox Judy top cap	35 inch-pounds
Rock Shox SID top cap	50 inch-pounds
Rock Shox brake post	60 inch-pounds
Rock Shox fork brace bolt	60 inch-pounds
Rock Shox Judy cartridge shaft compression bolt	60 inch-pounds
Rock Shox Judy neutral shaft compression bolt	60 inch-pounds
Rock Shox SID compression bolt, either leg	50 inch-pounds
Manitou 6-mm single fork crown clamp bolt	110–130 inch-pounds
Manitou 5-mm paired fork crown clamp bolt	60 inch-pounds
Manitou brake post	90–110 inch-pounds
Manitou fork brace bolt	90–110 inch-pounds
Manitou EFC/Mach 5/SX cartridge compression bolt	10–30 inch-pounds
Manitou neutral shaft compression bolt	10–30 inch-pounds
Manitou EFC/Mach 5/SX cartridge cap	30–50 inch-pounds
Marzocchi Bomber 26-mm top plug	106 inch-pounds
Marzocchi Bomber foot nut	106 inch-pounds
RST Mozo brake arch bolt	70–80 inch-pounds
RST Mozo fork crown clamp bolt	70–80 inch-pounds
Shoes	
shoe cleat fixing bolt	44–51 inch-pounds
shoe spike	34 inch-pounds

INDEX